ENERGENICS

ENERGENICS

M S RICHARDSON

ATHENA PRESS
LONDON

ISBN 978 1 84748 625 7

First published 2009 by
ATHENA PRESS
Queen's House, 2 Holly Road
Twickenham TW1 4EG
United Kingdom

Printed for Athena Press

This book is for my grandchildren

CONTENTS

LIST OF ILLUSTRATIONS AND CREDITS

INTRODUCTION

In October 1987 I attended a Workers' Educational Association evening course on parapsychology organised by the Department of Psychology of Manchester University. Early in 1988, a student I met on the course introduced me to spiritual healing and to dowsing. I knew nothing about either and their concepts amazed me. Working on the theory that the proof of the pudding is in the eating, and using myself as a guinea pig, I decided to try dowsing to see if I could discover the causes of the health problems I was experiencing and to put my findings into action. To my astonishment, my health problems rapidly disappeared. Shortly afterwards I used dowsing to learn how to use healing, and I was equally astonished when the healing worked. Since those small beginnings I have been privileged to be able to help in approximately 3,000 cases so far.

I have received wonderful support and encouragement on my journey as a dowser and as a healer. Unfortunately, I also discovered there was, and still is, much antipathy and prejudice against dowsing and spiritual healing, and particularly against the energy they both use. I quickly began to realise that if this form of energy and its allied therapies are to be taken seriously so that many more people can benefit from them, the questions that surround what they are and how and why they work needed to be answered more fully.

Energenics is my hypothesis about the origin, construction and organisation of all the wavelengths and frequencies of the life force energies and energy systems which fill the cosmos, the universe, the Earth and all life on Earth, including humanity. They are the energies which power all the processes of all physical matter of the Earth and of life on Earth, especially the human body, and give physical matter its ability to produce energy and power. They are also the energies used in dowsing and in spiritual healing. I devised the title 'Energenics' from the words 'energy' and 'mechanics' to create a word to describe the mechanisms and mechanics of all the energies and energy systems of creation, and how they connect with physical matter, especially the physical matter of the human body.

Energenics describes a separate and different energy system from the energy system known as the meridians. The meridians form the basis of traditional Eastern medicine and of the therapies of acupuncture, shiatsu and reflexology. My research has included meridians in order to understand how Energenics and meridians work together in partnership (see Part VIII).

Although I began to write this book in 1997, my research started in 1988 at the beginning of my work as a dowser, when I discovered that menaquinone (vitamin K_2) is vitally important to brain function (see Part V, Chapter III). With the exception of friends who are doctors or scientists, I could not find anyone in the establishments of science or medicine to take the idea

seriously. Energenics grew out of my quest to understand the energies involved, why they work and,
equally important, why they sometimes break down
and do not work. If it is to have lasting benefit, a
crucial part of the healing process is in discovering and
remedying why an illness or disease originally started. I
found the answers lie in the energy systems which
Energenics explores.

Experience from the beginning of my work has
shown me that my dowsing is accurate. I have used it
throughout my research to check and verify, or otherwise, my information, ideas and theories. I have
written *Energenics* as fact because I know and use it as
fact, and I find it works. At present my theories cannot
be tested by the conventional methods of today's
science because the energies involved cannot be
measured by the usual systems. Although great
advances have been made, as yet there are no scientific
instruments available which are as sensitive as a human
being using dowsing and/or healing to detect the very
subtle energies involved in the make-up of the state we
call 'life' and of the states which exist beyond what we
call 'life'.

I have used very few individual case studies because
Energenics is based on all the cases I have worked on
since 1988.

As my research developed, I began to realise the
information I was finding was not new, but a redis-
covery of very ancient knowledge. Clues to its secrets
are still scattered around the world in language, ancient
cultures, myths and legends. I have included some of
the historical background to how knowledge is lost

because I think it also helps to understand some present day attitudes to healing and to the 'E-word', energy.

Throughout the book I have called the source of all energy and creation the Creator-God, or 'God', because in my own vocabulary these are the words which sum up this concept in the most clear and simple way. If you are not comfortable with these words, I hope you will substitute your own definition of the source of the origins of your creation.

St Anselm (AD 1033–1109) was the leading early scholastic philosopher who formulated the ontological (i.e. metaphysical) argument for the existence of God. It states that if God is that which nothing greater can be conceived, then the existence of God is necessary, for it is possible to conceive of a greater entity than a non-existent God, or as the *Shorter Oxford English Dictionary* says in its definition of the explanation of this ontological theory, '[it is] the argument that the existence of the idea of God of necessity involves the objective existence of God'.

It is very important to understand that neither this book nor Energenics represent any form of religion or philosophy. Energenics may help to explain how they evolved and why humans worldwide seem to find it necessary to make up the rules, dogmas and codes of behaviour they call religion.

Although this book explains how and why healing and dowsing work, it is not about how to heal or how to dowse, or about labyrinths as such. There are already many excellent and detailed books on these subjects. A short summary of the history and uses of dowsing and details for drawing a classical labyrinth are included in the appendix.

Energenics is written for everyone. I hope you will find you can use the information for your own benefit, if you wish.

Not everything that can be counted counts, and not everything that counts can be counted.

Albert Einstein

PART I
PRELUDE

CHAPTER I
SCENARIO

Knowledge is passed on like a game of Chinese whispers. Imagine a huge game played worldwide over thousands of years. It probably started at least 14,000 years ago in very ancient Egypt and perhaps even earlier. As information was passed from generation to generation, it became altered and distorted. Each generation has its own way of accessing, using and discarding knowledge. Sometimes the most important parts are left out and subsequently lost because they seem so obvious it is taken for granted they are already known. The original whisper in this particular game contained the knowledge and understanding of the energies which underpin and power the cosmos, this planet Earth and all matter and life on the Earth, including humanity. Gradually the information became so fragmented the sense of it disappeared until, to many people, it became nonsense. It was labelled 'magic' or 'superstition'. At best it was called meta-physics. Now it is ignored by many people in our sophisticated society and by most of conventional mainstream science and medicine. There are a few exceptions: Albert Einstein realised there were forces at work which were beyond his knowledge at that time.

The ancient civilizations were not primitive. On the

contrary, their knowledge and understanding of all the wavelengths and frequencies of the energies which power the physical matter of creation gave some of them access to very advanced technologies which we have yet to discover and accept. I believe understanding these energies is the key to solving the remaining mysteries of how the human body works, why it sometimes does not work and the root causes of disease.

The basis of mathematics in ancient Egypt was One and the division of One was the Eternal Power. First the One was divided into two which, added to the original One, gives three. Thereafter the division goes on to infinity. From the division comes the multiplication. They also said that numbers control the universe. The Egyptians had a very detailed knowledge of the construction of the human physical body, gathered from the dissection of bodies in preparation for mummification.

The ancient Chinese concept of Oneness is remarkably similar. The Chinese Oneness is expressed as Tao. Tao is the source of all things, and the law of the universe. Lao Tzu's description in *Tao Te Ching* is:

> The Tao begets the One.
> The One begets the Two.
> The Two beget the Three.
> And the Three beget the ten thousand
>   things.
> All things are backed by the shade, faced by
>   the light,
> And harmonised by the immaterial breath.

The concept of Oneness, enshrined in ancient Egyptian mathematics and the Tao, has been distorted by Chinese whispers. When we start from all the divided parts of the whole instead of the One, we see only the multiplications and complications of creation.

According to the *Shorter Oxford English Dictionary*, the word 'energy' comes from two ancient Greek words. The first part *en* is a prefix used to transform a word into a stronger condition or state: it activates the word. For example, compass becomes encompass, fold becomes enfold. The second part of energy comes from an ancient Greek word meaning *work*, so the two parts together give the meaning of making something work. As far as we know, it was first used in this form by Aristotle, who lived from 384–322 BC. Through the centuries, it has been used in various ways. In 1599 it was used to mean force or vigour of expression. In the science of physics, energy is used to mean power actively and efficiently exerted, and the power 'of doing work possessed by a body or system of bodies'.

Part of the knowledge of an energy linking all creation has survived in the Eastern cultures of China, Japan and India, as well as in the culture of the Native Americans.

- The Japanese call this linking energy 'hado'.
- The Chinese call it 'chi'.
- The Hindus call it 'prana'.
- The Hebrews called it 'ruach'.
- The ancient Egyptians called it 'amun'.

The Egyptian concept of the Creator was known as 'Amun-Ra'. Ra was the sun. Amun was the name given to the creative power behind the sun. They gave equal status to Ra and Amun. Ra is also the name given to the sun by the Native Americans.

Hado, chi, prana, ruach and *amun* all loosely translate as the 'life force' or the 'breath of life': the power or force behind physical matter which makes it function. We do not have a special word for it in English so we use the word 'energy'. As well as its scientific definition, 'energy' in English also refers to the physical utility energies of gas, coal, electricity and oil to make things work, and this can lead to some confusion and misunderstanding. Throughout this book I shall use the words 'life force' and 'life force energy' to refer to the energy, the force, which supports, connects and powers all creation and the evolution of creation, all matter, all life, and makes it work.

One of the reasons why the knowledge of the life force aspect of the human body and its relationship with the Earth has survived in the Eastern cultures and in the few so-called primitive tribes still remaining in the world, has been the continued and continuing use of folk medicine. Even the Eastern cultures have been subjected to Chinese whispers and a large part of the 'how and why' has been lost. Nevertheless, these cultures and their healing systems hold enormous clues to guide us to knowledge which has disappeared over the millennia.

The knowledge of an energy system in the human body known as the chakras has been in existence in Eastern cultures for thousands of years. It is part of the yoga tradition of India and the ancient Chinese Buddhist tradition. The chakras are centred on various parts of the physical body. They are seen as powerful vortices of energy which bring together and maintain our mental, spiritual and physical states. The system was originally based on seven chakras. Recently it has been based on eight chakras. Each chakra has its own colour (i.e. its own wavelength and frequency of light) and its own mental and physical aspect. The traditional sequence of the first seven chakras in the body follows the sequence of the colours of the spectrum: red, orange, yellow, green, blue, indigo and violet, starting with red for the first chakra, situated at the base of the spine in the area of the coccyx, and ending with violet for the seventh chakra at the crown of the head. The eighth chakra is on the wavelength of turquoise. The chakra energy system is not theoretical or imaginary. It is widely used in vibrational, that is, energy, therapies. Many people can see and sense the energy and the colours of the chakras in their mind's eye. Some can see the colours with their physical eyes.

As well as radiating in various areas of the body, the chakras encompass the spine so all the chakras can be accessed via the spine. The yoga tradition tells us there is an important surge of energy which rises up from the base of the spine to the top of the head, like a tidal wave on a river. It is called the kundalini energy.

In his book *Living Energies*, Callum Coats (1996) notes that the German word for the spinal column is *wirbelsaule*, which translated directly into English means not 'spinal' but 'spiral' column, and that each of the vertebrae which make up the spinal spiral column is referred to as a whirlpool or vortex. As Coats points out, the German words show it appears they saw the spinal column as an energy structure rather than just a physical structure as we know it.

In the ancient Indian culture, the movements and breathing which form the yoga exercises are used to stimulate the prana of the body, and release any prana blockages and toxins from the body via the chakras. The Chinese use the slow rhythmic movements of t'ai chi, chi qong and kung fu in a similar way, although they have their basis in the Chinese martial arts. They build up the body's physical and mental strength and stamina, using energy exercises rather than physical exercises such as weight lifting, and so on.

In Chinese medicine, chi is the active energy which flows through the Earth and through all life on the Earth, including humanity. It is carried through the human body by lines of energy called meridians (see Part VIII). Chi is seen as the active force of nature, whether it is on land, in water, in the air or in the human body. The flow of chi varies with the phases of the sun and the moon, so it ebbs and flows as the tides of seas and rivers ebb and flow, and as the air ebbs and flows in the formation of wind and clouds.

The balance and equilibrium of chi is described by the Chinese as yin and yang. To achieve balance, harmony and equilibrium in all aspects of life, physical, mental and spiritual, yin and yang must be in balance, harmony and equilibrium. This applies as much to the Earth as to a human being. The Chinese concept sees the oneness of the connection between humans and their environment: the same chi flows through both.

The Chinese have always recognised the importance of the environment on the well-being of the people living there. If chi in the environment is out of balance and harmony, the chi of the inhabitants will be adversely affected, and vice versa. This is the basis of feng shui (which translates literally as wind, i.e. air, and water). Feng shui is the art of maintaining the balance of yin and yang in and on the Earth and in our homes, workplaces and schools.

Yin and yang become out of balance if there is too much of one and not enough of the other, whether it is the yin aspect or the yang aspect. Imbalance in the yin and yang of the chi will upset the flow of the chi, making it either too fast or too slow, which will have an adverse effect on the physical body. This can be treated by acupuncture, a remedy that has been in use for thousands of years. It is widely used today by the medical profession for pain relief.

The kidneys are considered to be of vital importance in Chinese medicine, both physically and in terms of chi. They are known as the root of life. They are considered to hold the key to birth, and development of the whole body throughout life. The kidneys control the water of the body and the distribution of air through the body. All disharmonies in the body stem to a greater or lesser extent from an imbalance of the yin and yang in the chi flowing through the kidneys. The chakra system shows the kidneys are in the area of the third chakra, which has a yellow vibration. In ancient China, only the emperor was allowed to wear yellow.

During the mummification process used in ancient

Egypt, only the kidneys and heart were left in the body. All the other organs, including the brain, were removed and stored in jars alongside the mummy.

Knowledge of the aura has also been preserved in Eastern medicine. The aura is the energy which surrounds the physical body of a human or a plant or animal, or the Earth itself. It also contains the chakras and their colours. The health or ill health of the body will show in the strength or weakness of the vibrations of the aura. Although to most people the aura is invisible, as with the chakras many sensitive people can literally see the aura. Usually it looks like a layer of coloured light surrounding the body (or plant or animal). The halo of light depicted in early European religious paintings of Christ and the saints and angels is an adaptation of the aura, but ordinary people were not allowed to have one.

A vast knowledge of herbs, using plants for medicinal purposes, still survives. Humans throughout the world have an instinctive knowledge about using plants for healing purposes. The native Canadian tribes who lived on Queen Charlotte Island off the west coast of Canada knew there was a plant on the island to heal every known human ailment. In the West, this natural alchemy has been distorted into chemical drugs, some good, some bad.

The ancient knowledge of the life force energy linking all creation was closely guarded by the men and women of the priesthoods of the ancient cultures. Some parts were probably handed down and taught by word of mouth. In ancient Egypt, the temples were also hospitals for treating the sick. Egyptian medicine followed the traditions of Thoth who, in addition to the concepts of science and knowledge, also represented writing and communication. He is reputed to have invented the Egyptian hieroglyphics.

Thoth and Maat, together in partnership, represented the highest ideals of ancient Egyptian philosophy. Thoth represented wisdom, and Maat represented truth and justice. They taught that wisdom and truth should never be separated. Thoth, also regarded as the father of dowsing, is shown as a man with the head of an ibis bird. The ibis bird always seeks out pure drinking water. Wherever the ibis drank, the people knew the water would be safe. Thoth holds a pitcher, with a stream of connected ankhs pouring from it, representing the life-giving properties of water. The ankh is the Egyptian symbol for life.

Gradually the power of Egypt diminished. From about 900 BC Egypt fell into decline and was invaded by the Greeks and then by the Romans. The Romans sacked Alexandria and its great library, with all the records of ancient knowledge, was burned and lost.

Hippocrates (c.460–30 BC), a Greek physician on the island of Kos, is generally regarded as the father of modern medicine. Knowledge of astrology was considered by Hippocrates to be vital to the study of medicine, but some of the knowledge of Thoth and the ancient world had perhaps already been lost. Hippocrates separated what he considered to be medicine and superstition. The symbol he used, the caduceus (Fig. 1), is still the symbol of the western medical profession today.

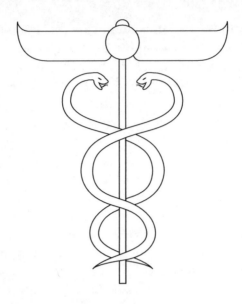

Fig. 1 The Caduceus

The caduceus was the symbol of the Greek god Hermes and the later Roman god Mercury, who both represented similar concepts to Thoth. They are usually known as messenger gods. A diagram of DNA has a similar construction to the entwined spirals of the serpents of the caduceus.

The ancient peoples of Northern Europe, and the Celts of Britain and Ireland had knowledge which ran parallel with the knowledge of ancient Egypt. They were traders, miners, farmers, and they were certainly not primitive. We can see from their legacy of stone circles and monuments such as Stonehenge in southern England, and New Grange in southern Ireland that they had a deep knowledge and understanding of the cosmos as well as of the Earth. The keepers of the secrets of this knowledge were the monks and druids, the equivalent of the priests of the Egyptian temples. As the druids gradually died out, much of their knowledge was lost with them.

By the eleventh, twelfth and thirteenth centuries in Europe the Chinese whispers had become even more distorted. Much of the how and why of the subtle energies of the Earth and the cosmos and of nature had been lost. When they were used, usually by simple country people using handed-down knowledge, the effect they produced was branded magic and sorcery.

The Christian church in Europe, under the Pope in Rome, ruled and controlled the whole of learning. Scholarship was not allowed to exist independently from the Church so scientific ideas were derived from theology and governed by what the Church approved of and what it did not. When Galileo invented his telescope in 1609 and then rediscovered that the Earth moved round the sun, he was tried, placed under house arrest and excommunicated by the Inquisition in 1633. To his lasting regret, Galileo changed his theory to placate the Pope and the Church.

By the twelfth century, men of science began to divide up the knowledge of science and medicine into the natural and the supernatural. Phenomena which could be explained were classed as natural. Phenomena which could not be explained were classed as magic and therefore were supernatural. It was decided that the natural was of God and the supernatural was probably not of God and therefore was 'the work of the devil' and was heresy.

The supernatural included knowledge of healing,

herbs, gems and crystals, and divination, which included dowsing. However, alchemy and astrology were not associated with magic and the supernatural and continued to be supported by the Church. So there were still small remnants left of the original Chinese whisper. Anyone who did not seem to agree with the dogmas of the Church was regarded as a heretic. From my own experience, this view still persists today. People who practised healing intuitively, without having 'studied' and without a licence, or who used a knowledge of plants, 'old wives' tales', and healing using 'magic' were particularly feared. They were classed as witches and therefore heretics and brought before the Inquisition. Women classed as witches outnumbered men by about ten to one.

The Inquisition was originally set up by the Church in 1022 to try heretics. It was re-established in 1208 to deal with the Cathars. The Cathars were a Christian religious sect who lived in southern France. They were probably descendents of the followers of Jesus who escaped from Palestine after his Crucifixion, and of the Essenes who were driven from Palestine by the Romans at the end of the first century AD. In what is known as the Albigensian Crusade, which continued for twenty years, the Cathars were eliminated. No one was spared, not even the children.

By 1235 the Papal Inquisition was firmly in place, and in 1252 Pope Innocent IV issued a 'bull', a Papal order with the full weight of the Church behind it, authorising the imprisonment, torture and execution of heretics on minimal evidence, and the seizure of all their worldly goods.

At the beginning of the fourteenth century, the Knights Templar fell foul of the Church and were wiped out in France by the Inquisition (see Part II, Chapter V). Only a few managed to escape to England and Scotland. The Inquisition was at its height in the fourteenth, fifteenth and sixteenth centuries and continued until approximately 1700.

The *Malleus Maleficarum* was a manual written by two Dominican Inquisitors. It was first published in 1486 and at least thirty editions of it appeared before 1669. It listed incriminations against witches, claiming women were the most likely candidates, and it detailed their means of torture.

The fate of people, most of them women, who were accused of witchcraft is indescribable, and they were eventually usually burned or hanged. The excesses of the witch-hunts were most severe in the fourteenth, fifteenth and sixteenth centuries. The Inquisition acknowledged burning 30,000 'witches' in 150 years. The true number may never be known but it is likely to be at least two million. They were usually ordinary men and women who were judicially murdered for having the knowledge and ability to heal. By far the greatest anti-witch crime hunts were committed in Germany.

Eventually, thoughts that the witch trials, as well as the witches, might be the work of the devil began to filter through the Church consciousness and it was decided they had better be stopped. In England, the last witch was officially hanged in 1684, in America in 1692, and finally in Germany as late as 1775.

In 1736, a law was passed in England which denied

the reality of witchcraft but provided for the prosecution of those who pretended to have magical powers. This law stayed in effect until 1951. Its influence is still present today in the *Shorter Oxford English Dictionary*'s definition of magic as 'the pretended art', or perhaps the definition only refers to the magic of conjurers achieved by clever illusion and manipulation.

In addition to the Inquisition, the twelfth and thirteenth centuries saw wars in Europe, and the Crusades against the Muslims in the Holy Land. The fourteenth century also saw famine, the Hundred Years War and the Black Death. In the fifteenth and the sixteenth centuries Europe, including Britain, was still ravaged by wars and plagues. It is no wonder that knowledge was lost in the ensuing din.

The Middle Ages, the eleventh to the fifteenth centuries, was also the time of the building of the great cathedrals of Europe, and the beautiful country churches of England. They arose like phoenixes out of the ashes. People never lost their unshakeable belief in God the Creator. A core piece of the Chinese whisper remained intact throughout.

Europe in the seventeenth century saw the teachings of the French philosopher Descartes, followed by Sir Isaac Newton (who was born in 1642, the year Galileo died). Between them, they further split the oneness. They separated the concept into philosophy and the physical, as the men of science in the twelfth century had split the natural and the supernatural.

Descartes and Newton developed a physical mechanistic view of the science of life on the Earth, and of the Earth itself. They have been immensely influential. Science and medicine have followed the pathway they set ever since. It has led to the study and recognition of the many parts of only the physical aspects of creation. However Descartes' theories are now being questioned by some mainstream scientists.

The aftermath of the turbulent centuries of the Middle Ages is still with us. One of the main reasons for the persecution of women who healed was fear, and some of that fear still persists today. The fear of so-called witchcraft has been perpetuated through the generations by children's stories of witches and wizards, usually wicked! One example is the fairy stories of the Brothers Grimm. Fear is a natural reaction to something we cannot understand or explain. There is also the fear of the empowerment knowledge gives to any individual human which might conflict with, or reduce, the power and influence of the ruling body, whatever that is. 'I can't count it, measure it or understand it, and therefore it does not exist' is still a fairly widespread scientific philosophy, even today. Healing and dowsing, and allied skills and arts such as homeopathy, herbal medicines and flower essences, are coming under attack again in the twenty-first century under the guise of 'safeguards' and EU directives.

In some ways we are still under the influence of the European medieval thinkers of 800 years ago. It really is time we moved on.

Fig. 2 A region in the centre of Saudi Arabia showing the effects of flash floods (satellite photograph)

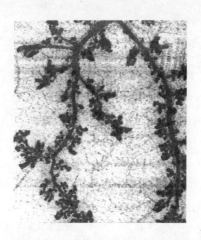

*Fig. 3 A seventy-day-old virgin mammary gland from a
stromelysin-1 over-expressing transgenic mouse*
© *Sympson et al., 1994. Originally published in* The Journal of
Cell Biology, *125(3): cover image*

*Fig. 4 Dendritic quartz, inclusion of rutile
The late Dr J Franks*

CHAPTER II

THE ENERGENIC CONCEPT

The more scientists explore the universe and the structures of the Earth, the more it is realised that everything is basically the same. The same basic geometry appears over and over again on this planet Earth and in space. The same chemistry occurs on a moon of Jupiter as on Earth. A fragment of Mars matches a fragment of the Earth. The Hale-Bopp comet is made of ice. Moon rock is the same as Earth rock. When a pebble is dropped into water, the outer ripple is almost the same shape as a spiral galaxy. Figures 2–4 show more examples of physical sameness (one-ness).

Energenics proposes that just as physical matter in the universe is basically the same, the basic structure of the energy systems of all creation in the universe and on the Earth are also the same.

The whole of the cosmos, the universe and all physical matter of creation, from an atom onwards, including the Earth and all life on Earth, is pulsating with an energy which is received, transformed and transmitted through a series of energy fields until it transforms into matter. It continues to be transmitted through the energy fields of matter, back into the energy fields of the cosmos in an unending eternal rhythm. The energy is pure thought and forms the cosmic life force. It is the one, same, basic ingredient of all creation. The source of it, the Creator-God, is the purest form of thought. All the energy fields of the cosmos, the Earth and of all life on Earth, especially humanity, evolve from it.

Consciousness evolves in the energy fields from the pure thought energy of the cosmic life force as it is processed through them. Although the energy field structures throughout the cosmos and creation are the same, every energy field develops and produces its own unique consciousness which in turn produces the uniqueness of physical matter within its sameness, within its oneness.

Interestingly, the law of physics which states that 'in every case in which energy is lost by resistance, heat is generated' can also apply to thought. It describes perfectly an argument caused by a clash of ideas based on human processed thought, especially a heated argument. When this happens, life force energy is also lost and the physical body is left weakened, the prover-bial 'weak at the knees' sensation.

The word 'heal' comes from the ancient German/Norse/Old English words meaning 'whole'. The word 'whole' implies completeness, oneness. As an energenic healer, I know I am a conduit, and the energy I sense flowing through me into the patient comes from the source of all energy, from the reservoir of the purest form of thought, the cosmic life force energy of the Creator-God. I know this energy heals. It restores shattered parts to wholeness and combines the whole parts into the oneness of the whole, whether it is a person, plant or animal, or the Earth itself. This implies that the cosmic life force energy is needed to bring about completeness, wholeness. Where it is missing, disease and fragmentation evolve.

Energenics also proposes that, in common with all matter, the Earth develops its own consciousness from the cosmic life force flowing through its energy field system. This Earth consciousness develops into the Earth's own life force. All life on Earth, including humanity, needs both cosmic life force and Earth life force in order to exist. Therefore the health of all life on this planet depends upon the health of the planet itself. Everything we do on or to the planet will affect humanity, for good or ill.

Everything created by humans begins with thought. The thought is processed into a consciousness and then into an idea of what is to be created. Thought energy of the originator of the idea remains with whatever has been created from that thought process. For example, dowsing shows that the consciousness of an artist is transmitted into and remains with his or her pictures. If the consciousness is positive and balanced, the dowser will receive a positive signal. If it is unbalanced, the dowser will receive a negative signal. Some people can sense the consciousness in a work of art, either positive or negative, without dowsing. Positive consciousness can have a pleasing and moving effect. If it is negative, it can have an unpleasant physical effect on a sensitive viewer. Consciousness in a work of art is a phenomenon recognised by some artists themselves. The Russian abstract expressionist painter Wassily Kandinsky wrote a book about it called *Concerning the Spiritual in Art*.

It is said that humans are made in the image of God. I believe this 'image' is the ability to create using thought. The original pure thought energy of the Creator-God is in, and remains with, every particle of all that has been and is being created. The purest form of thought is unconditional love. It is the spark of creation and powers the evolution of creation. It is the unifying life force energy of all creation, and 'the harmonising, immaterial breath' of the Tao. It is the basic common denominator of all creation from the farthest universe in the cosmos to an atom, and everything, including humanity, in-between. As in Egyptian mathematics and the Tao, the one divides into infinity. We are all variations on the same theme. We are all part of the Creator-God and the Creator-God is part of us. Whether it is a rock or a human being, ultimately all is one. As Plato said, 'we [humans] are a microcosm of the macrocosm'.

The paradox of the oneness of creation is uniqueness. Uniqueness, the only oneness, is an endorsement of oneness. It is oneness emphasised through every aspect of creation; simplicity and complication interwoven, especially in the part of creation we know as humanity. We need to know how the underpinning energy supporting oneness and uniqueness is organised. I believe clues to the answers to these questions are hidden in ancient symbols.

PART II
CLUES

CHAPTER I

SPIRALS

The spiral is one of the oldest patterns known to humans. It has been used for thousands of years worldwide and is still used today. Spirals form the basis of the paisley patterns of Scotland, Turkey, Iran and India, and the 'C' scrolls and 'S' scrolls of the rococco designs of the eighteenth and nineteenth centuries in Europe. The spirals of the traditional ogee patterns on fabrics are as popular today as they ever were.

Nothing in nature is static and the shape of the movement of nature is spiral, from the movement and shape of the galaxies to a leaf or a seed blown in the wind. The wind itself is spiral – ask any tornado! The emergence of a rose from its bud is spiral. Accelerated film of plants growing show the spiral movement of the growth of the plant. The orbital movement of the planets is spiral and the first shapes a child makes with a pencil are spirals. Scribble is spiral. The molecular structure of DNA is a double helix spiral. Spirals are inherent in our make-up.

The shape of the turbulence created in water when it flows past an obstacle is a pattern of alternating clockwise and anticlockwise spirals, as are the alternating spirals in the seed head of a sunflower. The vapour trail left by a high-flying jet aircraft forms into a series of interlocking spiral curves. A photograph of the Earth from a satellite shows the spiral of some cloud formations. Fossils and seashells are formed in the shape of spirals. Fingerprints are spiral.

The shape made by the ebb and flow of the tides is spiral, and it is also an ancient traditional pattern used by humans for decoration. This ebb and flow shape is also the shape of a learning curve: three steps forward and two steps back. Progress is only made after the two steps back. It is the same shape as the flow of water in the sea. After every wave breaks, the water recedes to form the next wave and continues in this rhythm for eternity. When the phases of the moon are plotted on to a paper over a period of years, the pattern produced is a spiral.

The triple spiral is another very ancient pattern, found worldwide. It is made of three spirals joined together in the shape of a triangle. It is found in jewellery designs from the Celts to the Vikings and is still used today. Often it was carved into stone. Perhaps the most famous triple spirals are carved on the stones of New Grange, the Neolithic monument in southern Ireland, dated 3200 BC (Fig. 5). The Hindu script for 'Om', meaning the eternal silence, is a triple spiral. It dates from before 3500 BC.

Why join three spirals together and what is their significance and meaning? We have a saying, 'everything goes in threes'. The most harmonious form of energy in an astrological chart is a trine, or triangle, formed by the positions of three of the planets. New plants and seedlings always thrive better if they are planted in threes in the form of a triangle.

This is a three-dimensional physical planet and

everything on it, and in it, is three-dimensional. Matter on Earth and in the universe is three-dimensional. Does each of the spirals represent a dimension of creation? When, and how, does a pattern become a symbol?

Fig. 5 Triple spiral engraving from chamber of the passage tomb,
Newgrange, Co. Meath, Ireland, c.3200 BC.
Reproduced courtesy of the Department of the Environment,
Heritage, and Local Government, Ireland

CHAPTER II
SYMBOLS

Although the triple spiral now looks to us like another form of decoration, its universal use over a long period of time, at least 5,000 years, implies it originally had an important meaning.

Ancient people understood the immense energy and power contained within symbols.

The word 'symbol' comes from the Latin and Greek languages. The Greek word is in two parts: the first part means 'a token, watchword, outward sign, a covenant'. The second part means 'a story' which represents a concept. So a symbol is an outward sign of the thought contained in the concept it represents. For example, a flag is a symbol of the nation or cause it represents. It is held in great esteem. To burn a flag is a symbolic gesture of destroying the power of the nation or cause the flag represents. The piece of patterned, coloured cloth in itself is nothing. It is the thought, the consciousness of the concept it represents which transforms it into something special. Held in front of an army, or a football team, it takes on enormous energy and power.

Letters of the alphabet are symbols of the sounds which make up words. The words represent our spoken thoughts and consciousness, our language. The symbols of the written letters enable us to record our thoughts and share them with others. They enable us to transfer our thoughts on to paper. Our signatures, each one unique as each human is unique, are our own symbols. Our entire thought energy, conscious and subconscious, is held and recorded in the way we write the symbols, the letters of our names in our signatures. This still applies to whatever symbol we use for our names. If someone is unable to write their name, the cross or mark they draw will contain the thought, the consciousness, of the energy of the person who made it.

Written music also uses universally recognised symbols. Great composers can hear the sounds of the music in their minds and transfer the sounds on to paper using the recognised symbol for each sound and rhythm. When great conductors read the symbols of the written music, they can hear in their heads, in thought, how the music should sound when it is played physically. Sir Malcolm Sargent said the first rehearsal he took with an orchestra was usually a disappointment because the sound it physically produced at that stage did not measure up to the sound he had in his head.

The circle-cross is an ancient symbol which appears in cultures across the world, from Ancient Egypt to the native North Americans (Fig. 6). It is made of three lines, one circular and two straight. The straight lines bisect each other and quarter the circle to form the cross within the circumference of the circle. The circle represents the cosmos, the whole, the oneness. The vertical line of the cross represents the Earth; the horizontal arm of the cross represents all life on Earth,

53

including humanity, interlinked with the cosmos (heaven) and Earth. Both the Earth and life on Earth are reaching out to, connected with and protected by the cosmos and the Oneness.

Fig. 6 Querino polychrome bowl c. AD 1125–1200

The Hopi people of North America believed the circle-cross represents life and balance in the universe. It also represents mother and child. They understood the circle and the cross should never be separated.

It is an interesting fact that for most of the past 2,000 years, a period of intense turbulence and strife, the symbol of the circle-cross has been split. The cross has been used without the circle to represent the sacrifice of Jesus, and ultimately man's inhumanity to man.

The Egyptian hieroglyph for a city is a circle-cross.

Cities and settlements were usually built in the shape of a circle-cross, with a surrounding wall and a gate or entrance at the north, south, east and west points of it. It is a format used worldwide for thousands of years. Is this because, like the spiral, it was instinctive for humans to use this symbol, this shape, which naturally gave protection to the inhabitants living in the settlement?

Fig. 7 The Classical Labyrinth (right-hand opening)

Fig. 8 Drawing of a three-dimensional Classical Labyrinth

Fig. 9 The Classical Labyrinth (left-hand opening)

Fig. 10 The Labyrinth of Chartres, the Circle-Cross Labyrinth

CHAPTER III
THE TWO LABYRINTH PATTERNS

The two most important ancient symbols still left to us are labyrinth patterns. Both are based on a cross in a circle. The most well known is called the classical or Cretan labyrinth (Fig. 7 and Fig. 9). It is an ingenious plan view of a complicated three-dimensional spiral (Fig. 8). It has nine parts: seven circular pathways leading to the centre, shaped like a finger. The base of the 'finger', the eighth part, is attached to the fifth pathway, and the tip of the 'finger', the ninth part, points upwards. The labyrinth can have a left-hand opening or a right-hand opening. The classical labyrinth is found in different cultures all over the world, from Crete to the Hopi Indians of North America, to Tintagel in Cornwall, and many places in-between. The classical Cretan labyrinth derives its name from the famous story of Theseus and the Minotaur in ancient Mycenaean mythology.

Theseus was the brave and handsome son of the King of Athens. He volunteered to be sent to Crete as part of the compulsory tribute of seven young men and seven maidens demanded annually by King Minos of Crete. They were sent to be sacrificed to the Minotaur, who lived in the centre of the labyrinth. Ariadne, the daughter of King Minos, fell in love with Theseus. To help him to escape, she gave him a thread to use on his way into the centre of the labyrinth and a sword to kill the Minotaur. Theseus slew the monster, rescued his fellow Athenians and, using the thread to guide him, led them safely out of the labyrinth.

The Minoan civilization existed in Crete from about 2500–1400 BC, and had affinities with the ancient Egyptian culture. It was a maritime and commercial power and eventually spread to include mainland Greece.

The second version of the labyrinth pattern is built into the floor of Chartres Cathedral in France and is often known as the Chartres Labyrinth (Fig. 10). It is more complicated than the classical labyrinth and has eleven pathways leading to the centre. Legend has it that to walk round the Chartres Cathedral labyrinth on your knees is the equivalent of a pilgrimage to Jerusalem. A similar labyrinth is built into the turf of the common at Saffron Walden in Essex, England.

The double axe, the symbol of power carried by the priestesses of the temple in the Minoan civilization, is a stylised version of the eleven-path Chartres labyrinth. It implies that both forms of the labyrinth were used by the Minoans. The eleven-path labyrinth seems to have been kept within the priesthood of the temple. The seven-path classical labyrinth was widely used and is found on seals and coins of the period, as well as being built into the ground.

It is important to understand that a labyrinth is not a maze and to know the difference. There are no choices of direction in a labyrinth. It is a single convoluted pathway, winding round before reaching the centre and returning back the way it came to the beginning. Provided Theseus had concentrated on the pathway and followed it carefully, he would not have needed a thread to find his way out. If he had been finding his way through a maze, he would certainly have needed a thread. The pathways of a maze present us with many choices of which way to turn before we can find our way to the centre and out again. A maze is complicated. The labyrinth only appears to be complicated because the beginning is halfway round, and just as we think we are nearly at the centre, the pathway takes us away again before leading us back to the centre. Then we have to carefully retrace our steps to return to the starting point.

Labyrinths, wherever they are found, are always special. They are not just used as part of decoration but always seem to have had a specific purpose, often connected with ritual or ceremony. The people making and using them seemed to have an innate understanding that the labyrinths connected them to unseen forces.

Often fishing communities would build a classical labyrinth by the coast. If they were built on an island, they were built on the west coast. To ensure good weather and a good catch, the women would walk round the labyrinth while their menfolk were fishing at sea. This ritual carried on until the beginning of the twentieth century on the island of St Agnes in the Scilly Islands.

CHAPTER IV

CONNECTIONS LINKING THE SEVEN-PATH STRUCTURE OF THE CLASSICAL LABYRINTH WITH NATURE AND OTHER SYMBOLS

When I was first exploring the importance and significance of the symbolism of the classical labyrinth and its seven pathways and centre, I began to notice how often seven appears in nature, whether it is animal, vegetable or mineral. The number seven also has a long tradition of being a magical and lucky number in many cultures. It is often regarded as the number of this planet Earth. Here are a few examples: a pebble dropped in a pool, or a drop of water dripping into a pool, produces seven ripples of water, each with its own energy, which can be detected by dowsing.

A stream of water from a tap or a waterfall has seven concentric rings of dowsable energy around it.

The Australian Aborigine tribes of the Gibson Desert used a pattern of seven concentric circles linked to pathways for body paintings which were used in a sacred ceremony to celebrate the meeting of man at the natural water holes (Fig. 11). Labyrinths are drawn in the ground and form part of ceremonial ritual, especially in New South Wales.

The usual rhythm of the surge of the strongest waves in the sea is either one in seven or one in five.

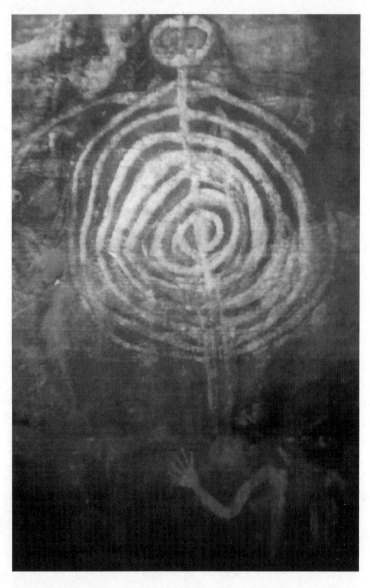

Fig. 11 'Water point' spiral, Aboriginal cave art, Australia

In the human body, both the larynx and the womb have seven layers of tissue surrounding the centre.

Every vertebrate animal, including the giraffe, has seven cervical vertebrae at the top of the spine, and eight cervical nerves. The ancient Egyptians considered these seven vertebrae to be the most important part of the spine. The giant Himalayan lily, *Cardiocrinum giganteum*, takes seven years from planting to come into flower. It then produces flowers every year which last for seven days. The leaves of the wild rose are divided into seven small leaves grouped on a stem.

There are seven colours of the rainbow and white light, or turquoise light, which resonates at the same frequency as white light.

In a diatonic scale in music, there are seven notes leading to the eighth note, the octave. The seventh note added to any three-note chord is significant in changing the character of the sound.

Seven occurs over and over again in fairy stories and in mythology. The magic seven-league boots of the hero, who was often the seventh son and also had magical powers, enabled him to encompass the world, usually in three strides. King Minos demanded seven young men and seven maidens.

There are seven chakras in the traditional Indian yoga and Chinese Buddhist teachings. There are eight planets, seven planets and the Earth, in our solar system. On 24 August 2006, Pluto was demoted from a planet. It was not known as a planet in the ancient world.

The classical labyrinth can be drawn with either a right-hand or left-hand opening: the cells of the human body can be either right-handed or left-handed. The rare Chinese reishi mushrooms were believed to confer immortality (Fig. 12). They look like a classical labyrinth.

The area which links the inner ear to the brain is called the labyrinth area.

Fig. 12 Red reishi mushrooms – Gandoderma lucidum

Symbols within the Classical Labyrinth

In his lecture to the British Society of Dowsers' Diamond Jubilee Conference in York, England, July 1993, Richard feather Anderson showed that the classical labyrinth also has within it the structure of other symbols.

If the classical labyrinth is drawn with straight lines instead of curved lines, it emerges as a plan view of a pyramid (Fig. 13).

Fig. 13 A Pyramid Labyrinth

The tip of the pyramid is at the top of the cross, the top part of the centre of the labyrinth. This is the shape of the step-pyramid at Saqqara in Egypt. It appears to have six steps and the apex. However, the first step (or first pathway of the labyrinth) is built underground and was originally lined with beautiful blue ceramic tiles. The entrance to the pyramid is above ground level, in the position of the third pathway (the second layer above ground). It is in the position of the entrance to the labyrinth.

When Pharaoh Zoser (2770 BC) asked his architect, scientist and doctor Imhotep to build the pyramid at Saqqara, the reason for building it was to help to save Egypt from a disastrous famine which had lasted for seven years.

To make the working plans, Imhotep studied and used all the ancient knowledge and wisdom of Thoth, kept in the library at Heliopolis. He was not finding his way through a learning curve. The pyramid needed to be built quickly if it was to relieve the famine, so he must have also used a known technology to achieve this.

Imhotep was greatly revered and was later deified, the ancient equivalent of sainthood. Presumably he succeeded in his mission to end the famine.

In addition to the circle-cross and the pyramid (Fig. 16), there are other interesting symbols and structures to be found within the classical labyrinth.

The stylised tree of life pattern is also the formation of the children's game of hopscotch, which is played worldwide (Fig. 14). The ancient symbol of the Tree of Life is usually associated with the Essenes (see Part II, Chapter V). It had seven branches reaching up to the cosmos and seven roots reaching down into the Earth. Humanity is shown in the centre, in the trunk of the tree, representing our connection with both the Cosmos (heaven) and the Earth.

Additionally, there is the zigzag shape of lightning (Fig. 14).

The six-pointed star, known as the Star of David, is also found in the labyrinth (Fig. 15). Traditionally, it has been seen as the symbol of the energies of heaven coming down to Earth and the energies of the Earth reaching up to heaven (as above, so below). The shape of the centre meeting place of the triangles is a hexagon, the shape of a bees' honeycomb. Scientists often use the hexagon in diagrams to show molecular structures and chemical reactions.

The game of Chinese chequers is based on the six-pointed star pattern.

Although the Star of David is a six-pointed star, it is a different shape from the star in the labyrinth. The Star of David is made of two equilateral triangles, each angle measuring sixty degrees. The star in the labyrinth is an isosceles triangle with two equal sides. The approximate measurement is seventy-two degrees for the two base angles, and thirty-six degrees for the apex angle of each triangle.

The shape of the triangles found in the classical labyrinth is also the shape used for the traditional pointed hats of witches and wizards in fairy stories, and for the dunce's hat. Was the dunce's hat originally a healing device, to clear the brain of harmful, disrupting energies, so that thought could flow freely and the brain would be able to function efficiently again?

The sign for infinity is contained in the labyrinth (Fig. 16). It is the shape of the movement of the hula dance of the Polynesian peoples of the South Pacific. It is also the shape of the dance performed by bees outside the hive before they fly off to search for honey, and before re-entering the hive on their return.

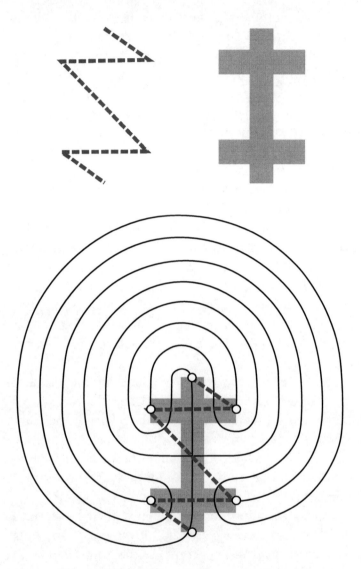

*Fig. 14 Patterns within the Classical Labyrinth:
the zigzag of lightning, the 'Tree of Life' and the game of hopscotch*

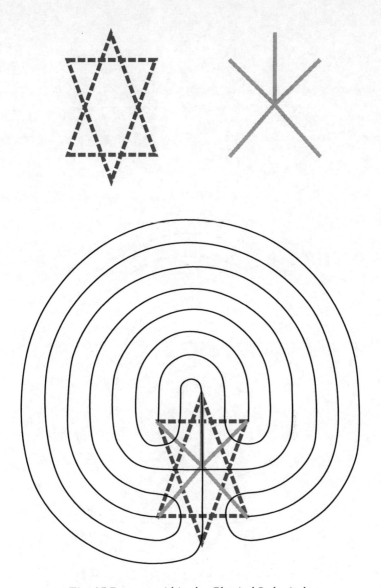

Fig. 15 Patterns within the Classical Labyrinth:
the six-pointed star and the star sign for Sirius

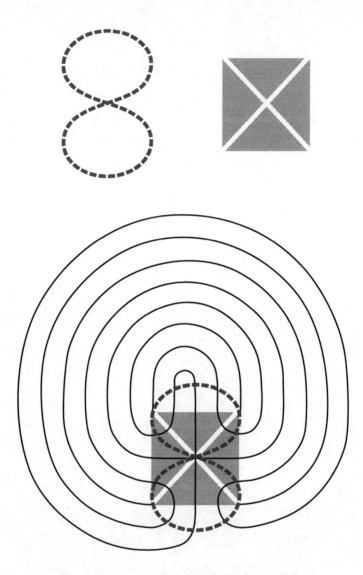

Fig. 16 Patterns within the Classical Labyrinth:
plan view of a pyramid, and infinity and the Hula dance

The symbol of the pharaohs of ancient lower Egypt was the bee. The coronation ceremony for the pharaoh was held at the pyramid of Saqqara. The pharaoh was considered to be the link between the gods and the Earth. In front of the pyramid there is a labyrinth structure of stones where the newly crowned pharaoh performed a ceremonial dance in the shape of the figure of eight, re-enacting the dance of the bees. This ceremony was performed every thirty years of the pharaoh's reign as an act of reconnection to the gods.

A diagram of a quartz crystal lattice (molecule) consisting of a balance of one silicone atom and two oxygen atoms (SiO_2) is contained within the labyrinth (Fig. 17). It is made up of a plan view of a pyramid and a three-dimensional elevation view of the pyramid, a hexagon, a five-pointed star, the six-pointed star and a cube.

The ancient Egyptian symbol for the star Sirius is made with five lines drawn in a star shape (Fig. 15 and Fig. 20). It is used to represent the cosmos in all the paintings on the tombs and in the temples.

For example, it covers the ceiling of Nefertari's tomb in the Valley of the Queens (eighteenth dynasty c.1550 BC). Nefertari was the favourite consort of Rameses II. Sirius was very important to the ancient Egyptians. The fertility and the prosperity of Egypt depended on the flooding of the Nile. The heliacal rising of Sirius (when Sirius rises in the sky at the same time as the sun) coincided with the beginning of the annual flood of the Nile and marked the start of their calendar year.

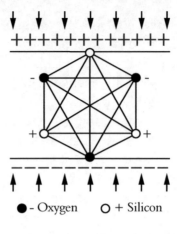

● - Oxygen   ○ + Silicon

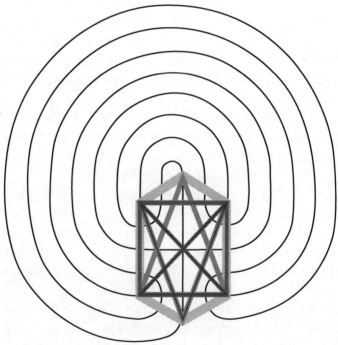

Fig. 17 Patterns within the Classical Labyrinth:
quartz crystal lattice (SiO₂)

When the Sirius star symbol is placed in the classical labyrinth, all the lines meet at the centre point of the cross. Four lines pass through all the turning points and the fifth line reaches up to the top of the cross at the top of the centre of the labyrinth. Is it reaching up and out into the cosmos, to Sirius, and beyond?

The five-pointed star, unlike the six-pointed star, and the five points of the symbol of Sirius, does not include the top of the cross which forms the tip of the centre section of the classical labyrinth (Fig. 18). We have found, through dowsing, that the symbol of the five-pointed star has strong, unbalanced, turbulent energy.

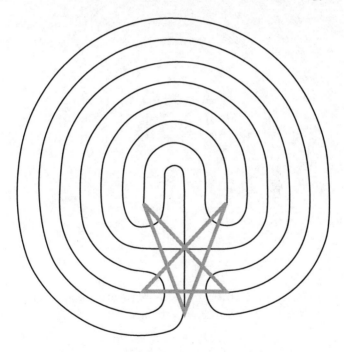

Fig 18 Patterns within the Classical Labyrinth:
the five-pointed star, the pentacle

The movement round the classical labyrinth shown by the arrows in the diagram (Fig. 19) appears to be chaotic, especially near the centre, until we realise the arrows are all moving in the same direction, along a single pathway to the centre and out again. We can see each pathway has a two-way movement, forwards and backwards, or right and left, depending on the outward or inward movement. It gives a centrifugal movement and a centripetal movement.

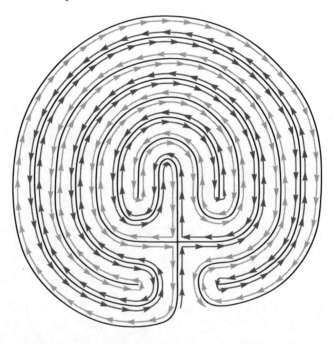

Fig. 19 Diagram showing the two-way flow of the pathways of the Classical Labyrinth

0 _____ 50 cm

Fig. 20 An architectural relief fragment of a naos (shrine) of
Nekhthorheb from Bubastis, thirtieth dynasty c. 343 BC
Nekhthorheb, wearing the blue crown, his two arms extended to
support heaven, represented by the Sirius star signs © The Trustees
of the British Museum. EA1106 Drawing by Claire Thorne

CHAPTER V

THE CIRCLE-CROSS LABYRINTH AND ITS CONNECTION WITH THE KNIGHTS TEMPLAR AND THE LEGENDARY HOLY GRAIL

The meanderings of the pathways of the eleven-path labyrinth of Chartres Cathedral form a circle-cross pattern (Fig. 10). I shall refer to this form of labyrinth as the circle-cross labyrinth to distinguish it from the classical labyrinth. Its entrance and exit is through the third pathway of one of the four sections of the labyrinth which are formed by the pattern of the pathways. In order to walk from the entrance to the seven-part centre and back to the exit, the eleven pathways have to be walked twice, making a total of twenty-two pathways.

Chartres is one of five great cathedrals built in France in the twelfth and thirteenth centuries. The others are at Toulouse, Orléans, Notre Dame and Amiens. They are built on very ancient sacred sites which were known in pre-Christian times as places of enlightenment, due to their planetary connection with Venus. Venus in ancient mythology was the goddess of love. All five cathedrals are built on very strong Earth energy lines, with Chartres at their pivotal point.

The cathedrals were built after the Knights Templar

returned from Jerusalem in 1128. The man most connected with the building of Chartres was St Bernard of Clairvaux, the Abbot of the Cistercian Monastery at Clairvaux. He was also one of the founders of the Order of the Knights Templar. As Bernard de Fontaines, he joined the struggling Cistercian Order in 1120. The Cistercian Order flourished under his leadership and he rose to become one of the most influential men in Europe.

In 1118, on the instigation of St Bernard, nine French Knights travelled to Jerusalem and presented themselves to the King of Jerusalem, Baldwin II. They said their mission was to protect pilgrims and the public highways from criminals. They would be soldiers of Christ and live a monastic life although they were not monks. They took vows of chastity, obedience and non-possession of personal property, showing they were totally trustworthy and could not be bribed. They were given a house on the site of King Solomon's Temple, and were known as the Knights of the Temple, or Templars.

Although their mission was enormous – the land was infested with robbers and brigands – they were completely independent and they took no part in fighting. Eventually they were given the sole use of Solomon's Temple. We can only assume, therefore, they must have succeeded in their mission…

It is thought the Ark of the Covenant was hidden in the Temple of Solomon for safekeeping. Its hiding place was always kept a closely guarded secret. We are told in the Book of Exodus in the Bible that the Ark was built by Moses to contain the Ten

Commandments and the Law (the Testimony), Exodus 40:20–21, written with 'the finger of God' on two tablets of stone which were given to Moses when God spoke to him on Mount Sinai for the second time (Exodus 34).

It has always been thought that nine Knights working alone could not possibly safeguard the Christian pilgrims in and around Jerusalem, especially as they did not fight. So it must be just another myth… Or did the Knights have another motive for being in Jerusalem? Was it to find the Ark of the Covenant and its treasure?

There is a legend that Mary Magdalene and some of Jesus of Nazareth's friends fled to Egypt and then to France after Jesus' crucifixion, and ended their days there. Jesus, John the Baptist and John the Beloved (Jesus' brother) were members of the Essene Brotherhood. Moses was also an Essene. The origins of the Essenes are lost in the mists of antiquity but certainly date back thousands of years. Their principles form the basis of all the great religions and were taught in Sumeria, Persia, Egypt, India, Tibet, China, Palestine and Greece. They were healers and astronomers and had a deep, fundamental knowledge of the cosmos and the Earth. The Essenes were also the authors of the Dead Sea Scrolls, written at the end of the first century AD, just before the Essenes in Palestine were wiped out by the Romans.

Perhaps some of them escaped the Roman slaughter and went to France to join their friends and their descendants, taking with them the knowledge of the secrets of the Ark and its hiding place.

Were these the people who founded the sect which came to be known as the Cathars? The Cathars lived in southern France until they, too, were wiped out on the orders of the Pope, another Roman, at the beginning of the fourteenth century.

Did the Cathars retain the knowledge of where the Ark and its contents were hidden, and is this the knowledge which somehow came to Bernard de Fontaines (St Bernard of Clairvaux)? Is this why he sent nine Knights to Jerusalem, and why the order of the Knights Templar was founded?

I am proposing that by the time the Knights Templar returned to France in 1128, they had discovered the Ark of the Covenant and had learned its secrets. They used the knowledge to build Chartres, most probably by using dowsing to guide them. The design and measurements of Chartres are based on sacred geometry, as is the great Temple of Karnak in Egypt. The building of Chartres and the other great Gothic cathedrals is like a miracle itself. The knowledge seems to have sprung from nowhere. There is no evidence of a learning curve. Suddenly, it seemed, the stonemasons were immensely skilled. Even today, modern architects and engineers say they do not have all the knowledge to be able to build Chartres.

To make sure the secret formula would never be lost, it was built into the floor of the cathedral, but its meaning, its instructions, were still kept hidden within the 'temple', with the Knights Templar. The secret formula is the circle-cross labyrinth. However, they left a clue: it was said that to walk round the labyrinth on your knees was the equivalent of a trip to

Jerusalem. Perhaps the purpose of Chartres Cathedral was to house the circle-cross labyrinth, well disguised among the many splendours of the building.

Within a relatively short space of time, great Gothic cathedrals were being built across Europe, and especially in England.

The Knights Templar grew to be an immensely powerful and rich organisation, but one that always used its power and riches ethically, for good. Eventually the King of France wanted to acquire their wealth, and they fell foul of the Church, the Inquisition and the State. On Friday, 13 October 1307, the senior Grand Masters were arrested in Paris simultaneously with thousands across France. A few escaped and fled to England and Scotland, but the Templars' 'treasure' and fleet seemed to vanish without trace before the King could take them over. After years of imprisonment, the Grand Master, Jacques de Molay, and the Preceptor of Normandy were burned at the stake in 1314. Both the King of France and the Pope were dead within the year.

Is the search for the Ark of the Covenant and its secrets encapsulated in the legends of the search for the Holy Grail?

Were the circle-cross labyrinth and the classical labyrinth kept together in the Ark? Do they hold the codes for accessing secret sacred ancient knowledge about the Earth and the cosmos? Are they the Law, written on two tablets of stone by 'the finger of God' and given to Moses on the mountain? Aaron's rod, kept in the Ark, was a dowsing rod, a means of accessing, verifying and activating the Law, the knowledge held within the code of the two labyrinths. My dowsing gives a 'yes' answer to all these questions.

Legend has it that Rosslyn Chapel in Scotland was built to house the lost Holy Grail, brought there for safekeeping by the Knights Templar who escaped from France.

We have discovered through dowsing that the simple diagram of a circle enclosing a cross is a shorthand symbolic version of the Chartres labyrinth. In Rosslyn Chapel there is a window which is a perfect, simple circle-cross. A window of this shape is very unusual in a church building of the fourteenth century. When the Knights Templar fled from France, did they encode the circle-cross labyrinth into the circle-cross window in Rosslyn Chapel, to let in the light and energy of the source of all energy, the essential cosmic life force energy for all life and all creation. Is this circle-cross window the legendary Holy Grail of Rosslyn? Is the circle-cross labyrinth it represents the Holy Grail, the Holy Grail being the key for breaking the code for creation?

If knowledge needs to be safeguarded, one way is to encode it and give only very few initiated people the key to break the code. The knowledge is safe provided the key is not lost. If the initiated are unable to pass on the code adequately and accurately, their knowledge will eventually disappear and lie buried somewhere in the universal consciousness in the energy fields of the cosmos.

CHAPTER VI

THE RELATIONSHIP BETWEEN THE CLASSICAL AND CIRCLE-CROSS LABYRINTHS AND THEIR HEALING PROPERTIES

The classical nine-part, seven-path labyrinth has been used, and is widely found, around the world. It is known to have special healing properties. The circle-cross labyrinth, except in the form of the simple cross in a circle, was not widely known or found. Each labyrinth on its own is effective. However, to be fully effective, to complete the puzzle, do they need to work together? Together they are extremely powerful so were they kept separately for safety's sake, perhaps to retain the knowledge and the power, in every sense of the word, in the hands of the initiated? It was like the situation of a woman who is asked to share her favourite cake recipe. She agrees, but to retain the secrets of her recipe, she leaves out a crucial ingredient.

The diagram of an eleven-path labyrinth is reflected in the drawing of the interference pattern of a macroscopic molecule of light within a quartz crystal (Robert Webster, *Gems*, cited in *Pi in the Sky* by Michael Poynder, 1992). It shows the pattern of the true Maltese cross and a circle-cross. One of the two symbols of the Knights Templar is the Maltese cross in a circle. The other symbol is of two knights on one horse. Is this a coded reference to the two labyrinths and their interrelationship?

The symbol of the Celtic cross which pre-dates Christianity, and the symbol of the early Coptic Christian Church, were circle-crosses similar to the Maltese cross.

The circle-cross labyrinth, with its eleven pathways leading to the centre, appears to have connections with the sun and therefore with the cosmos. The polarity of the sun alternates and the energies change from electric to magnetic every eleven years. The whole cycle takes twenty-two years. The sunspot activity takes eleven years to complete: five years to build up and six years to fade away. Interestingly, in ancient times the tilt of the Earth's axis was twenty-two degrees. It is now twenty-two and a half degrees.

In recent years, labyrinths have been widely studied, especially in America, and many excellent books and articles have been written. There is even a labyrinth website on the Internet. Many people have found great benefit from walking to the centre of a labyrinth and out again and healing has taken place in the centre of the labyrinth. The classical labyrinth used by fishing communities has already been mentioned. These were busy, hard-working people. It is doubtful they would have wasted their time if they could not see and feel the advantages of what they were doing.

All living matter, including humans, is surrounded by an energy known as an aura. It has within it all the colours of the spectrum. Although it is not visible to most people, many sensitive people can see this energy vibrating around a person, and it can easily be detected and measured by dowsing. Using dowsing to measure the extent of their auras, I asked about forty people to walk round a classical labyrinth marked out on the ground. I also drew a classical labyrinth on a piece of paper and asked about twenty people to follow the labyrinth pathways with a finger of whichever hand they were comfortable to use. Both methods are known as walking the labyrinth.

In every case except one, I found the auric energy field expanded by two or three times its original size after walking the labyrinth. If there was a colour imbalance in the aura, it was rectified. If there was any damage to the aura, it was healed. This happened regardless of whether the person knew anything about labyrinths or not, and most didn't. Scepticism made no difference either, and there have been a few sceptics!

In the one exception, the person walked a few steps round the classical labyrinth and stopped for several seconds, then walked a short distance further and stopped again. She continued her journey to the centre and out again in this disjointed way. When her aura was measured after she had completed the labyrinth, it had not changed or expanded. After she had repeated the exercise, this time walking smoothly in and out, her aura had doubled in size.

I asked other dowsers to repeat the experiments. Some of the dowsers knew nothing about labyrinths. They had similar results to mine.

Using dowsing to check the results, to our surprise we found that a small diagram of a classical labyrinth or a cross in a circle attached to the main electricity meter of a house neutralised harmful (i.e. unbalanced) electromagnetic energy being emitted from the electrical appliances in the house – the fridge, the kettle, the microwave and so on. When a small circle-cross is attached to a television set or to a computer and to its mouse or to a mobile phone, harmful radiation emissions are also significantly reduced.

We have found that to activate the energy encapsulated in the labyrinth for a specific healing purpose, the specific thought for that purpose is needed. The labyrinth protected the fishing communities because this was the thought of the people when they used it. When they stopped thinking why they were using the labyrinth, nothing happened. The labyrinth did not appear to work. Gradually, labyrinths became the victims of Chinese whispers. However, the symbols of the labyrinth patterns retain within them the original thought and knowledge of the people who worked out their format. When the labyrinths are used for healing, not only is matter itself healed, but the labyrinths are also re-energised by the thought, the consciousness, of the people using them.

As a healer, it is perfectly feasible to me that the nine original dedicated Knights Templar (one for each of the parts of the classical labyrinth) used the two labyrinths for healing and for protecting Jerusalem and the Christian pilgrims. They would have needed to live and work together but in isolation, and they would have had no need to fight. I suggest the nine original Knights Templar were in fact a powerful team of nine healers.

I find the two labyrinth patterns are very efficient healing tools, but how can a diagram heal? Why are they the shapes they are?

PART III
THE COSMIC AND EARTH LIFE FORCE ENERGIES

CHAPTER I

THE FORMATION OF COSMIC LIFE FORCE, THE COSMIC ENERGY FIELDS AND MATTER

Energenics proposes that the keys to the knowledge of how the energy which powers physical matter is constructed are found in the two ingenious codes of the circle-cross labyrinth (Fig. 10) and the classical labyrinth (Fig. 7 and Fig. 9).

I believe the circle-cross labyrinth is a diagram of the structure of the pure thought energy which originates from the Creator-God and flows through all creation. It is the diagram of the actual spark of creation. The thought process is continuous and ever growing; the universe is expanding and will continue to expand as thought expands and grows.

Thought is the ultimate energy. It is the basis of all creation. It is outside of time, outside of space. We can be on the far side of the world in a thought, or on the outer edges of the universe. We can travel back into history or into the future in a thought.

We know from our own experience of conscious thinking that thought contains both sound and light. We can hear and see our own thoughts with our mind's ear and our mind's eye. During meditation, many people can see wonderful clear colours which cannot be replicated in the physical world. Both sound and light are known properties of the universe in their denser frequencies associated with matter. In their frequencies within thought, sound and light are also outside of time and space.

The pure thought of the Creator-God, the source of all thought, has three wavelengths: the thought itself, the pure sound and the pure light of that thought. Together they form the cosmic life force, the sea of energy which fills the cosmos.

The concept of the three wavelengths of thought, sound and light, of and from the Creator, forming the cosmic life force, is encapsulated in the ancient symbol of the triple spiral which later emerges in Christianity as the Holy Trinity: God the Father, God the Son and God the Holy Spirit.

The original pure thought of the Creator-God, the source of the cosmic life force, is unconditional love. At the end of the fourteenth century, St Julian of Norwich was shown, through her visions and her subsequent meditations, that God is Love. She wrote, 'Love was His meaning.'

It seemed to me that in our sophisticated twentieth- and twenty-first century world, the word 'love' has become contaminated by innuendos of sex, control and desire, and its original meaning has become obscured, so I meditated and asked to be given the right words and the best way to describe the pure thought of the source, of the Creator-God. The words I received were 'kindness', 'respect' and 'compassion'.

Three cosmic energy fields evolve from the three wavelengths of the original thought energy of the

Creator-God at the source, to form the original eternal cosmic energy fields of soul, of spirit and of mind of the Creator-God at the source.

All other energy fields of soul, of spirit and of mind evolve from them and are connected to them.

A fourth energy field, the energy field of matter, evolves from soul, spirit and mind to form physical matter. Physical matter emerges and develops as the energy field of matter is completed.

Today, soul and spirit are regarded with some suspicion and scepticism, especially spirit. At best they are seen as nebulous, philosophical and religious concepts. In Energenics, the energy fields of soul, spirit and mind, together with the energy field of matter are all essential integral parts of all physical matter.

Each and every part of matter, from an atom onwards to the Earth itself, has its own energy field system of the four energy fields of soul, spirit, mind and matter. The energy fields are connected to each other and to their physical matter by the cosmic life force. The purpose of the energy fields is to receive, transform and transmit the cosmic life force into and through the energy field system and into and out and through its associated physical matter. Each of the four sections of the circle-cross labyrinth represents an energy field.

As well as being a map of the flow of the cosmic life force, the circle-cross labyrinth is also a map of the energenic structure of the energy field system of matter, all matter in creation including humanity. It even encapsulates the simultaneous aspect of all the energy fields working together outside of time, inter-woven by the pure thought of the Creator-God.

Energenics proposes that the classical labyrinth is a diagram of the formation of the energy fields which underpin all matter, including our own human bodies. The classical labyrinth is a plan view of the three-dimensional spiral structure and flow of each and every energy field of creation. The entrance and exit of every energy field is through the third pathway. When we are walking a classical labyrinth, we are directly in touch with all the component parts of our own energy fields. We are directly in touch with the Earth's energy fields and the cosmic energy fields, and the energy fields of the One, the Creator-God.

The flow of both the circle-cross and the classical labyrinths is two-way: into the centre, and out from the centre. The classical labyrinth shows how the life force flows into, through and out of each energy field. The circle-cross labyrinth shows how, and where, the cosmic life force enters the four energy fields, flows through to physical matter and comes back through the four energy fields and out again into the cosmos. It also enables us to see the detail of the interrelationship of the four energy fields (Fig. 21).

Dowsing shows:

- The first quarter of the circle-cross labyrinth, where the entrance/exit to the labyrinth is placed, represents the energy field of soul.

- Moving clockwise, the second quarter represents the energy field of spirit.

- The third quarter represents the energy field of mind.

- The fourth quarter represents the energy field of matter.

- The centre of the labyrinth represents physical matter itself.

- The energy field of matter leads into and out of the centre, i.e. into and out of physical matter.

- The centre is surrounded by six symbols, three on each side.

- The three on the left of the centre circle represent the thought, sound and light of the cosmic life force.

- The three on the right represent the thought, sound and light of the consciousness of matter which evolves from the cosmic life force flowing through the four energy fields into physical matter.

The formation of the pathways of the circle-cross labyrinth shows that the energy fields of soul and spirit are linked by five conjoined pathways.

The energy fields of spirit and mind appear to be mirror images of each other. They are connected by three joined pathways.

Mind and matter energy fields are almost a mirror image of the energy fields of soul and spirit. They are linked by five conjoined pathways.

The pathways of the circle-cross labyrinth do not give soul direct access to mind or to matter but it has to communicate with them through the spirit energy field, and the spirit energy field's connections with the mind energy field. However, the energy fields of soul and matter are almost mirror images of each other.

Fig. 21 The relationships between the energy fields of soul, spirit, mind and matter, and physical matter in the Circle-Cross Labyrinth. The six 'petals' surrounding physical matter at the centre represent the thought, sound and light wavelengths of the Cosmic and Earth life-force energies. C/L – Cosmic Light; C/S – Cosmic Sound; C/Th – Pure Thought of the Cosmos; E/L – Earth Light; E/S – Earth Sound; E/C – Earth's own Consciousness

Since the energy fields evolve from thought, and thought contains sound and light, each energy field and each pathway of every energy field has its own wavelengths and frequencies of light and of sound. The light wavelengths of the seven pathways are the seven wavelengths of colour of the spectrum. At the centre is white light, and turquoise, which is on the same wavelength as white light but vibrates on a different frequency.

The sound wavelengths and frequencies of the seven pathways and centre are the wavelengths and frequencies of the sound of the notes of the octave of the tonic sol-fa.

The seven junctions at the bends of each of the pathways of the energy fields shown in the classical labyrinth show the positions of the seven chakras. These are the spiral vortices of energy known for thousands of years through the Hindu and Buddhist traditions (described in Part I). The centre of the labyrinth shows two more parts – the top and the bottom of the centre pathway. This gives two more chakras, making nine chakras for each energy field (centre pages) – see Part IV, Chapter III.

The function of the chakras is to receive, transform and transmit the life force energy through the energy fields from one pathway to the next, enabling the life force energy to make a smooth transition through the wavelengths and frequencies of the energy field pathways, into the centre and out again into the next energy field, eventually into matter and back again into the energy fields, on and on into infinity and eternity.

Energenics proposes that each chakra is itself an

energy field and has its own classical labyrinth. Therefore each chakra has its own nine chakras and eight pathways. Each pathway of the chakra energy fields also has its own consciousness and frequencies of colour and sound based on the spectrum and the tonic sol-fa. The chakras play a vital role in maintaining the balance, harmony and equilibrium of the whole energy field system.

The classical labyrinth of the energy fields can have either a right-hand entrance/exit, or a left-hand entrance/exit. Dowsing indicates that the energy fields of soul and of matter have right-hand entrances/exits; spirit and mind energy fields have left-hand entrances/exits. The chakra energy fields have left-hand entrances/exits. The chakras of the chakras have right-hand entrances/exits. The energy field of the ninth chakra has a right-hand entrance and exit.

Thought and thought-energy exist outside of time, and the energy fields of soul, spirit, mind and matter are also outside of time. When they are attached and connected to physical matter, they become encapsulated in the time frame of that matter. Matter is finite. When matter 'dies', finishes, its energy fields are released and are reabsorbed into the infinite wavelengths and frequencies of the source, the cosmic energy fields.

The four energy fields bring to their matter its general and individual characteristics of uniqueness and its eternal connection to the oneness. They receive, transform, transmit and circulate the cosmic life force energy into and through the physical matter they support, ensuring its continual connection to the oneness, to the Creator.

During this process the cosmic life force, and its sound and light, absorbs the sound and light of the energy fields through which it is travelling, forming the consciousness, i.e. the processed thought of each energy field and its chakras and the physical matter which evolves, from the atom onwards.

The labyrinths show us how all the building blocks of creation are constructed from the one original thought through every dimension, wavelength and frequency of creation in the cosmos, the Earth and everything on and in the Earth, including humanity.

So what is the significance of a maze?

Perhaps a maze is a representation of our journey through life as we live it. Life is a series of choices and the paths we take in our lives are determined by the choices we make. Make the wrong choices and we are lost in the maze. Make the right choices and we quickly and easily arrive at our goal. Even if we make the wrong choices, eventually we will arrive at our goal and find our way out of the maze.

The labyrinth can also be seen as a pattern of events which make up our lives. There are twists and turns: we think we are getting somewhere and suddenly find we appear to be moving further away from our goal. Then, suddenly, everything comes together after all. We reach the centre and perhaps rest a little, because we still have to move on. Reaching the centre is only half the story, beautifully illustrated in the story of Theseus and the Minotaur. If the tune created from the labyrinth pathway sequence of sounds is played or sung, the tune created is unfinished at the centre (me, ray, doh, fah, te, lah, soh, doh; soh, lah, te, fah, doh, ray, me).

On 1 March 1980 a mathematician at the IBM Research Institute in upstate New York, Dr Benoît B Mandlebrot, discovered a very simple equation which became known as the Mandlebrot. The Mandlebrot Set was formed when it was put together with fractals, discovered by Professor Ian Stewart of Warwick University. Fractals are the geometric figures of the patterns in nature. They are continuing fractions.

The Mandlebrot Set produces a series of inter-locking spirals which seem to evolve from nowhere and which grow and spread, inter-spiralling into infinity. The colours of the spirals, which are all the colours of the spectrum of the rainbow, are not arbitrary. They are like a contour map, defining different areas of calculation. The Mandlebrot Set was described as 'the thumbprint of God'. When I first saw it, I realised I was looking at an accurate representation of the interwoven labyrinths which make up creation and its supporting cosmic life force energy. The spirals were described as islands in a sea of chaos but it is not chaos: it is labyrinthian, an amalgamation of the circle-cross and classical labyrinths.

As these ideas on the labyrinths were formulating, I began to wonder 'What *are* numbers?' We know they are a means of identifying and measuring and quantify-ing how many, how much, but that alone did not seem enough to justify the ancient Egyptian concept that numbers control the universe, a view shared by Pythagoras and Galileo. In ancient times all numbers were made from symbols for one to nine. Suddenly I realised that each of the symbols we call numbers one to nine represents the energy of a part of the classical labyrinth. So each number represents a wavelength and frequency of a pathway of the energy fields in the universe, and on and of the Earth, so numbers would hold the secrets of the universe.

Once we begin to understand these energies, we will begin to understand the universe and ourselves, as Plato and Einstein said we would.

As the cosmic life force energy enters the four energy fields and travels through them into matter and back again, it is both giving and receiving thought and its sound and light to and from the energy fields and their chakras. There is a constant two-way transforming and transmission of thought being processed into consciousness, between the energy field's physical matter and the life force energy.

Here on Earth, the effect of stars, planets, the moon, the sun, on each other and especially on the Earth and everything on the Earth, including humanity, has been known and studied and respected for many thousands of years. It is known as the art of astrology.

Astronomy is the study of the physical matter and geography of the universe and the cosmos. Modern astronomers have rarely recognised there is energy filling the universe, and therefore fail to understand astrology. Astrology uses the knowledge of the physical structure of the universe and cosmos in order to be able to study and interpret the effects of its energy structures, especially in relation to the Earth and everything on the Earth, including humanity.

Astronomy shows us that matter is spinning in space. We know the Earth revolves on its axis and moves with the other planets around the sun, and the moon moves around the Earth. The energy to produce all of this movement comes from the life force energy which fills the cosmos and links and flows through all the labyrinths of the energy fields of the cosmos and its matter, including the Earth. The basis of this cosmic life force energy is the thought energy of the Creator-God – pure unconditional love.

Creation is basically as simple as the combination of the classical labyrinth and the circle-cross labyrinth. It is, literally, love that makes the world go round!

CHAPTER II

INTRODUCING EARTH LIFE FORCE AND THE COSMIC LIFE FORCE CONNECTIONS WITH THE EARTH

Cosmic life force is essential for all creation, including our planet Earth and all life on the Earth, animal, vegetable and mineral. However for aeons the Earth has been looked on as 'Mother' to all life on Earth. The Earth is referred to as 'goddess' in the myths and legends of cultures worldwide. All physical life as we know it evolves from the Earth, is sustained by the Earth and eventually returns to the Earth.

Our mother Earth needs the cosmic life force from the source, the Creator-God, to enable her to develop and maintain all life of the Earth. Life on Earth needs both cosmic life force and the energy of the Earth which evolves from the cosmic life force in order to exist and thrive. Is this why God is seen as a father figure – 'Our Father' – and is instinctively given a masculine gender, and why the Earth is given a feminine gender?

I shall refer to this vital Earth energy, which evolves in the Earth's own energy fields from the cosmic life force, as Earth life force.

The knowledge of the Earth life force and cosmic life force coming together in balance and harmony to create and maintain all life on Earth is at the heart of the ancient Eastern concept of yin and yang, and the ancient Egyptian symbol of life, the ankh (Fig. 22).

Fig. 22a The ankh – the Egyptian symbol of life

Fig. 22b The symbol of yin and yang

The circle of the ankh represents the One and the cosmic life force. The horizontal line represents the Earth life force, linked to the cosmic life force, and the vertical line represents life which evolves from both the cosmic and Earth life forces.

The traditional symbol of balance and harmony between the Earth and the cosmos – 'as above, so below' – is the six-pointed star which is found in the classical labyrinth (see Part II, Chapter III and Fig. 15).

Triangles are the symbols of balance and harmony. The two triangles making the star, one pointing upwards and the other downwards, overlap to form a hexagon at the centre. They neatly illustrate the concepts of the cosmic life force coming to the Earth, and the formation of the Earth life force. They both reach out again into the cosmos after combining in the centre to produce life on Earth represented by the hexagon.

In Energenics, the three sides of the downward-pointing triangle represent the three component parts of the cosmic life force: thought, sound and light. Energenics proposes that the thought-sound wave-lengths of the cosmic life force are transmitted to Earth via the star Sirius, and the thought-light wavelengths are transmitted to Earth via the sun. These two wave-lengths of cosmic life force merge with pure cosmic thought energy as they enter the Earth's own energy field system of the four energy fields of soul, spirit, mind and matter, resonating simultaneously around and within the physical planet.

CHAPTER III

THE SOLAR AND THE SIRIUS CONNECTIONS WITH THE COSMIC LIFE FORCE AND THE EARTH

Human beings worldwide have always recognised the sun as vital to our lives and to the lives of everything on the Earth. The sun has been worshipped since time immemorial. The ancient Egyptians encapsulated their understanding of the life force energy coming into the sun from the cosmos in their concept of Amun-Ra. Amun is the power behind the sun; Ra is the sun. The symbol for the sun is a circle with a dot at the centre which sums up this concept beautifully. It is still used today as the sun sign in astrology. On the other side of the world, this same symbol for the sun was used by the Native Americans. They also called the sun 'Ra'.

As well as the symbol for the sun, ancient people's knowledge of the sun and the cosmos is apparent in the measurements of the pyramids and in the eleven-path circle-cross labyrinth (see Part II, Chapter VI).

The second pathway of the cosmic life force coming to Earth is represented by the second side of the downward pointing triangle of the six-pointed star, and comes to Earth via Sirius, the Dog Star.

Sirius is the forgotten star. It is one of the nearest stars to Earth, being eight to nine light years away (another connection with the classical labyrinth of the energy fields). We see it as the brightest and the most twinkling star. It is directly in line with, and below, the three stars of Orion's Belt in the southern sky. The ancient Egyptians knew the importance of Sirius. Their calendar was based on the start of the heliacal rising of Sirius, which occurs every 365 and a half days, almost the exact time it takes for the Earth to move round the sun. 'Heliacal' means the star rises and sets in the sky at the same time as the sun. Paradoxically, at that time, Sirius cannot be seen.

The start of the heliacal rising of Sirius occurred on 19–20 June, close to the summer solstice, and coincided with the start of the annual flooding of the Nile. For over 3,000 years this date did not change, in defiance of the progression of the equinoxes. The heliacal rising of Sirius now starts a little later, around the beginning of July.

'Sirius' in ancient Egyptian text means 'gives life'. The Nile is/was the lifeblood of Egypt, until the building of the Aswan Dam broke its back. The flooding gave annual regeneration, both to the Nile and to Egypt. It lasted for a period of forty days, known as the 'dog days'. Forty days is a period of time which reoccurs in many stories and legends. If it rains on St Swithin's Day (15 July), it is said it will rain for the following forty days. The New Testament tells us Jesus went into the wilderness for forty days.

Whenever the starry sky was painted in ancient Egyptian tombs, in temples or on coffin lids, the five-pointed symbol of Sirius was always used (Fig. 20).

Osiris ('of Sirius') and Isis (the wife of Osiris), two

of the earliest and most important gods or concepts of the ancient Egyptians, were closely connected with Sirius. Osiris represented life and regeneration and Isis is the regenerator. Both were seen as great healers. Osiris was also linked to the constellation of Orion. The three stars of Orion's Belt point the way to Sirius. The three Great Pyramids in Egypt are built as a replica on the Earth of the three stars of Orion's Belt. They also point the way to Sirius, as does the main shaft inside the Great Pyramid of Giza.

The Dogon and Tutsi tribes in Africa still have knowledge of Sirius and its companion star, known as Sirius B, embedded in their culture and knowledge. Sirius B is a white dwarf star and is not visible to the naked eye. It was not discovered, rediscovered, until 1862. The ancient Egyptian symbol for the Nile was the lotus flower. The flower head represents the delta; the long stem represents the river flowing into the delta.

The five arms of the Sirius symbol converge at a centre point. This is not the same symbol as the five-pointed star, made of five lines which intersect each other and known as a pentacle (Part II, Chapter III and Fig. 18).

When the symbol of Sirius is drawn in the classical labyrinth, its lines pass through and link all the turning points of the labyrinth, i.e. the positions of all nine chakras of the energy fields (Fig. 15). The link upwards with the ninth chakra, which connects directly with the cosmic life force, is particularly important. I will look at the energenic chakra system and the ninth chakra in detail in Part IV.

Briefly, the ninth chakra transmits cosmic life force directly into the eighth chakra at the centre of the classical labyrinth of the energy fields, and maintains the correct quantity and flow of the cosmic life force into each energy field and throughout the energy field systems.

I believe Sirius is connected to the Earth's own ninth chakra.

The theory of Energenics proposes that the energy fields of Sirius are used to transform and transmit the cosmic life force, enabling it to reach the Earth in exactly the correct wavelength and frequencies to achieve complete balance and harmony in the Earth's energy field system. The adapted cosmic life force will therefore be used by the Earth and all life on Earth with the maximum efficiency. Is this why Osiris and Isis were seen as healers?

Perhaps too much undiluted cosmic life force would be too strong for the Earth's own energy and for life on Earth and its 'voltage' needs to be reduced, just as electricity has to be transformed at various levels to match its usage. The origin of electricity is in the cosmic life force.

To summarise: the pure cosmic life force is the vital pure thought energy and its sound and light from the source of all energy, the Creator-God.

The sun adapts the colour – i.e. light wavelengths – and frequencies of the cosmic life force for the Earth. Sirius adapts the sound wavelengths and frequencies of the cosmic life force for the Earth.

These three components, Sirian-adapted cosmic life force, solar-adapted cosmic life force and pure thought from the Source, form the cosmic life force as it enters the system of the Earth's own four energy fields, vibrating in the Earth's aura and within the Earth itself.

CHAPTER IV

HOW EARTH LIFE FORCE EVOLVES FROM COSMIC LIFE FORCE

Earth life force evolves as the Earth itself evolves, both physically and energenically. The energy field structure of all matter, including the Earth, is the same. All matter from an atom onwards has four energy fields which act together as a vehicle to carry cosmic life force energy into and out of physical matter, providing the energy to power all the physical processes of matter.

Each and every individual energy field is a spiral in the format of a classical labyrinth.

Each and every combination of the four energy fields which form the energy field system is woven into the pattern of the circle-cross labyrinth by the cosmic life force flowing through them. This is the oneness of creation.

The uniqueness of creation is in each energy field system, which holds the programme and formula for the existence and development of its particular physical matter. It is transmitted into and through the physical matter by the cosmic life force. This applies to all matter from an atom onwards: the oneness again.

Atoms are the basic physical building blocks of all matter in the universe. They are the basic building blocks of the sun and of our solar system, of Sirius, and of the Earth and all life on and in the Earth.

The physical Earth develops from the atoms of all the ninety-two natural elements known in the universe. A vast amount of knowledge about atoms and molecules has been amassed since the nineteenth century.

Very simply and briefly, every atom is made of three types of particles, neutrons, protons and electrons. They are known as subatomic particles. The number of protons in an atom is exactly equal to the number of electrons. Neutrons have no charge, i.e. they are neutral. Protons have a positive charge. Electrons have a negative charge. The neutrons and protons together form the nucleus of the atom, and the nucleus has a positive charge.

The negatively charged electrons circulate at random around the nucleus. The nucleus is tiny in volume compared with the volume of the atom, and it is the heaviest part of the atom: it has the most mass. Although equal in number and equal in charge to the protons in the nucleus, the electrons have hardly any mass. The rest of the atom is regarded as empty space. The atoms of each of the ninety-two natural elements have different numbers of subatomic particles (neutrons, protons and electrons).

Molecules are the smallest part of matter (including gases) which form from the bonding together of two or more different atoms.

The most important and the simplest molecule of the Earth and all life on Earth is made from two atoms of hydrogen and one atom of oxygen, which bond together to form the molecule of water.

Energenics proposes that, in common with all matter, each atom has four energy fields, evolved from the energy fields of the Creator. They are soul, spirit, mind and matter, leading to the physical matter of the atom itself. The individual structure of each energy field is a classical labyrinth.

The four energy fields resonate around and within the nucleus of the atom. They are held together within the atom by the cosmic life force, in the energy pattern of the Creator and the pattern of the movement of the cosmic life force: a circle-cross labyrinth.

Therefore the movement of the neutrons, protons and electrons within the atom is not random; it is in the formation of the two-way flow of a circle-cross labyrinth. The space around the nucleus and the subatomic particles in the atom is not empty. It is filled with the thought, sound and light of the cosmic life force circulating through the energy field system of the atom, creating the consciousness – i.e. the processed thought – of the atom.

The blueprint and programme for each atom is held in the soul energy field, which provides the entrance for the cosmic life force into the energy field system and the physical matter of the atom. The blueprint gives the atom its own individual characteristics and determines the numbers of subatomic particles in the atom and its ability to bond with other atoms to form molecules. The programme is transmitted through the atom's energy field system, into and out of the nucleus by the cosmic life force.

The sound and light of the two-way flow of the cosmic life force through the circle-cross labyrinth of the energy field system of the atom produces the movement of the electrons, protons and neutrons within the atom and its nucleus. The negative charge of the electrons and the positive charge of the protons also evolve from the two-way flow of the cosmic life force.

The negative charge of the electrons evolves from the inward flow of the cosmic life force, and the positive charge of the protons from the outward flow. The inward flow produces electric energy. The outward flow produces magnetic energy. In other words, each atom behaves like a mini sun. The ancient symbol for the sun, a circle with a dot in the middle, is also a neat diagram of an atom showing the nucleus at the centre with the electron 'cloud' surrounding it.

The cosmic life force prevents the negatively charged electrons from merging with the positively charged nucleus. Usually opposite poles attract in electromagnetic energy. However, in thought energy (the thought, sound and light of the cosmic life force) like attracts like – negative attracts negative and positive attracts positive.

The four energy fields of each atom resonate around and within the nucleus of the atom. Energenics also proposes that the energy field systems of all matter formed from the combination of atoms, from the simplest molecule, to the Earth, and all life on the Earth, also resonate around and within their physical matter. The energy fields resonating around matter form that matter's aura.

The aura acts as a reservoir of cosmic life force for the energy field systems resonating within matter, and also reflects them. Any fault in the energy field systems within matter will be transmitted into the aura.

Each individual energy field system of each individual piece of physical matter, from an atom to the Earth itself, develops its own consciousness from the cosmic life force flowing through.

In common with all physical matter, the Earth and the Earth's own energy field system and the Earth's own consciousness are formed from the sum of all its parts from atoms onwards, physically and energenically. The Earth's own four energy fields hold all the programmes needed for the formation and combinations of all the water and minerals which make up the entire physical Earth.

The Earth's own consciousness forms the Earth life force. It also flows in the formation of the circle-cross labyrinth. The Earth life force, with the cosmic life force, is essential for all life on Earth. If either cosmic or Earth life force is deficient or out of balance or harmony with the other, life on Earth suffers, including human life.

Earth consciousness, with its sound and light wavelengths and frequencies, evolves from the pure thought of the cosmic life force and its sound and light as they are processed through the Earth's energy fields. Based on the Chinese concept of chi, meaning life force, and the principles of yin and yang, meaning the balance and harmony of the cosmos and the Earth, I have named the light wavelength of the Earth life force, which evolves from the light of Earth consciousness and the cosmic life force transmitted to Earth via the sun, 'electromagnetic chi'.

I have named the sound wavelength of Earth life force, which evolves from the sound of the Earth consciousness and the sound of the cosmic life force transmitted to Earth via Sirius, 'yiang energy' because it is a balanced mixture of the yin of the Earth and the yang of the cosmos.

The inward journey through the circle-cross labyrinth to the centre represents the flow of cosmic life force through the energy field system to the centre which represents the formation of Earth life force and the formation of matter. The outward journey from the centre represents the flow of the Earth life force through the energy field system.

The circle-cross labyrinth shows the cosmic life force enters the energy field systems of all matter from atoms to the Earth via the third chakra of the soul energy field. It returns through the energy field systems to soul, back into the cosmos, carrying with it consciousness it has absorbed from the energy field systems.

The Earth life force enters the energy field systems of all life on Earth via the third chakra of the energy field of matter. It returns through the energy field systems back to the Earth's own energy field system, carrying with it consciousness it has absorbed from the energy field systems of all life on Earth.

The cosmic life force and the Earth life force therefore flow in opposite directions through the energy field systems of all matter of the Earth and of life on Earth, from atoms and the essential molecule of water onwards, i.e. the Earth life force is a mirror image of cosmic life force.

The constant uninterrupted flow of the cosmic life force is essential to ensure the cleansing, balance and harmony of the Earth's own energy fields, and is therefore essential for maintaining the quality of the Earth life force.

Both cosmic and Earth life force are needed to keep all the energy fields of all life on Earth in balance, harmony and equilibrium. If either cosmic or Earth life force is contaminated in any way, or out of balance with each other, life on Earth suffers, including human life.

Thought, both the pure thought of the source and the cosmic life force and the processed thought of the consciousness of the Earth, powers all the processes of creation and evolution on and of the Earth. It weaves through the 'threads' of the pathways of the energy fields of the Earth and of life on Earth, like the warp and weft of woven cloth. If we could see the pattern of the weave, it would be a circle-cross labyrinth.

The circle-cross labyrinth is a very powerful tool for cleansing, balancing and healing the cosmic life force and the Earth life force, as well as for healing whole energy field systems, including the collective energy field systems of all the natural atoms which make up the Earth life force, and the synthetic atoms which contribute to it but also unbalance it.

The healing of the cosmic and Earth life force energies is very important. My dowsing indicates that the huge increase in the use of mobile phones and satellite communications since the 1980s is having a very harmful effect on the Earth, the environment and all life on Earth including humanity. It is also preventing the natural absorption of carbon dioxide into the Earth's atmosphere.

CHAPTER V

THE PHYSICAL EFFECTS OF COSMIC AND EARTH LIFE FORCE ENERGIES ON THE EARTH

There were several people in the twentieth century who discovered an energy of the Earth and the cosmos, and showed how it could be harnessed and used. Their efforts were not met with accolades!

One was Nikola Tesla, who was born in Croatia in 1856 and died in 1943. He moved to America in 1884. Tesla was a genius. He invented the AC induction motor, which is still the basis of the electrical power industry. He made many other inventions, including an invention which would have enabled anyone to access electricity without power lines, wiring and cables. His funding was cut off and his laboratory destroyed.

In the 1930s another scientist, Dr T Henry Moray, from Utah, USA, invented a mechanism for accessing electricity called the Radiant Energy Device. It was powered from 'the sea of energy in which the Earth floats'. This was also the title of a paper he wrote, published by Cosray Research Institute, Salt Lake City. His apparatus was destroyed and he was thanked with bullets but fortunately survived.

Another man was a psychiatrist, Wilhelm Reich,

again in America. In the 1950s he discovered an energy in the human body which he called 'orgone' energy. He recognised it was also an energy of the Earth. Using apparatus he had invented, he was able to generate energy without using fossil fuel – coal or oil – apparently from nothing. In 1954 he was ordered to appear in court by the Food and Drug Administration of America. The judge decided Reich was a confidence trickster and ordered him to stop his researches. When he continued his work, he was re-arrested in 1956 and jailed in March 1957. He died in prison in November 1957. That year, the Food and Drug Administration obtained a court order for Wilhelm Reich's books and research to be officially destroyed. They were still being burned by the New York authorities in 1960.

The Earth's own energy field system and its conscious-ness vibrate both within and around the physical structure of the Earth. The forces created by the cosmic life force flowing and circulating through them produce all the physical movement of the planet. This includes the movement of the Earth on its axis and through space, all the movement within the Earth, the movement of the Earth's crust and the heat which is generated by the friction caused by these movements.

The movement of the Earth's crust was only accepted by scientists in the 1960s and 1970s.

Two early pioneers of the geophysical theory of plate tectonics were Alfred Russell Wallace and Alfred Lothar Wegener.

Alfred Russell Wallace was a Leicestershire school-master, born in 1823. In 1854 he went to the West

Indies and then, inspired by Philip Sclater's book *Birds in the East Indies*, he moved to the East Indies to study and observe all the birds, animals, insects and plant life there. He wrote a paper on evolution, and the idea of 'the survival of the fittest' before Charles Darwin published his theories.

From his observations he realised that species in the west, for example monkeys, apes and thrushes, lived in the west but not in the east; and wallabies, kangaroos, cockatoos and platypuses, lived in the east but not in the west. Studying their habitats, he plotted a line which distinguished their biological and geological zones. It is called the Wallace Line. When the theory of plate tectonics was introduced in 1965, it was found that the Wallace Line follows the boundaries between the Indo-Australian and Eurasian plates.

The second pioneer was a German astronomer, meteorologist and Arctic explorer, Alfred Lothar Wegener. He noticed how the eastern coastline of South America seems to fit into the south-western coastline of Africa, between Nigeria and Angola. He put forward the idea of the movements of the Earth's crust and the sinking into the sea of some areas of the crust. In 1915 he published his book *On the Origins of the Continents and Oceans*. It was not well received. When he died in 1930, he was still being ridiculed as a notorious heretic.

However the discoveries of geophysicists in the 1950s and early 1960s led to the theory of plate tectonics, and we now know our seemingly solid Earth is anything but solid. Not only is it spinning in space and on its axis, the whole fabric of the Earth is constantly moving. The 'plates' are the shifting pieces of the Earth's crust which form the landmasses of the islands and continents, and the beds of the oceans. As they move and push against each other, the volcanoes and mountain ranges and valleys are formed. Volcanoes occur where subterranean movements of parts of the Earth's crust collide together, one pushing the other under. These areas are called 'subduction zones'. The volcanoes release the immense pressures which build up in the subduction zone. If the pressure is too great, the volcano explodes, or there is an earthquake.

Krakatoa, the world's most notorious volcano, is an island off the west coast of Indonesia. It sits on the subduction zone at the edge of the Indo-Australian plate and the Eurasian plate. The pressures created as these two plates crash together caused the volcanic eruptions leading to the explosion of Krakatoa in 1883.

The news of the explosion of the volcano of Krakatoa was the first huge natural catastrophe which could be recorded worldwide. The telegraph had been invented in the 1830s and its network of international cables linked east with west by the 1870s, using the Morse code invented by Samuel Morse in 1844. Helped by the telegraph and Morse code, Mr Reuter began his news gathering operation in 1858 and it was worldwide by the 1870s.

The final part of the eruption and explosion of Krakatoa produced two kinds of shockwaves, airwaves and sea waves. Although it was invisible, the airwave showed as a sudden burst of pressure on barographs worldwide, including the Royal Observatory at

Greenwich. When all these recordings were examined, they showed the airwave bounced round the world seven times.

There were two types of sea waves produced by the explosion: long waves and short waves. They fanned out westwards from Krakatoa, across the oceans of the world. The east was blocked by a landmass, which bore the brunt of the massive tsunami waves produced as the island of Krakatoa disappeared into the sea. The short waves travelled in a sequence of fourteen waves. They were first noticed at Galle, on the southern tip of Ceylon.

The long waves travelled in a sequence of seven waves and were recorded by automatic tide gauges around the world, as far away as Socoa near Biarritz in France and, finally, at Devonport in England.

Recent research into the complicated movements of the Eurasian plate and the Indo-Australian plate as they push towards each other shows the plates are moving in a direction which turns around a pole of rotation located a few miles to the south and east of Cairo in Egypt, in the area where the Pyramids are built.

When dowsing over a map of the world to pinpoint the physical location of the chakras of the Earth's energy field of matter, we found the eighth chakra – i.e. the centre of the classical labyrinth formation of the energy fields and the chakra which links directly with the ninth chakra connecting with the cosmic life force – was centred on the area of the Great Pyramid of Giza, just outside and south of Cairo. There are several pyramids in this area of Egypt, including the Pyramid of Saqqara (c.2700 BC).

Was one of the reasons for building the pyramids where they are, in the format they are in, to maintain sufficient cosmic life force from the sun, and especially from Sirius, to keep the Earth's own energy and energy fields, especially the energy field of matter, in balance and harmony to protect the Earth in this area of complicated plate and seismic activity?

It would appear the ancient Egyptians, in addition to their superior knowledge of the cosmos, also had a superior and intimate knowledge of the Earth and all its energenic and physical systems.

Perhaps the movement of the plates is not complicated after all but in the shape of the seven pathways of a classical labyrinth, with its centre south of Cairo.

Geophysics shows the movements of the Earth's magnetic energy fields seem to flow north to south, up and down. Do they follow the spiral pattern of the classical labyrinth with the entry and exit near the equator, where magnetic energy appears to be lowest?

The colours of the southern and northern auroras also correspond to the colours of the bottom (south) and top (north) pathways of the classical labyrinth spiral. Red, orange, yellow and green are the colours of the southern aurora; turquoise, blue, indigo and purple are the colours of the northern aurora.

CHAPTER VI

THE PYRAMIDS AND ANCIENT EGYPTIAN CONNECTIONS TO ENERGENICS

I think the pyramids of Egypt were built to access not only the cosmic life force transmitted to Earth via the sun but, especially, the cosmic life force transmitted to Earth through Sirius.

The formation of the pyramid is a classical labyrinth, built in a square form instead of a round form. The pyramid at Saqqara has the first pathway underground. The entrance is therefore on the third level, not on the second level, as it appears to be. The top of the pyramid represents the ninth chakra and forms a direct link with the cosmic life force. In the Great Pyramid of Giza, the centre of the pyramid labyrinth is in the centre of the pyramid at the end of the shaft. The position of the shaft leads to the King's Chamber within the Great Pyramid and points directly to the star Sirius. The three pyramids of Giza are built in the exact formation of the three stars of Orion's Belt: they are built on the Earth to link with Sirius.

The proportions of the pyramids of Egypt are based on sacred geometry, i.e. measurements which have their basis in the measurements of the Earth and of the sun and of the moon, and measurements found in nature. Research has shown that the proportions used for the measurement of each side of the base of the pyramid evolve from the measurement of the diameter of the Earth, i.e. the radius of the Earth x 2. The radius of the Earth is 3,960 miles; therefore the diameter of the Earth is 3,960 x 2 = 7,920 miles. Each side of the base of the pyramid is based on 7,920 miles.

The measurement of the proportions for the height of the pyramid evolves from the measurement of the radius of the Earth plus the measurement of the radius of the moon. The radius of the Earth is 3,960 miles; the radius of the moon is 1,080 miles. Therefore the height of the pyramid is based on 3,960 + 1,080 = 5,040 miles.

When the numbers of these measurements are brought down to their lowest common denominator to give the proportions of the pyramid, we have the radius of the Earth as 11, the diameter of the Earth as 22 and the radius of the moon as 3. Therefore the proportions of the pyramid are: each side of the base 11 x 2 = 22, and the height 11 + 3 = 14.

We can see from these numbers the pyramids have a strong connection with the circle-cross labyrinth and the classical labyrinth.

In 2006, modern astronomers decided Pluto is not a planet. The ancient astronomers did not include Pluto as a planet, and without Pluto the Earth, Mercury, Mars, Venus, Neptune, Uranus, Saturn and Jupiter, plus the sun, the moon and Sirius equals eleven. Using dowsing to plot on a world map where the ley line from Sirius connects with the Earth, the point coincides with the Earth's eighth chakra in the position of the pyramids of Giza.

When the pyramids were originally built, they were

clad in large slabs of white polished limestone. They were placed with a precision greater even than the outer cladding of today's space rockets. Limestone is a porous rock which easily absorbs water. The top section of the pyramid was covered in gold, representing the sun, and the tip was covered in turquoise. The colour turquoise has a neutral polarity, the same as the pure white light of the cosmic life force, the pure thought energy of the Source, the Creator-God, the power behind the sun. For thousands of years, turquoise was highly prized by the native tribes of North America.

I am suggesting that the pyramids were built as very important power generators, to access and use all the energy available in the cosmic sea of energy which surrounds the Earth.

The pyramids are not tombs and never were tombs. The pharaoh was seen as the supreme representative of the gods on Earth. The pyramid would have been the only fitting place to put the pharaoh when he died.

Knowledge of the true function of the pyramids was probably a closely guarded secret between the priests and the pharaohs. As the knowledge became distorted and lost over the centuries, the efficacy of the pyramids was gradually lost, but they still have remarkable healing properties.

Was the special secret knowledge kept by the priests the code of the circle-cross labyrinth? It is the cipher for decoding the interlocking sequences of the energy fields of physical matter and the movement of the cosmic life force, the cosmic sea of energy, and of the Earth life force. It holds the secret of matter; it is a map of the energy within an atom.

Without the map, the movement inside an atom appears to be random. The circle-cross labyrinth is a journey to the centre and out again, along one single convoluted pathway, one thread. To access the energy, including the light and sound within an atom, the atom need not be split with all the attendant damaging side effects. It could simply be unwound.

The ancient Egyptians had knowledge of, and used, sonar and light technology which we have not yet accessed.

When the pyramids and the huge temples were built, was sonar energy used to cancel gravity, so that the heaviest stones were reduced to the weight of feathers, making the building process very easy, quick and accurate?

The interior of the pyramids, the inner depths of the temples and the inner depths of the tombs in the Valley of the Kings would have been in complete darkness. The tombs are tunnelled deep into the hillsides yet the walls and ceilings are covered with intricate, delicate paintings, especially in the burial chamber in the deepest part of the tomb. There must have been some form of electricity to give the painters the light to do their work. Candles and burning torches would certainly not have been sufficient; they would have used too much oxygen as well as leaving sooty deposits. Did they use the light within the cosmic life force?

Were the technologies the ancient Egyptians used developed from unravelling the atom and using the cosmic sea of energy?

When the unending eternal energy of the cosmic

life force is harnessed, all the energy problems of our civilization will be solved. We will no longer need to plunder and ruin the planet to the detriment of it and of us all.

CHAPTER VII

THE ROLE OF WATER AND OF CRYSTALS IN ENERGENICS

One of the simplest and most important molecules of planet Earth is made from two atoms of hydrogen fused with one atom of oxygen to produce the molecule of water. Water covers four fifths of the Earth's surface. Our own human bodies are also made of seventy to eighty per cent water. We know all life on Earth depends on water, but it is not just the wetness of water and the physical minerals dissolved in the water that make it essential.

We also know water is a very good conductor of electricity, which is one of the components of the life force energies. Energenically, water is used for conducting and connecting the life force energies of the cosmos and the Earth into, and through, the physical planet and the physical matter of all life on this planet, whether it is animal, vegetable or mineral. Experiments have shown there is virtually no difference in the basic compositions of blood, sap and seawater.

Other experiments have shown that when a snow crystal is thawed and then refrozen, it freezes back into its original shape, demonstrating that water has memory, i.e. it holds and stores consciousness.

The water formed as vapour in the Earth's atmosphere absorbs and remembers all consciousness received from the Earth's aura. The atmospheric water vapour eventually joins with the water vapour received from water which has evaporated from the Earth's surface, and clouds are formed. When the water vapour condenses and falls as rain or snow, it still carries within its energy field system all the thought, consciousness, sound and light it has received and absorbed and brings them directly to the physical Earth, as well as bringing the cosmic and Earth life forces within the water.

The life force energies transmitted through the rain and the water are used directly by the Earth's vegetation, by the soil and rocks of the Earth, by the Earth itself and by the seas and rivers and by all life in them.

The yiang wavelength of the Earth life force contained in the rain is needed to start the processes of building the molecules needed for growth. The electromagnetic chi wavelength of the Earth life force absorbed by the rain is needed to maintain the growth.

Each raindrop is a circle-cross labyrinth system of the four classical labyrinth energy fields which spiral to Earth. In effect, energenically, each raindrop is a miniature Earth. The raindrop also stores within its own consciousness the consciousness of all the other energy field systems it contacts on its journey.

Unfortunately, water remembers *all* the consciousness it contacts. It not only stores the two life force energies, it also stores human thought and consciousness and the distorted consciousness of polluted life on Earth. Acid rain is not only caused by physical pollution, but by the polluted thought energy, consciousness of the Earth and especially of humanity.

Recent work by Masaru Emoto in Japan, using frozen water crystals, shows the effects of pollution on water, and the effect of human consciousness on water in the form of words and music, i.e. thought sound, either written or audible. His experiments have produced some remarkable results. They confirm the actual physical effect of consciousness on water. Since seventy to eighty per cent of the matter of all life on Earth, including the human body and the human brain, is made of water, Masaru Emoto's work confirms the physical effect of consciousness, thought, on matter. The photographs in his book (Copyright © 2004, from the book *The Hidden Messages in Water* by Dr Masaru Emoto, reprinted with permission from Beyond Words Publishing, Hillsboro, Oregon) show the effect on the frozen crystals formed from water exposed to positive and contra written words and phrases. The frozen crystals of water labelled 'You Fool' are shattered. The frozen crystals of water labelled 'Love and Appreciation' are beautifully formed.

We know we cannot exist without oxygen, air and water. The air we breathe, as well as being a collection of essential atoms and molecules, also contains both the cosmic and Earth life force energies. We literally breathe them into our physical bodies. The thought, sound and light of the cosmic life force and the consciousness, yiang, and electromagnetic chi of the Earth life force in the air and in the Earth are needed to start and maintain the processes of photosynthesis which release oxygen and carbon dioxide from the surface of the Earth, and all the chemical processes needed to build and maintain all life on Earth.

Water plays an essential role in the formation of all crystals found in rocks and minerals. Crystals have a vital energenic function in the physical Earth. They are formed in three main ways.

The first is by the cooling of molten rock, known as magma, for example as in the formation of granite, a crystalline rock. Water tends to lower the temperature of the magma. The more slowly the magma cools, the larger the crystals of the various minerals which form. If the magma cools quickly, as for example with lava from a volcano, the crystals can only be seen clearly under a microscope. Sometimes as the magma cools near the surface, cavities are formed within it by the steam and other gases escaping. The cavities gradually fill with water, which eventually evaporates leaving, inside the cavity, crystals of minerals which had dissolved in the water. This is how amethyst crystals are formed.

Secondly, crystals are formed from a solution of various minerals dissolved in water, deep in the Earth. Due to the pressure beneath the surface of the Earth, the water cannot become steam and at the very high temperatures involved, up to 850 degrees Celsius, these substances are able to be dissolved in the water. The hot solutions of water and minerals are shot through the rock, forming 'veins'. Gradually, as the solutions cool and the water content evaporates, layers of crystals are formed, including metals such as silver and gold.

Thirdly, there are crystals which have grown very

slowly in rocks which have basically been cooked under pressure, very deep in the Earth, at least twelve kilometres below the surface. The rocks have been subjected to intense heat and pressure. If the rock cools quickly enough, crystals will be preserved. For example, garnets and other gemstones are formed in this way.

Energenically, crystals have a clearing and cleansing role to play in the Earth's energy systems. Within the Earth, they have a similar function to glands in the human body.

A few crystals, for example quartz, have pyramids incorporated into their shapes. The atoms of the minerals in the crystals are arranged symmetrically in a lattice formation (for example, like neatly stacked oranges on a market stall). This lattice symmetry of the atoms gives the crystals their uniform crystalline physical structure. The crystals subjected to the high pressures deep in the Earth have the greatest symmetry in their formation.

The symmetrical formation of their atoms enables the crystals to directly transmit cosmic life force through the physical Earth, to ensure the physical Earth itself receives cosmic life force and a correct balance of sound and light. Therefore the crystals are used to maintain the balance and harmony and equilibrium of yiang and electromagnetic chi of the Earth life force throughout the planet and especially deep in the Earth. This is the essence of their healing properties, which have been known and used by humans for thousands of years.

The origins of jewellery began from finding ways of

attaching crystals to our bodies or our clothing so that their healing powers could be carried around with us. As well as their usefulness, they are very beautiful, and some are very rare. Gradually we forgot how and why they were useful and concentrated only on their beauty and rarity and therefore their value in terms of money.

Their usefulness diminished as our conscious knowledge of their life-force-enhancing properties was lost in the thousands of years of Chinese whispers. As that consciousness is renewed, the consciousness within the crystals can be reconnected to us. Today, many healers use crystals to assist in transmitting healing cosmic life force. This aspect of the energenic properties of crystals is being rediscovered and used again. There are many excellent books on the healing properties of crystals.

Trees have a very important energenic function on the Earth. In addition to water, trees draw up huge amounts of Earth life force from the Earth, eventually discharging it into the air and the atmosphere through their own energy field systems, which are programmed to act as Earth life force cleansers, in addition to the programmes needed for the trees' own lives.

If the Earth life force absorbed by a tree is polluted, or out of balance, the cosmic life force flowing through the tree's energy field system acts as a cleanser and neutraliser for the unbalanced Earth energy. The neutralised Earth energy is eventually discharged harmlessly from the trees' energy fields into the air, the atmosphere, of the surrounding landscape. Trees also provide reservoirs of Earth life force for the flora and fauna living in and on them. Without the energenic function of the trees, deforestation can eventually lead to desert and famine. Trees should be valued and preserved and planted in town and city environments where they are of great healing value to the health and well-being of the human population.

CHAPTER VIII
LEY LINES AND GEOPATHIC STRESS

In addition to the energy fields of the Earth, there is a separate and important network of lines or pathways of energy which covers the Earth's surface. They are known as ley lines. The equivalent in the human body are known as meridians.

There is a major difference between ley line pathways on the Earth and the energy field pathways of the Earth and of life on Earth. The pathways of the energy field systems carry the two life force energies throughout the energy field system into and through and out of physical matter. The consciousness of the physical matter evolves from these processes. The pathways of the Earth's own energy field system flow throughout the Earth from its deepest depths to and through the surface, back into the depths of the Earth, and into and out of the Earth's aura.

Ley lines lie on the surface of the Earth and *reflect* the consciousness which is created in the energy fields of the Earth and of life on Earth.

Ley lines do not contribute to the making of consciousness but they can, and do, affect the consciousness of the Earth life force and, subsequently, the consciousness of life on Earth, especially human life.

The strongest ley lines and the ley lines which most

affect humans evolve from the thought, sound and light of the consciousness discharged by and from humanity. For example, using consciousness, the Aborigines in Australia laid down pathways of consciousness from waterhole to waterhole. The consciousness pathways, the ley lines, became physical pathways enabling them to find their way across the deserts.

Most ley lines were laid down by the consciousness of generations of people, stretching back into very ancient antiquity. The strength or weakness of the ley line is increased or lessened by the consciousness of succeeding generations living, working, playing and fighting on or near the ley lines, constantly adding to the mesh of reflected consciousness covering the Earth's surface.

Ley lines are also strongly affected by the consciousness enfolded into the structures built by humans, including road building. Human-made structures on the Earth have an added energy complication. As well as a consciousness within the matter of the materials used to build them, they also absorb and reflect out into the ley lines they create the consciousness of the humans who designed and built the structures. They reflect the consciousness of the purpose of the structure, and the consciousness of the humans using them.

Provided the consciousness within the human-made structures is in balance and harmony with the Earth and its landscape, these structures will contribute to the well-being of the Earth and its life force.

If the design and use of the human-made structures are unbalanced and inharmonious with the Earth's own consciousness, the consciousness they discharge will distort the ley line. The Earth life force will be polluted in its area with potentially harmful consequences for the people living there. Human beings are particularly vulnerable to the effects of distorted ley lines and the resulting polluted Earth life force.

The collective unbalanced consciousness caused by excess fear, and its spin-offs of anger, cruelty and hatred reflected into the Earth's ley lines, has a very damaging effect on the Earth and the Earth's life force. Consequently, this damages the physical and mental health of humanity, and eventually damages all life on the Earth.

A ley line may be in balance and harmony with the Earth but sometimes it may be too strong for the people living over it. It will interfere with the balance of the Earth life force they receive, making it either too strong or too weak; an example of how it is possible to have too much of a good thing.

Water absorbs the consciousness transmitted through the ley lines, as well as absorbing and remembering the consciousness evolved from the Earth's energy field systems and the life force energies. If a ley line happens to follow the path of an underground stream, the water of the stream will absorb the consciousness of the ley line and reflect it back to the ley line. The effect of this is a doubly strong ley line in an area of underground water. Some life may thrive on this extra-strong energy, but some will not.

If a human habitually sits, sleeps or stands over a too strong or unbalanced ley line, producing unbalanced absorption of life force, whether it is at home, at work, at school or in hospital, that person's own energy field system will gradually be disrupted, eventually leading to his or her physical and/or mental ill health. The delicate energy fields of children are particularly vulnerable. This phenomenon is known as geopathic stress. It is one of the key factors in the cause of ill health, cancer and cot deaths, as published research carried out in Germany since the 1930s has shown.

Gustav Freiherr Von Pohl began his research in 1929. The Central Committee for Cancer Research in Germany published his findings and in 1930 he read a paper to the Medical Congress in Munich. His book *Earth Currents – Causative Factors of Cancer and Other Diseases* was published in 1932.

In Germany, architects and builders regularly use dowsing to check that houses are built in areas of safe, i.e. harmonious and balanced, Earth energies, avoiding strong ley lines (see Bibliography and Further Reading for more books on this subject).

The scientific establishment in the UK does not recognise or accept that geopathic stress exists. Research into it and its effects is not included in any cancer, leukaemia, or cot-death research in this country.

Geopathic stress was a factor in one hundred per cent of the cases I have been involved with since the beginning of my work as a healer in 1988. Occasionally geopathic stress has been the only cause of the disease.

Digging and tunnelling to build new transport systems disturbs the ley lines at that place and can also unbalance the energy fields of the Earth and the Earth life force energies there. However, left to its own devices, the Earth seems to recover. Unfortunately, human intervention can make a bad situation worse if it is done on a purely physical level, without knowledge or reference to the underlying ley lines and energy structures involved.

The ley line of a human-made structure is drawn towards and links with the nearest structure on land or water, human-made or natural. The people who built Stonehenge, Silbury Hill and all the stone circles, standing stones and wood henges had a deep knowledge and understanding of the cosmos and of the energy structures of the Earth and how they connect and work together.

They used their knowledge of the energenics of the stone used to construct the monuments. The energy fields of the stones (or the wood) would receive and then transmit the cosmic life force into the surrounding Earth in that area. The ley lines formed from the reflected consciousness of the monuments and the people who made and used them carried this extra cosmic life force across the surface of the Earth, enhancing its fertility, making it more beneficial for the people living and working in its vicinity. The nearest analogy we have is of the multifaceted mirrors of the lantern of a lighthouse which hugely enhance and reflect the power of the light inside the lantern.

Stone circles, including Stonehenge and wood henges, were usually built with a stone called the heel (or heal?) stone placed nearby. Its purpose was to direct the ley line created by the monument, and to reflect cosmic life force, from the circle into the required direction to enhance the Earth life force in the surrounding land and area where it was needed. These monuments worked, provided the consciousness held within the structure included the processed thought of the knowledge underlying their construction and purpose. Once it is lost, the structure is 'switched off'.

The people building Stonehenge had the knowledge needed to use the sound wavelengths of the cosmic life force energy transmitted via Sirius to neutralise gravity, enabling them to easily move and manoeuvre the huge stones.

Ancient earthworks and barrows perform a similar function to standing stone circles. Glastonbury Tor and Silbury Hill are two famous examples. They were also sometimes used as burial chambers for the leaders of the local community, providing the best energy to speed a soul and its spirit into their right dimension but, as with the pyramids, this was not the main purpose and function of the monuments.

The Irish round towers, church spires and the obelisks of ancient Egypt were all built to connect with cosmic life force to enhance Earth life force.

As the stone circles and monuments have become damaged, dismantled and their main purpose forgotten, so the consciousness, sound and light they continue to emit becomes disjointed and ceases to be of any benefit to the Earth. They may even become detrimental by upsetting instead of enhancing the balance and harmony of the Earth life force.

The Chinese have understood geopathic stress and its implications for centuries. Their philosophy of feng shui is based on their knowledge of Earth energies and ley lines and ways of making them work for our benefit. However, it is not always possible to avoid unbalanced Earth life force so it is helpful and useful to know that healing using energenics can easily restore balance and harmony.

Feng shui consists of a set of general rules about the positioning and maintenance of objects in the house and the colours, i.e. light wavelengths, to be used so that their energy field systems will be in balance and harmony with ours. To be fully effective, each environment needs to be tailored as far as possible to the general needs and energies of the people using it. For various reasons, this is not always possible or practical.

The solution to all energy problems and to most physical problems is healing. Just as we can heal people, so we can heal the Earth, our homes and workplaces. Earth healing is especially effective if a group of healers work together to connect to the source of all energy, the Creator-God, and using meditation ask for the clearing and cleansing of all polluted energy, for the cause of pollution to be healed and for replenishment with pure cosmic life force energy to restore balance, harmony and equilibrium. Ideally, we need Earth healing groups in every town, city and village. Since the foot and mouth disaster of 2001, it is needed in the countryside, too (see also Part VIII, Chapter II).

CHAPTER IX

THE STRUCTURE OF THE ENERGY FIELDS AND LEY LINES AND THE ENERGENIC EQUATION

At present, the only instrument available to find out about ley lines and all the subtle energies of the cosmos, the Earth and life on Earth, is the cosmic computer of dowsing, using the ultimate scientific instrument – a human being with all its energenic and physical components.

Dowsing shows us that every ley line is divided into seven parts. When the line is in balance, the dowsing signals for each of the seven parts correspond exactly with the dowsing signals of each of the seven pathways of the classical labyrinth pattern of the energy fields.

The light energy of each pathway of the energy fields, and each part of the ley lines, corresponds to the colours of the spectrum. Their sonar energy corresponds to the tonic sol-fa scale in music (doh, ray, me, and so on).

The structure of a ley line is a simple spiralling, striped, rainbow-patterned ribbon.

There are three dowsing signals: positive, negative and neutral.

- The first pathway of the classical labyrinth of the energy fields and the first part of the ley line gives a positive signal.

- The second gives a positive signal.
- The third gives a negative signal.
- The fourth gives a neutral signal.
- The fifth gives a positive signal.
- The sixth gives a positive signal.
- The seventh gives a negative signal.
- The eighth part of the labyrinth, the centre, dowses as neutral.

If this is written as an equation, with the fourth neutral part as the equals sign, and excluding the eighth neutral part, we have two positives plus one negative = two positives plus one negative:

$$2P + N = 2P + N$$
$$2N = 4P \text{ therefore } N = 2P$$

Therefore, two positives are needed to balance one negative.

Putting the light, sound and polarity of the energy field pathways and the ley lines together we have:

- 1st pathway and part = red = doh = positive.
- 2nd pathway and part = orange = ray = positive.
- 3rd pathway and part = yellow = me = negative.
- 4th pathway and part = green = fah = neutral.
- 5th pathway and part = blue = soh = positive.
- 6th pathway and part = indigo = lah = positive.

- 7th pathway and part = violet = te = negative.
- 8th centre = turquoise = top doh = neutral.

This polarity applies to every frequency of the wavelengths of light and sound of every energy field in creation, and every ley line.

It shows the spectrum gives the same polarity equation, and the tonic sol-fa gives the same polarity equation. The seven pathways of each energy field give the same polarity equation: $2P = N$.

Both black and white contain within them all the colour wavelengths and frequencies of the spectrum. Therefore both black and white have within them positive, negative and neutral, so the energy equation for black is the same as the energy equation for white: $2P = N$.

The dowsing responses for each of the three parts of the cosmic life force are:

- Pure thought from the source is positive.
- Cosmic life force transmitted via Sirius is positive.
- Cosmic life force transmitted via the sun is negative.

Therefore, cosmic life force, to be in balance and harmony, needs two positives and one negative within it.

The dowsing responses for each of the three parts of the Earth's own energy, the Earth life force, are:

- The Earth's own consciousness is negative.
- Yiang energy (from Sirius) is positive.
- Electromagnetic chi (from the sun) is positive.

Therefore Earth life force also has two positives and one negative within it.

Although the polarity within the cosmic and Earth life forces differs, the energy equation $2P = N$ also applies to the composition of both cosmic and Earth life force. The polarity of the pure thought of the cosmic life force is positive, and the polarity of the consciousness of the Earth life force is negative.

The colour, i.e. the light, of the cosmic life force dowses as white. The colour, i.e. the light, of the Earth life force dowses as black. Both black and white contain the energy equation $2P = N$. When the energy equation within black and within white is in balance, both black and white dowse as neutral.

Dowsing shows that the polarity of the Earth life force taken as a whole is negative, and the polarity of the cosmic life force taken as a whole is positive. This shows the correct ratio between cosmic and Earth life force to achieve the optimum balance, harmony and equilibrium needed for all life on Earth is: two parts cosmic life force to one part Earth life force, i.e. $2P = N$. This is the same as the energy equation for the balance of the energy fields and ley lines. Too much of one results in not enough of the other. Similarly, a deficiency of one leads to an excess of the other.

The energy equation $2P = N$ shows clearly that positive and negative are essential to each other in the correct proportions.

Yin and yang are the ancient Chinese symbols for the concept of the perfect balance between the Earth (yin) and the cosmos (yang). The symbol itself shows yin and yang are inseparable.

144

Yin is represented by the dark side of the symbol, and has light within it.

Yang is represented by the light side of the symbol, and has dark within it.

The polarity of yin dowses as negative, and the polarity of yang dowses as positive.

In the Chinese tradition, either one out of balance, by excess or deficiency, will upset the balance and equilibrium of the other.

Traditionally, the Earth is regarded as 'the Mother', and therefore female. The Creator is regarded as 'Father', and therefore male. So the Chinese concept of yin has also come to be regarded as female, and yang has come to be regarded as male.

Traditionally, black is associated with yin, the dark side of the symbol, and white is associated with yang, the light side of the symbol. However, dowsing shows that both black and white have a neutral polarity, created by the balance of the energy equation $2P = N$.

- The dowsing response for 'imbalance' is negative.
- The dowsing response for 'balance' is positive.

Is this why, in our language, we have come to interpret negative as bad, and positive as good?

The interpretation of negative as bad (and therefore undesirable), and positive as good (and therefore desirable), has led to the mistaken perception that:

- Yin = Earth = black = feminine = negative = bad.
- Yang = cosmos = white = male = positive = good.

The concept of yin and yang has become distorted in Chinese whispers and has come to be interpreted as symbols for opposites, i.e. duality.

Used as a description of the interrelationship, complete balance, harmony and equilibrium between the Earth and the cosmos and their life force energies, the partnership of yin and yang gives a wonderfully concise and accurate symbol. However when it is used as a general description for the alternate energies in the duality of the Earth it has led, and still leads, to distortion and misunderstanding, which has infiltrated and become fixed into the psyche of human males and females to the detriment of both.

This flawed interpretation of yin and yang has led to centuries of repression and unequal treatment of women, by both men and women, to the detriment of both men and women. The sooner this flawed perception and its consciousness is corrected, the better it will be for humanity and the Earth itself and therefore all other life on Earth. Its flawed consciousness is upsetting the balance, harmony and equilibrium of the consciousness of the Earth life force, and polluting the cosmic life force as it is transmitted through the energy fields of the Earth and of all life on Earth, especially humanity.

Some dowsers have found when healers are giving healing that the patient and the healer (usually female) are both over an area of Earth energy which dowses as negative and black. On the face of it, with our usual interpretation of negative and black equalling bad separately and especially together, it seems as though the (female) healer can only be doing her patient harm;

'black magic' springs to mind. Four hundred years ago she would have been branded a witch and, at best, burned or drowned.

Now with the knowledge that the Earth's own life force energy resonates as black, and has a negative charge, we can see that as well as accessing and channelling cosmic life force from the source into her patient, the healer is channelling into the Earth's own energy field; she is also bringing the recharged, balanced Earth life force into the patient, restoring balance and harmony to both life force energies. She has instinctively chosen an area for her healing which will benefit both her patient and the Earth.

Perhaps 'black magic' originally meant the Earth's own magic, the Earth's own life force. Traditionally the Black Madonna represents the Earth, the most famous being in Chartres Cathedral. By working only with the Earth's energy, without the double balance of the cosmic life force energy from the Source, from the Creator, the balance, harmony and equilibrium is upset and the result is bound to be detrimental.

CHAPTER X

THE ENERGENIC EQUATION AND THE BALANCE OF CONSCIOUSNESS

The Energenic equation shows one negative = two positives, $2P = N$. Put another way, negative consciousness weighs twice as much as positive consciousness. Therefore it requires only a little extra negative thought consciousness to tip the scales and upset the equilibrium and balance between and within the energy fields, with potentially harmful consequences for physical matter. Twice as much positive as negative is needed to keep the balance. Twice as much cosmic life force is needed than Earth life force to keep the two life force energies in balance.

The thought energy of the Creator, the basis of the cosmic life force and all consciousness, is pure, unconditional love: kindness, respect and compassion.

The basis of the processed thought, i.e. the consciousness of the Earth's own energy, the Earth life force, is fear, the sense of danger. In balance, it is the natural safeguard and defence for all life on the planet, and in the correct proportions keeps the equilibrium of safety and therefore of security and comfort. Life full of kindness, respect and compassion, safety, security and comfort is the ideal our Creator has for all life, especially human life.

Because of the 'heaviness' of fear, the consciousness

within the Earth life force is very easily thrown out of balance and tipped into excess fear, which generates the emotions of hate, anger, prejudice, guilt and, as Julian of Norwich said, 'Impatience and doubtful dread, the two pestilences our Lord would have us be without.'

The concept of the equilibrium and balance of consciousness was symbolised by the ancient Egyptians in Maat. Maat's symbols are a set of weighing scales, a plumb line and bob, and a feather. She also represents truth, balance and harmony, justice and music, i.e. sound. The scales represent the equilibrium of, and between, the energy fields. She shows it takes only a feather to tip the scales from balance to imbalance, and vice versa. The plumb line and bob, i.e. a pendulum, is one of the tools of dowsing, a way of accessing the truth. Knowledge of truth keeps fear in equilibrium. Fear of the unknown, the 'perhaps, could, maybe', the 'doubtful dreads', easily upset the balance of consciousness. Doubtful dread is pedalled daily by all forms of our modern media, by many politicians, by religions of all persuasions and by science.

Insufficient cosmic kindness, respect and compassion will result in too much Earthly fear, as the concept of yin and yang shows. Similarly, the equilibrium can be upset by insufficient fear. Too much positive is as unbalancing as too much negative!

Since negative and positive are both essential parts of processed thought, consciousness, I shall use the word 'contra' instead of the usual 'negative' to describe unbalanced, inharmonious and therefore potentially harmful consciousness.

Earth consciousness, and the Earth life force, becomes polluted if the contra-consciousness from the energy fields of life on Earth, especially humanity, becomes absorbed into the Earth's own energy fields within the Earth. We can see how humanity contributes to the ill health and malfunction of its own and other species, and the planet itself, simply by the contra way we process thought energy through our own energy fields!

The subliminal heat generated by the excess of our contra-consciousness and its effect on the Earth's life force contributes as much to physical global warming as the excess of carbon dioxide.

The sound and light components of the Earth life force energies are tangible and measurable. They are already used in medicine and science in the form of electricity, ultrasound, lasers, radiography and radiotherapy, and in computers, and so on. However it is the thought energy within the cosmic life force, and the consciousness produced from it, which is the essential essence, amalgam and activator.

Without the cosmic life force energy, nothing 'is'. We cannot 'be', and neither can the Earth. But at present it cannot be measured, except by dowsing.

If the Earth and its life force is out of balance and harmony, due to a deficiency of cosmic life force, like any other physical matter it will malfunction and fall sick. When the Earth is sick, *all* life on Earth suffers to a greater or lesser extent.

Originally the Kabbalah was the secret, unwritten tradition of learning handed down from Moses to the rabbis by only word of mouth, and kept secret by them. In 1592, a Kabbalist was 'one skilled in the mystic arts and learning'. Later, after Newton and Descartes, the dictionary describes it as 'the pretended tradition of the mystical interpretation of the Old Testament of the Bible'. The Kabbalah is now written down.

When verbal traditions were first published in the Middle Ages, punctuation was introduced. However, punctuation can drastically change meanings. Did the first punctuators unintentionally change original meanings in the Kabbalah and other oral traditions?

The medieval alchemists also unwittingly corrupted the concepts of creation and enlightenment which had been handed down from ancient knowledge. They equated them, literally, with material gold and matter and therefore with material wealth and riches. This, in turn, led to the most horrendous working conditions for the people involved in the quest to change lead, base metal, into gold.

They did not realise their clues were encoded in the language of our material world but referred to energy structures. They did not understand that 'base' consciousness could be balanced, healed and restored to golden consciousness by the addition of sufficient quantities of cosmic life force.

PART IV
THE ENERGY FIELD SYSTEMS AND
THE CHAKRAS IN HUMANS

CHAPTER I

OUR HIDDEN DIMENSIONS AND HOW THEY WORK

The energenics of human beings is basically the same as any other physical matter on the Earth, of the Earth, of the universe. We all have the same basic energy structures. We are part of the oneness of creation, yet each human is unique. The unifying energy of the oneness is the thought, sound and light of the Creator-God. All energy fields and the cosmic life force evolve from it. The cosmic life force is transmitted through all the energy fields of creation, and is essential for all physical matter and physical life.

The Earth life force is also essential for all life on Earth. It evolves from the cosmic life force and therefore also contains the thought energy of the Creator.

The formation of every energy field is a classical labyrinth spiral. The flow of the labyrinth is in and out. It can have either a right-hand or left-hand entrance. The flow of the life force energies along each pathway of the energy fields appears to move in the opposite direction to the next pathway. In fact, they are moving in the same direction, towards the centre and out again. Fig. 19 shows the seeming chaos of the movement. Remembering the labyrinth is one pathway, it is not chaotic at all, and not even complicated.

The circle-cross labyrinth shows how the four

classical labyrinths of the energy fields of soul, spirit, mind and matter of every energy field system integrate with each other to carry the cosmic and Earth life force energies to form physical matter, represented by the diagram at the centre of the labyrinth.

The in-and-out, to-and-fro rhythm of both labyrinths also shows how the four energy fields carrying the two life force energies vibrate in the aura and within the physical body *simultaneously*. The inward flow of the labyrinth represents the energy fields in the aura. The outward flow represents the energy fields vibrating within the physical body. They demonstrate how the energy fields affect the physical body, and how the physical body affects the energy fields.

The inward flow of the circle-cross labyrinth represents the cosmic life force entering the system of the four energy fields through the third chakra and pathway of the soul energy field in the aura.

The centre diagram and the outward flow of the circle-cross labyrinth from the centre represent the Earth life force entering the energy field system through the third pathway of the energy field of matter within the physical body. It shows how the two life force energies, although flowing together in the same pattern, flow in opposite directions through the energy fields.

The exit from the energy field system represented by the circle-cross labyrinth is the same as the entry. The cosmic life force exits through the third chakra of the soul energy field and returns to the cosmos. The Earth life force exits through the third chakra of the energy field of matter and returns to the Earth.

It is difficult to describe the interaction of these subtle energies and energy fields, which are outside of time, in a framework of language of our physical world which is bound by time. However, the interaction and relationships of the energy fields is particularly important for understanding human energenics and ultimately the human body and our physical lives.

If there is a block somewhere in the energy fields of the aura, the inward flow of the cosmic life force will be disrupted and depleted, leading to an excess of Earth life force flowing into the energy field system the opposite way.

If the connections between soul and spirit with mind and matter are disrupted or unbalanced, this will eventually lead to disruption and imbalance in the physical body.

The circle-cross labyrinth shows that before physical matter is formed, there has to be an interaction of first soul then spirit, then mind and lastly the energy field of matter.

In the energenic build-up to physical matter, there are five connections, backwards and forwards between the energy fields of soul and spirit, and between the energy fields of mind and matter. There are three connections between spirit and mind.

The circle-cross labyrinth illustrates how soul and matter (for example, the human body) almost mirror each other, and how spirit and mind do mirror each other.

Although they reflect each other, matter and soul have no direct contact. Their contact and connections have to come via the spirit and mind energy fields.

The consciousness of the soul energy field contains the complete programme, the blueprint, for its whole physical matter, for example a human being. In a human, it forms our deep sub-subconsciousness. It includes all the programmes needed to activate and maintain all the molecules, cells, organs and liquid/water content of the physical body.

The soul of a human being contains the consciousness of each lifetime of that soul's existence in the universe. It could have accumulated over aeons of our physical time, bearing in mind that the source of our energy fields of soul, spirit, mind and matter, to which all energy fields belong, is eternal and outside of time.

The spirit energy field receives and transforms the soul's consciousness so that it can be transmitted and assimilated into the mind energy field. In a human, it forms our deep subconsciousness and the vital two-way link between soul and mind, the energy field of matter and the physical body. The physical body cannot access spirit and soul directly, except through mind. Soul cannot access mind and matter directly except through spirit. Soul and spirit contain the 'essence' of the human being. Mind transmits that essence into the energy field of matter. The energy field of matter transmits it into the physical life.

In addition to its own consciousness, the mind energy field provides access to and from the deep sub-subconsciousness of the energy fields of spirit and soul, as well as to and from the conscious consciousness of the energy field of matter and therefore physical matter itself.

As processed consciousness from mind and matter

is transmitted back through the energy field system to spirit and soul, it can eventually affect the blueprint and programmes held in the soul for its physical matter, for good or ill. For example, the residual contra-consciousness of contra events in babyhood and childhood can affect the functioning of the physical body later in life.

Provided the energy equation $2P = N$ is maintained in the energy field system and in the cosmic and Earth life forces flowing through, the balance, harmony and equilibrium of physical matter will also be maintained.

It is vital for the physical and mental health and well-being of a human being that the three wave-lengths of consciousness – i.e. sub-subconscious, subconscious and conscious-consciousness of the mind energy field's own consciousness – are in balance, harmony and equilibrium. This enables us to consciously alter our thinking to bring in more of the kindness, respect and compassion of the cosmic life force to neutralise excess fear and its adverse effects.

The fourth energy field shown in the circle-cross labyrinth is the energy field of matter. It leads directly to physical matter and transmits into physical matter, via the life force energies, all the programmes for all the chemical processes needed for the complete functioning of physical matter, from a molecule to the whole physical body. The cosmic and Earth life forces also provide the energy to power and maintain all these physical processes.

Simultaneously with the cosmic life force, the Earth life force enters the energy field system but through the third chakra of the energy field of matter. The energy field of matter has direct access to the Earth life force as the soul has direct access to the cosmic life force.

The circle-cross labyrinth shows that the energy fields of mind and matter are inseparable, and the energy fields of spirit and of soul are also inseparable.

As well as contributing to our everyday thinking in the mind energy field, we experience the consciousness of the energy field of matter as emotions. Provided the energy field of matter is in balance, harmony and equilibrium and its energy equation $2P = N$ is maintained, our emotions will also be in balance and harmony and the equilibrium between the mind and matter energy fields will be maintained.

The consciousness of the energy fields is continually evolving and changing as the cosmic and Earth life forces enter and circulate through them, into the physical body and back into the energy fields. When the life forces circulate back into the cosmos and the Earth and the air we breathe, they carry with them an imprint of the consciousness of the energy field systems they have passed through.

This imprinted consciousness contributes to the atmosphere of a place, which in turn becomes part of the Earth life force of and in that place. A group consciousness builds up which may be harmonious or discordant for the individuals living or working there. All is well, provided there are adequate amounts of cosmic life force getting through. If cosmic life force is blocked for any reason, the Earth life force is further unbalanced. This can have a detrimental effect on some of the inhabitants or occupants, especially if their energy fields are already processing their own contra-consciousness. This is why it is so important to have schools which fit the children attending, rather than a 'one size fits all' system, i.e. making the children fit the schools, which will inevitably lead eventually to discord. The consciousness from the children who are not in their right environment will have a detrimental effect not only on those children but also on the school environment and *all* the children there. Although some will be more resilient than others, sensitive children and children who are already vulnerable will suffer most.

Human beings have been created with a unique programme enabling each individual human to choose how to consciously think and act: we have been given free will. The duality of the Earth created by the two life force energies of the cosmos and the Earth gives us our basis for choice: no duality, no choices. There would be nothing for us to choose between. Without choices we would have no opportunity to use, to exercise, our unique free will which contributes to our individual uniqueness, energenically and physically.

With free will comes responsibility. Using the consciousness of our own energy fields, and the thought content of the cosmic and Earth life forces, we are each individually responsible for the choices we make and for the actions we take as a result. Only each individual can decide how he or she will think and subsequently act, contra or balanced, harmonious or discordant.

A human being is the sum of all the energy fields of all the atoms, molecules, cells, organs, not only of itself but of the water and organisms living in the body. In other words, each human being is like a miniature planet or star.

CHAPTER II

THE INTERACTION OF OUR ENERGY FIELD SYSTEMS WITH OUR PHYSICAL BODIES AND OUR PHYSICAL LIVES

The energy equation $2P = N$ applies to all energy and energy fields, and their chakra energy fields, including human energy fields. We need twice as much cosmic life force as Earth life force to keep balance and harmony and equilibrium in and between the energy fields, and therefore in the physical body.

The programmes for the functioning of all aspects of the physical body from molecules onwards are held in the consciousness of the soul energy field. They are transmitted by the life force energies through the whole energy field system and into matter. The soul has the closest and most direct access to the Creator-God via its direct access to the cosmic life force. This is perhaps why the soul is so highly regarded in all cultures and is so closely linked with religion. It has led to the Chinese whispers which have relegated it to a philosophical concept, especially in Western cultures, instead of the factual, vital core of our existence. When it is functioning correctly – in the balance, harmony and equilibrium of $2P = N$ – the soul carries the thought, sound and light of the Creator-God, the cosmic life force, into spirit, where it is held as our reservoir of kindness, respect and compassion for ourselves and for everything we have contact with, physically, mentally and spiritually. Through spirit it is transmitted into mind, into the energy field of matter, and then into the physical body and into our physical lives.

The soul and spirit energy fields hold and store all the thought processes we regard as sub-subconscious and subconscious. These wavelengths of consciousness include the programmes for our autonomic nervous systems and for the processes needed in physical life which we do 'without thinking'. The circle-cross labyrinth shows how this subconsciousness, i.e. the consciousness we are not aware of, is carried forward by the life force energies from soul into spirit into the mind energy fields, where it mingles with the conscious mind. The colour, light and sound of the subconscious affects the light and the sound of the conscious mind energy field, and is carried forward into the physical body by the energy field of matter. Events and thoughts which lead to laughing and crying are two simple examples of this.

Similarly, the consciousness of events in our physical lives, and events which affect our physical bodies, are carried back through the labyrinths, through mind, back to spirit and then to soul, where it becomes absorbed into our programmes and eventually influences our spiritual, mental and physical reactions and actions. All is well provided the energy equation $2P = N$ is maintained in the energy fields.

All the energenic components of physical matter are outside of time and space. Simultaneously, i.e. outside of time and space, as cosmic life force is entering the energy field system through soul in the aura, the Earth life force enters the energy field system through the third pathway of the energy field of matter, resonating within physical matter, i.e. within the physical body. The two life force energies are travelling together through all the energy fields but in opposite directions.

Since the mind energy field controls our conscious thinking and consciousness and is integral with our physical bodies, it follows we could consciously control our mind energy field as we control our bodies. As a baby learns to control its physical movements, we can learn to control our mind movements. Some people are very adept at being able to consciously control the changes in wavelengths and frequencies of the mind energy field in order to access other parts of the energy field system. It is a form of mental gymnastics.

We do not think it is strange to see people do amazing things with their bodies in Olympic gymnastic competitions. Why should we think it strange, weird or unbelievable when some people can easily use their skills to access the consciousness flowing through other parts of their energy field system, which also gives them access to other energy field systems? EEG tests carried out on dowsers show the rapid changes which take place in the brain when they begin to dowse, when dowsing and at the end of dowsing. Dowsers are very agile mental gymnasts.

The information received and transmitted by the life force energies is essential for the correct programming and maintenance of all the molecules, cells, organs and liquids (water systems) which make up all the physical matter of the physical human body. If, and when, the life force energies are blocked and cease to flow, the physical matter ceases to function efficiently and eventually dies.

This applies to the Earth itself and all life on Earth, from the single cell of an amoeba to a human being.

The highly efficient, intricately simple communications network built up between the life force energies and all the energy field systems of humans, of humanity, of all life on Earth, of the Earth and everything on the Earth, extends out into the universe and the cosmos, back to the source, the Creator-God.

The four main energy fields of soul, spirit, mind and matter, and their chakra systems, provide all the programmes within the energy field systems of all the molecules, cells, nerves, organs, muscles, blood, bone, water, liquid, tissue which make up all the component parts of the physical human body. These subsidiary energy fields and their programmes are part of the four main energy fields of a human being, as the main energy fields of a human being are part of the energy fields of the Creator. All the subsidiary energy fields and the four main energy fields are connected to each other by the two life force energies flowing through.

The energy fields resonating in the aura around the body act as a reservoir of life force energies and consciousness for the energy fields resonating within the physical body, including all the subsidiary energy fields. If the main energy fields, or any of the subsidiary fields, are out of balance or synchronicity and therefore out of equilibrium for any reason, eventually the effect of this will be felt throughout the energy field system and in that part of the physical body related to it. Similarly, if the physical body is out of balance and harmony, or physically damaged, the energy fields may eventually be weakened and damaged.

We can use physical exercise to keep the physical body supple and in good order. We can also use the mental exercise of meditation to enable us to keep control of the mind energy field to give us mental agility and flexibility. This will enable us to change wavelengths so we can consciously access the sub or superconsciousness of the spirit and soul energy fields, and the higher wavelengths of the mind energy field near its centre.

In order to be fully connected to the life force energies, and therefore functioning perfectly, all the energy fields and their chakras need to be aligned together and in balance, harmony and equilibrium with each other. Any one disconnected or out of alignment, and therefore malfunctioning, will adversely affect the whole energy field system. The resulting imbalance will be reflected in the main chakra system of the main energy field system.

The nine main chakras show us when and where there are any faults anywhere in the system, and they show us when the faults are corrected. The simplest way to correct the chakras is by fine-tuning their colours and sound using dowsing and/or energy medicine, i.e. healing and meditation. This is why meditation has been proved to be good for our physical health.

CHAPTER III

THE ENERGENIC CHAKRA SYSTEM

The ancient Indian and Chinese knowledge of the main chakra system has been handed down almost intact. The colours of the chakras are based on the colours of the spectrum and are immensely important. They show us the wavelengths and frequencies of the light of the individual pathways of the energy fields. In the ancient traditions, the chakras are shown in sequence numbering one to seven consecutively.

In Energenics, the function of the chakras is to receive and transform the cosmic and Earth life forces, and to transmit them through the wavelengths and frequencies of each of the energy field pathways, and into and out of the energy fields themselves. It is very similar to the action and effect of breathing.

The information received and transmitted by the life force energies is essential for the correct programming and maintenance of all the molecules, cells, organs and water systems which make up all the physical matter of the human body. If, and when, the life force energies are blocked and cease to flow, the physical matter ceases to function efficiently and eventually dies.

The chakras are also energy fields, formed in the spiral of the classical labyrinth. They therefore have their own pathways and chakra systems, the chakras of the chakras.

Although the position of the main chakras in relation to the physical human body is very similar to the Eastern traditions, in Energenics the sequence of the flow of the life force energies through the chakras follows the sequence of the pathways and the two-way flow of the classical labyrinth. Therefore the entrance and exit of the energy fields is through the third chakra, and the third pathway. On the inward flow, the pathway leads out to the second chakra and its pathway, and then to the first chakra and its pathway. The first pathway leads directly up to the fourth chakra and pathway, and from the fourth directly up to the seventh chakra and pathway.

The seventh pathway leads to the sixth chakra and pathway. The sixth pathway leads to the fifth chakra and pathway.

The fifth pathway leads directly to the eighth chakra at the beginning of the centre pathway of the energy field. The eighth chakra leads through the centre to the ninth chakra at the top of the centre pathway.

The return sequence is as important as the inward sequence. It is the same for all energy fields, including the energy fields of the chakras themselves. To sum up, the sequence is: 3, 2, 1, 4, 7, 6, 5, 8 and 9, and returning 9, 8, 5, 6, 7, 4, 1, 2 and 3.

Dowsing shows that in all classical labyrinths the area of greatest energy is not at the centre, as might be expected, but at the turning point where the fourth pathway meets the seventh pathway i.e. at the seventh chakra.

The wavelength of consciousness of each pathway and its chakra, and its sound and colour, remains the same for every energy field of the energy field system from molecules onwards, for all life on and within the Earth, especially humans, and the Earth itself. However the frequencies of the wavelengths, the nuances of consciousness, vary from energy field to energy field and show in the varying frequencies of the colours and sounds of the pathways and their chakras.

I have found we each seem to have a 'key' colour. It may show as our favourite colour. Sometimes we feel drawn to a colour perhaps because, at that time, that wavelength of light has become depleted in our energy fields and needs to be recharged, like recharging a battery.

Our own 'key' sound will be the note we choose to sing at any given time, whether aloud or in thought. When we sing sound in thought, in our heads, we access all the frequencies of that sound from audible to subliminal.

Recharging the colours and sounds of the energy fields and chakras has a very healing, beneficial effect. It helps to return them to integrated balance and harmony. It restores the equilibrium between the energy fields and the free flow of the life force energies.

Community singing is an immensely powerful source of sound energy. It brings together an enormous range of wavelengths and frequencies of sound. Behaviour and achievement in schools has diminished since the communal singing of songs and hymns has been abandoned, or reduced.

Remembering our bodies are seventy to eighty per cent water, the varying effects of sound and music on physical matter are shown very graphically in the photographs of water crystals in Masaru Emoto's book (Copyright © 2004, from the book *The Hidden Messages in Water* by Dr Masaru Emoto, reprinted with permission from Beyond Words Publishing, Hillsboro, Oregon).

Energenics correlates the pathways and chakras of the three-dimensional classical labyrinth spiral with the human body. Using dowsing to verify the connections, it shows that some organs and parts of the body are connected to more than one chakra and pathway. The starting point is the third chakra and pathway because this is the *simultaneous* entry for the Earth life force in the energy field of matter within the physical body, and the cosmic life force in the soul energy field in the aura around the body.

The cosmic and Earth life forces flow together, but separately, through the energy fields and they flow in opposite directions. The third chakra also forms the junction between the energy fields, enabling the life forces to flow freely through all the energy fields of the whole energy field system, and physical matter.

To be in complete balance and harmony, all the energy systems within and around the body need to be synchronised. Therefore the definition of the chakras and the pathways relates to the main chakra system and the pathways of the main energy fields of soul, spirit, mind and matter of the whole human body. This encompasses the chakras and pathways of all the subsidiary energy field systems of the human body, from molecules onwards.

Time forms a climbing spiral and is part of the

physical aspect of creation. It is related to the frequencies, the vibrations, of the energies of physical matter. The slower the frequency, the denser the matter. And Earth has the highest density in the universe. Our physical lives in our physical, finite world are bound by time. Our language, both written and spoken, reflects this. Although we can think outside of time and space, we cannot read or speak outside of time. We need to remember this when describing the flow of the energy fields, the life force energies and consciousness vibrating simultaneously, eternally and outside of time.

To simplify the description of these simultaneous movements, I shall start at the entrance of the inward flow to the centre of the energy fields and then describe the reverse, outward flow. The spectrum colours and tonic sol-fa scale of sound encompass and symbolise all the frequencies of all their wavelengths.

CHAPTER IV

THE ENERGENIC CHAKRA SYSTEM OF THE HUMAN BODY (Figs. 23 and 24, centre pages)

The main energy field system mirrors all the subsidiary energy field systems of all the molecules onwards which make up the fabric of the entire physical body. Similarly, the subsidiary energy field systems mirror the main energy field system. Therefore a fault in one will show as the same fault in the other. The following descriptions of the energenic chakras relate to all the energy fields of the main energy field system of the human body. The sequence follows the pathways of the classical labyrinth.

The area of the body encompassed by each and every pathway and chakra includes, in addition to the organs, *all* the molecules, cells, neurotransmitters, nerves, blood, water and lymph systems, gland and muscular systems, and the skeletal and skin framework, i.e. all the physical matter of the body from atoms and molecules onwards in that area.

The Third Chakra and Pathway

The third chakra resonates on the wavelength and frequency of *yellow*, and the sound of *me* in the tonic sol-fa scale. It is centred on the kidneys. It receives, transforms and transmits the life force energies into the third pathway of the energy fields. The third pathway encompasses the area of the body connected to the part of the spinal cord passing through the sixth to the eleventh dorsal vertebrae of the spine, and their relevant pairs of spinal nerves. The organs in this area are:

- the kidneys;
- the stomach;
- the pancreas and duodenum;
- the spleen and diaphragm;
- the base of the lungs;
- the adrenal glands;
- the ureters.

I have already mentioned the importance given to the kidneys in ancient Egypt and ancient China. In Chinese medicine and acupuncture, the kidneys are considered to be the root and source of life and contain our 'essence'. They control the yin/yang balance of the whole body (i.e. the energy balance), and therefore the development and well-being of the whole physical body and its vital water content.

The third chakra and the third pathways of the energy fields connect with our instincts, our instinctive behaviour and characteristics, our 'gut' feelings and responses which are automatic to us as individuals, and which also govern our fight-or-flight responses to danger. If these wavelengths and frequencies of consciousness are out of balance and harmony, the physical body in that area will eventually also become unbalanced and inharmonious. The disruption or discomfort, i.e. the *dis*ease, caused to the consciousness may become some form of physical disease. The third chakra and pathways of the energy fields are vitally important to the whole energy field system. They control both the entry and the exit of the life force energies, in and out of each energy field. If they are blocked in any energy field, anywhere in the energy system, the flow of both Earth and cosmic life force will be distorted, adversely affecting the whole energy field system.

The Second Chakra and Pathway

The third pathway of the energy fields leads to the second chakra, which resonates on the wavelengths and frequencies of *orange*, and the sound of *ray* in the tonic sol-fa. The energy field of the second chakra is centred on the appendix and the cecum, the start of the large intestine. It receives, transforms and transmits the life force energies into the second, orange, pathway which is connected to and encompasses the whole area of the body which contains the twelfth dorsal and first and second lumbar vertebrae, and their relevant pairs of spinal nerves. It is a relatively narrow section, but it is also the area of the spine where the spinal cord ends and where ten pairs of spinal nerves are clustered together. These are four of the five lumbar nerves, the five sacral nerves, and the one coccygeal nerve. The roots of these ten nerves extend from this small area of the spinal cord to govern the end of the vertebral column (the spine) from second/third lumbar vertebrae to the coccyx at the base of the spine. The organs of the body connected into the second pathway are:

- the appendix and cecum;
- the middle part of the abdomen from the umbilicus, or navel;
- part of the small intestines;
- part of the colon;
- the ovaries and fallopian tubes;
- the ureters.

The second chakra and second pathways of the energy fields connect with our emotions. These are our thoughts and feelings which arise spontaneously from events which occur within, and outside of, our own lives; the thoughts which make us laugh or cry, which make us happy or angry. These thoughts are connected directly to the Earth's life force which, when it is in balance and harmony, is protecting and nurturing, leading to happiness and contentment, and Earthly sexual love. When the content of the Earth life force is overloaded, leading to excess fear, it leads to emotions of worry, anxiety, hate, lust, anger, frustration, impatience, and all the thought processes which lead to excess stress. This happens when the balance of the Earth life force with cosmic life force becomes distorted. Given the area of the body which will be physically affected by the stress, it shows a reason why so many people have back problems.

The First Chakra and Pathway

The second pathway leads to the first chakra and its associated pathway. They resonate on the wavelengths and frequencies of *red*, and the sound of *doh*, the first note of the scale of the tonic sol-fa.

The first chakra is centred on the uterus, the womb in a female, and the prostate gland in a male. It receives, transforms and transmits the life force energies into the first pathway. This is the widest and longest pathway of the energy field. It is connected to and encompasses the whole of the lower part of the body from the area of the second and third lumbar vertebrae of the spine, and includes the legs, ankles and feet. Although the spinal nerves for this lower part of the spine 'rise' in the spinal cord in the second pathway, their roots extend to their relevant vertebrae in the first pathway. The first pathway is connected to:

- the sex organs;
- the uterus;
- the bladder;
- prostate gland;
- the remainder of the colon and large intestine;
- the rectum and anus.

The consciousness of the first, red, chakra and pathway is connected to the physical aspects of our bodies and lives, to the physical cleansing and sexual functions of the body, to our Earthy, practical thoughts and emotions, and our innate common sense on a conscious level which enables us to organise our lives. The common sense comes from the thought energy of the balanced mixture of cosmic and Earth life force, flowing through the first chakra and pathway in the ratio of $2P = N$, combined with the chakra and pathway's own wavelengths and frequencies of consciousness. Common sense literally keeps our feet on the ground, physically, energenically and metaphorically.

The Earth and cosmic life forces reach the first chakra and pathway after passing through the consciousness of the third and second chakras and pathways. Their processed consciousness, balanced or unbalanced, will affect the functioning of the physical body in the area of the first pathway. We know intense emotion can make us feel 'weak at the knees'. Extreme stress or fear can cause incontinence. These are just two examples of how all the chakras and pathways of the energy fields affect each other, and how they affect the physical body.

The Fourth Chakra and Pathway

The first pathway leads directly to the fourth chakra and its associated pathway. They resonate on the wavelengths and frequencies of *green*, and the sound of *fah* in the tonic sol-fa scale.

The fourth chakra covers the heart and the spleen. The spleen produces all the lymphocytes needed by all cells. It creates the lymph system, which carries water in the form of lymph throughout the body. The heart controls the blood supply to the whole body. The fourth chakra receives the life force energies from the first pathway and transforms and transmits them into the fourth pathway.

The fourth, green, pathway encompasses the whole of the area of the body from the second dorsal vertebrae to the eighth dorsal vertebrae, and includes the spinal cord and spinal nerves in this part of the spine. The fourth pathway includes:

- the heart;
- the spleen;
- the upper arms;
- the blood and arteries;
- the lungs;
- bronchial tubes;
- the pleura;
- the chest, breast and nipples;
- the gall bladder;
- the common duct;
- the liver.

The fourth pathway overlaps the third pathway in the area of the sixth to the eighth dorsal vertebrae inclusive. It therefore also includes the stomach, pancreas and diaphragm.

The fourth, green, chakra and pathway is the balancer of the energy fields. It is the area where the cosmic life force entering the energy field through the ninth chakra merges with the Earth life force entering the energy field through the third chakra. The consciousness of the fourth pathway therefore merges cosmic love and wisdom with the Earthly emotions of the first three chakras and pathways.

The fourth chakra and pathway bring the unconditional love, i.e. the kindness, respect and compassion of the cosmic life force, into our instinctive emotions and therefore balances excess fear and contra-consciousness which may have crept in.

Is this the reason why 'love' is traditionally represented by a heart?

The fourth chakra is represented by the equals sign in the essential energy equation $2P = N$. The importance of the heart – physically, emotionally, intellectually and energenically – was well known to the ancient Egyptians.

The physical link between the sex organs in the first two pathways and the breast is well known. When a new mother is given her baby to suckle, it facilitates the shedding of the placenta from the womb. A newborn baby suckling at the mother's breast can produce contractions of the muscles in the uterus and cervix.

The basis of breast milk is water, which will have absorbed the mother's consciousness. If the mother's consciousness has been, and is, in balance and harmony, the baby will benefit both physically and energenically.

The Seventh Chakra and Pathway

Continuing the inward flow of the life force energies through the labyrinths of the energy fields, the fourth pathway leads directly up from the heart and spleen area of the body to the seventh chakra and the seventh pathway at the top of the head. They resonate on the wavelengths and frequencies of *violet*, and the sound of *te* in the scale of the tonic sol-fa.

The energy field of the seventh chakra, known as the crown chakra, is centred on the pineal gland, a tiny gland of immense importance to both the physical and energy structures of the human body. It is positioned in the deep centre of the brain, and its energy field system holds and transmits the programmes for the functions of all parts of the brain, physically and energenically. The pineal gland is our essential 'micro-chip'. The seventh chakra receives the life force energies from the fourth pathway and transforms and transmits them into the seventh pathway. The seventh pathway encompasses:

- the pineal gland;
- the beginning of the spinal cord;
- the first cervical vertebrae and its spinal nerve;
- the area of the crown of the head and the brain that includes the pituitary gland and the middle ear;
- the heart.

The consciousness, the processed thought, of the seventh chakra and the seventh pathway is associated with intellectual wisdom, i.e. wisdom connected with conscious reasoning. When it is in balance and harmony, it combines the Earthly thought energy of the Earth life force and the thought energy of the cosmic life force, brought together within the pineal gland. The Egyptians knew the importance of the role played by the pineal gland. It was represented by the cobra, poised ready to strike, on the crowns of the pharaohs. The crown encompassed and enclosed the area of the seventh pathway on the head of the pharaoh. The position of the cobra was in the position of the pineal gland, i.e. the position of the seventh chakra.

The cobra, an animal which has exceptional vision, also represented protection. When we have, and use, our inner vision as well as our outer vision, we are given the means of 'seeing' far horizons. We can be prepared for the dangers and pitfalls of life and life's events, and take the right and necessary steps to avoid and prevent them and, most importantly, to assess the implications of our decisions correctly. This knowledge is one of the sources of wisdom. It empowers us, giving us the opportunity to make informed choices and accept the responsibility which goes with them. The ability to access wisdom, which is available to everyone, is a particularly key attribute in a leader.

Our traditional illustration, the symbol, of the crown of kings and queens, especially in children's books and the paper crowns in Christmas crackers, is made of a series of triangles, linked together to fit on the top of the head above the ears, in exactly the position of the seventh pathway, and in the same position as the crowns of the pharaohs. Triangles represent the most harmonious form of energy. Perhaps the triangles represent true protection for the seventh chakra and pathway to ensure that the wearer of the crown can access true, harmonious, balanced wisdom needed to make the wisest decisions for the community.

Dowsing shows that in all the energy field labyrinths, the area of the strongest energy is situated at the joining of the fourth and seventh pathways; the position of the seventh chakra.

In two 'strides', the life force energies are transmitted from and to the first chakra at the base of the spine via the heart and spleen, the balancing fourth chakra, to the top of the head, the seventh chakra and the pineal gland.

Is this the basis of the kundalini energy rising up from the base of the spine to the head in the ancient Hindu concept?

As well as its importance in the physical body, the heart has an essential, pivotal role in the energenics of the human body. It links the brain with the lower part of the body. In terms of consciousness, it links the intellectual with the physical. The physical connection is already known. If a deep vein thrombosis in the leg reaches the heart, the result is catastrophe for the physical body.

A block in the energy of the lower chakra at the base of the spine would prevent sufficient life force energy rising up via the heart to the head, to the essential pineal gland which stores and governs all our programmes, physical, intuitive, intellectual and instinctive. The block would prevent the pineal gland from working at full efficiency and would therefore be detrimental, disrupting the transmitting of the correct programmes.

The Sixth Chakra and Pathway

The classical labyrinth pattern shows the seventh pathway is the smallest and shortest and appears to be nearest to the centre. However, it moves away from the centre and leads instead to the sixth chakra and the sixth pathway.

The sixth chakra and its pathway resonate on the wavelengths and frequencies of the colour *indigo* and the sound of *lah* in the scale of the tonic sol-fa. It is centred on the olfactory bulb and the hippocampus, the two most ancient parts of the brain. They store our memory banks, including our deep subconsciousness, transmitted into them from the pineal gland and its energy fields. The sixth chakra receives the life force energies from the seventh pathway and transforms and transmits them into the sixth, indigo, pathway.

As well as the olfactory and hippocampus areas of the brain, the sixth pathway encompasses:

- the area of the head from, and including, the centre of the forehead;
- the eyes;
- the cheekbones;
- the nose and sinuses;
- the outer ears;
- the tongue;
- the associated areas of the brain for the above listed.

Within the brain, the sixth pathway connects with all the cranial nerves and the four lobes of the brain in both right and left brain hemispheres. It includes all the brain tissue, fluid and neurotransmitters in these areas. It also connects with the second and third cervical vertebrae, and with their section of the spinal cord and with their spinal nerves.

The forehead, just above the eyes, is the area of the head we instinctively hold if we are trying to remember something, beautifully illustrated in Rodin's famous statue, 'The Thinker'. It is as though we are instinctively trying to connect and communicate with inner knowledge.

The consciousness of the sixth chakra and pathway gives us our 'sixth sense', our intuition, our ability to 'know' and to 'see' further than the logic of our physical, practical world. It enables us to quickly work out the best way to respond to events and situations which may be outside our control. It is the area of the 'third eye', which the ancient Egyptians called the Eye of Horus. Their god, Horus, is represented as a hawk. Like the cobra, the hawk's eye has amazing vision, enabling it to see its quarry from great distances. However, unlike the cobra, the hawk is able to fly and to hover in flight, to cover great distances and to keep still in the air. So the bird's-eye view of the third eye of Horus gives us even better information than the Earthbound snake's eyes give us. It gives us the ability to have an overview, a bird's-eye view of events, and enables us to 'see' in all directions, past, future, and all the twists and turns of the present. It is closely associated with the seventh chakra and pathway. The third eye of intuition needs the pineal gland to activate it. The wisdom associated with the seventh pathway is enhanced by the intuitive consciousness of the sixth pathway, and vice versa. The crown of a leader should encompass both the sixth and seventh chakras and pathways.

The colour indigo of the sixth chakra and pathway is a mixture of the wavelengths of violet and blue. It is a mixture of the purple of the seventh chakra and pathway, and the blue wavelengths of the fifth chakra and pathways, and indicates its close links with both.

The Fifth Chakra and Pathway

Continuing the inward journey through the energy field labyrinth to the centre, the sixth pathway leads to the fifth chakra and pathway, which appears to be moving even further away from the centre. The energy field of the fifth chakra and its associated pathway resonate on the wavelengths and frequencies of *blue*, the colour of a clear blue sky, and the sound of *soh* in the scale of the tonic sol-fa. It is centred on the larynx and the thyroid gland. The physical construction of the larynx is very similar to the construction of the womb. They both have seven layers of tissue surrounding the centre, i.e. they both have a classical labyrinth construction. The fifth chakra receives the life force energies which have absorbed consciousness from the sixth pathway, and transforms and transmits them into the fifth blue pathway.

The fifth pathway encompasses:

- the larynx;
- the thyroid gland;
- the lips, mouth, upper and lower jaw and teeth;
- the Eustachian tube;
- the throat, neck, neck glands, pharynx and tonsils;
- the shoulders and elbows;
- the area of the neck and spine, and spinal cord from fourth to the seventh cervical vertebrae and their spinal nerves (it does *not* include the eighth cervical spinal nerve).

The consciousness of the fifth, blue, chakra and pathway is associated with all aspects of communication and creativity, on every wavelength and combination of wavelengths of soul, spirit, mind and matter, and physical matter. The fifth chakra and pathway are closely associated with the intuitive consciousness of the sixth chakra and pathway.

The fifth chakra and pathway and its consciousness are immensely powerful and important to humanity. We cannot exist as a human race without creating, and our existence would be greatly impaired without the ability to communicate. Problems always arise among humans when lines of communication break down or are blocked, or become overloaded with contra energy. The fifth pathway holds within it all the transformed wavelengths and frequencies of the consciousness of the previous pathways. Just as it seems to move further away, it carries them to the centre of the energy field and to the eighth chakra.

The mathematical ratio 5:8 gives us the 'golden mean', the visual, physical proportions in nature of balance, harmony and equilibrium. There are five sides (including the base) and eight triangles in a pyramid (the four triangular sides and four triangles in the base).

The Eighth Chakra and Pathway

In Energenics, the eighth chakra at the beginning of the centre of the energy field holds the balanced and harmonious integration of all the different wavelengths and frequencies of the chakras and pathways of the energy field system. It resonates on the wavelength and frequencies of *turquoise*, and the sound of top *doh* in the scale of tonic sol-fa. Turquoise resonates on the same wavelength as white light, but on a different frequency. The eighth chakra is centred on the thymus gland. It also encompasses:

- the oesophagus;
- the trachea;
- the lower arms and wrists, and hands;
- the eighth cervical spinal nerve, the first dorsal or thoracic vertebrae, and its section of spinal cord and its spinal nerves.

The small area of the eighth chakra and the centre of the labyrinth form the datum point in the physical body for the synchronisation of the four energy fields: soul, spirit, mind and matter, and all their chakras. Energenically, its role is vital.

All the consciousness of all the energy field pathways and chakras come together at the centre. The thymus gland, although small, plays an essential role in keeping the balance and equilibrium of the physical body, both physically and energenically.

It is very interesting that the lower arms and the hands are included energenically into the centre of the energy field, where all the consciousness of all the pathways meet. The structure of our physical hands, with all their lines, is like a physical, coded book which records our programme as it unfolds and develops from birth and throughout life, and therefore tells all about us. Reading hands is a skill which has been practiced from time immemorial. Today, hands are used as diagnostic tools by some doctors, especially in mainland Europe. Hands are also used in reflexology as a map and guide to the whole body.

Physically, hands are linked to more parts of the brain than any other part of the body. Our programme and all our consciousness, recorded and transmitted through all the energy fields, from soul to matter and to physical matter, is also transmitted via our hands into our handwriting and, especially, into our signatures. When we make our own mark, using our hands or a hand-held tool, the mark or signature contains a coded summary of the entire consciousness of our soul, spirit, mind and matter energy fields, whether we are literate or not. It is possible to learn how to break the code and read all about a person from their signature. As we know, fingerprints are unique to each individual human being.

The centre of the energy field labyrinth appears to point upwards and the eighth chakra leads directly to the energy field of the ninth chakra.

The Ninth Chakra

The position of the peak of the ninth chakra is approximately two feet (approximately sixty centimetres) above the head, just beyond the aura and directly above the seventh chakra, centred on the pineal gland in the deep centre of the brain.

The ninth chakra energy field directly connects with and receives the pure cosmic life force and transmits it directly into the centre of energy field, and into the eighth chakra, making a direct link of cosmic life force to the eighth chakra.

The ninth chakra vibrates on the wavelength and frequency of *white* light and *top, top doh*, i.e. one octave higher than 'top doh' of the eighth chakra in the scale of the tonic sol-fa. The eighth, turquoise chakra and the white light of the ninth chakra vibrate on the same wavelength but at slightly different frequencies.

All the chakras are crucial but the ninth chakra is absolutely crucial to the well-being of all the energy fields, and therefore of the physical body. It protects the whole energy field structure and its physical matter. The ninth chakra ensures there is sufficient cosmic life force circulating through each energy field to keep the Earth life force in balance and harmony as it also circulates through the whole energy field system.

The main direct connection to the cosmic life force in all the energy field systems of matter is through the third chakra of the third chakra of the soul energy field. In addition to this constant main supply of cosmic life force, every energy field, including soul and including all the chakra energy fields, has its own direct access to cosmic life force through its own ninth chakra.

Provided the ninth chakra is fully open and is working efficiently, it will transmit into its energy field enough cosmic life force to balance any excess Earth life force or contra-consciousness which has been absorbed by the cosmic life force flowing through the system. The ninth chakra is the Creator's 'failsafe' device to keep the energy equation $2P = N$ intact throughout the energy field systems. It maintains the balance, harmony and equilibrium of matter, especially the human body and every aspect of its health. Problems arise energenically and physically when this ratio changes.

The structure of the cosmic life force energy is the circle-cross labyrinth. The ninth chakra of each energy field has to connect the classical labyrinth structure of every energy field with the circle-cross labyrinth structure of the cosmic life force. Therefore the structure of the ninth chakra has to be able to encompass and fit both.

The format produced to achieve this is a four-sided classical labyrinth i.e. a labyrinth drawn as a square instead of a circle. Each side, as in the circle-cross labyrinth, represents an energy field. The result is a pyramid (Fig. 13).

Taking a human being, the nine chakras of the ninth chakra's own energy field each connect with its corresponding main chakra in the main energy fields of soul, spirit, mind and matter of the whole physical body. For example, the third chakra of the ninth chakra connects with the third chakra of the main energy fields. Its second chakra, with the second chakra, and so on. This ensures the cosmic life force can be received, transformed and transmitted throughout the main chakras' own energy fields, through all the pathways of the main energy fields, and also throughout all the subsidiary energy field and chakra systems of all the component parts of the physical body.

Apart from its shape and construction, the ninth chakra differs from the other chakras in its size. It is large enough to cover the entire auric field of its physical matter. It forms a protective energy membrane of cosmic life force, spreading around outwards, above and below the aura. It extends to approximately two feet (sixty centimetres) below the feet, i.e. into our physical surroundings.

The ninth chakra is therefore able to ensure there is a sufficient supply of cosmic life force, and its sound and light, to maintain the correct balance of yiang and electromagnetic chi energies within the Earth life force where we are. Paradoxically, it is the ninth chakra which keeps us *grounded*. It 'fixes' us to the Earth, providing the cosmic life force energy we may need to neutralise any unbalanced Earth energies we encounter. It keeps the energy equation in balance in both our physical bodies and in the Earth. If the ninth chakra is malfunctioning, the harmful effects of geopathic stress, caused by unbalanced Earth life force, will be greater.

The concept of the ninth chakra is echoed in the Essene symbol of the tree of life. It shows a human in the lower trunk of the tree. The branches of the tree reach up to the sky, to heaven. The roots reach down into the Earth. The strength of the tree surrounding the human figure symbolises the protection given by the ninth chakra.

The effect of 'grounding' is also a protection for our lives as well as our bodies on this planet. It ensures our energy fields absorb Earth life force in the correct balance to give us enough caution to allow us to live our lives in security, and therefore in peace. Too much Earth life force tips the balance of caution into too much fear, with all its contra-allied emotions of anger, hate, frustration, impatience and doubtful dread. However, not enough Earth life force can mean we go blithely on in a well-meaning way, regardless of danger, only to find ourselves in awkward and difficult situations.

Regular use of meditation and visualisation will keep the ninth chakras fully connected to their energy fields, and the main ninth chakra connected to the main chakras of the entire main energy field system of the physical human body, and this will show in the aura. Measured by dowsing, before and after meditation, the dowsing response demonstrates the aura is strengthened and expanded after meditation.

The Reverse Sequence of the Chakras

The outward journey of the life force energies from the centre of the energy field labyrinth is in the reverse sequence of the inward journey to the centre. They flow from the ninth chakra, connected to the centre, and the eighth chakra, also connected to the centre. From the eighth chakra they flow to the fifth pathway and chakra, to the sixth, to the seventh, down to the fourth, then down to the first, up to the second, and out of the energy field through the exit at the third chakra, and into the next energy field entrance at its third chakra, and so on. The life force energies will have absorbed consciousness and programmes from the previous energy field, and will transmit them into the next energy field.

Summary

Some organs of the body – for example the brain, lungs, heart, stomach, pancreas and spleen – are covered by more than one of the main pathways and main chakras. The lungs span five chakras and pathways; the spine is completely connected into the whole energy field system.

Some organs of the body which appear unimportant in the physical functioning of the body are very important in the energenics of the body. For example, the thymus gland, the appendix, the spleen and above all, literally, the pineal gland in the brain. The uterus and the prostate gland are also very important beyond their roles in the reproductive cycle. Once their

Fig. 23 Classical Labyrinth: The circled numbers show the positions of the chakras in the energy field labyrinth. The colours and sounds show the wavelength of the pathways and the chakras. Important: the flow of the energy field in the body is in the rhythm of the Classical Labyrinth. It starts at the third chakra and flows in the sequence of 3 2 1 4 7 6 5 8 9 and returns 9 8 5 6 7 4 1 2 3

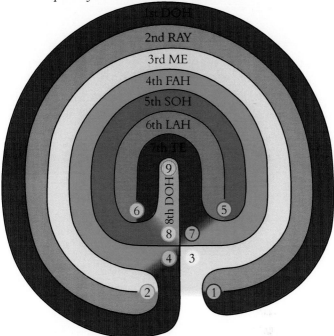

1st DOH
2nd RAY
3rd ME
4th FAH
5th SOH
6th LAH
7th TE
8th DOH
9

Fig. 24 [overleaf] shows the relationships of the spine, the spinal cord (shown in black) and the spinal nerves to the pathways, chakras, colours and sounds of the four main energy fields: soul, spirit, mind and matter. Each pathway includes all the organs in that area of the body. Note the areas where the pathways overlap. The chakras are centred on the areas of the body as shown. The spinal cord ends between the first and second lumbar vertebrae in the area of the second pathway and chakra. The area of strongest energy is the seventh chakra, which is centred on the pineal gland in the brain. The meanings of the pathways and their chakras in relation to a person's life are shown on the left of the diagram. Imbalance in a person's life may eventually show up in the corresponding pathway/chakra area of the person's body. The body cannot be fully healed unless the life aspect is balanced and healed

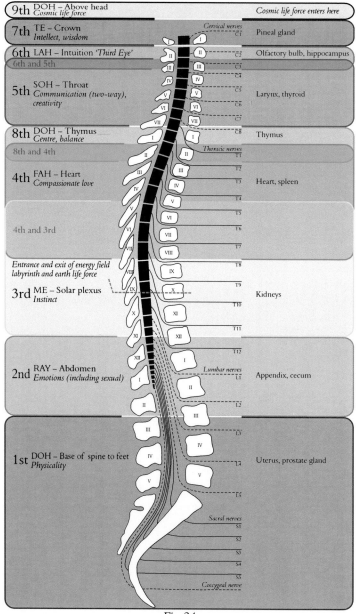

9th DOH – Above head *Cosmic life force*		Cosmic life force enters here
7th TE – Crown *Intellect, wisdom*	*Cervical nerves* I — C1 II — C2	Pineal gland
6th LAH – Intuition 'Third Eye'	III — C3	Olfactory bulb, hippocampus
6th and 5th	IV — C4	
5th SOH – Throat *Communication (two-way), creativity*	V — C5 VI — C6 VII — C7	Larynx, thyroid
8th DOH – Thymus *Centre, balance*	I — C8	Thymus
8th and 4th	II — *Thoracic nerves* T1	
4th FAH – Heart *Compassionate love*	III — T2 IV — T3 V — T4	Heart, spleen
	VI — T5 VII — T6	
4th and 3rd	VIII — T7	
Entrance and exit of energy field labyrinth and earth life force	IX — T8 T9	
3rd ME – Solar plexus *Instinct*	X — T10	Kidneys
	XI — T11	
	XII — T12	
2nd RAY – Abdomen *Emotions (including sexual)*	I — *Lumbar nerves* L1 II — L2	Appendix, cecum
	III — L3	
1st DOH – Base of spine to feet *Physicality*	IV — L4 V — L5	Uterus, prostate gland
	Sacral nerves S1 S2 S3 S4 S5	
	Coccygeal nerve	

Fig. 24

Fig. 23 Classical Labyrinth: The circled numbers show the positions of the chakras in the energy field labyrinth. The colours and sounds show the wavelength of the pathways and the chakras. Important: the flow of the energy field in the body is in the rhythm of the Classical Labyrinth. It starts at the third chakra and flows in the sequence of 3 2 1 4 7 6 5 8 9 and returns 9 8 5 6 7 4 1 2 3

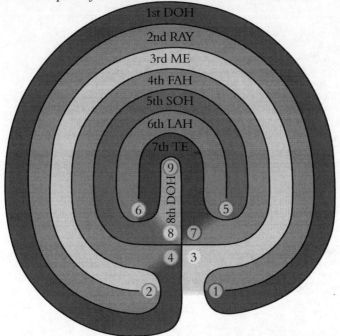

1st DOH
2nd RAY
3rd ME
4th FAH
5th SOH
6th LAH
7th TE
9
8th DOH
6   5
8   7
4   3
2   1

Fig. 24 [overleaf] shows the relationships of the spine, the spinal cord (shown in black) and the spinal nerves to the pathways, chakras, colours and sounds of the four main energy fields: soul, spirit, mind and matter. Each pathway includes all the organs in that area of the body. Note the areas where the pathways overlap. The chakras are centred on the areas of the body as shown. The spinal cord ends between the first and second lumbar vertebrae in the area of the second pathway and chakra. The area of strongest energy is the seventh chakra, which is centred on the pineal gland in the brain. The meanings of the pathways and their chakras in relation to a person's life are shown on the left of the diagram. Imbalance in a person's life may eventually show up in the corresponding pathway/chakra area of the person's body. The body cannot be fully healed unless the life aspect is balanced and healed

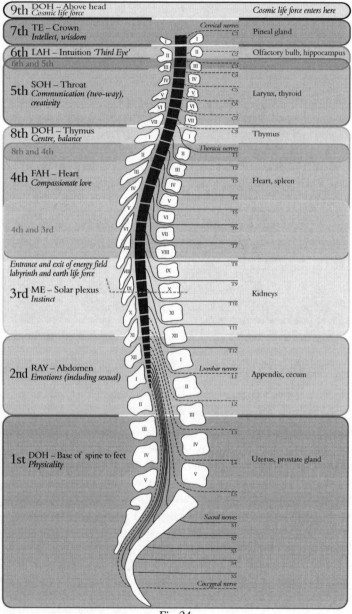

9th DOH – Above head
Cosmic life force — *Cosmic life force enters here*

7th TE – Crown
Intellect, wisdom — Pineal gland

Cervical nerves

6th LAH – Intuition *'Third Eye'* — Olfactory bulb, hippocampus

6th and 5th

5th SOH – Throat
Communication (two-way), creativity — Larynx, thyroid

8th DOH – Thymus
Centre, balance — Thymus

8th and 4th

Thoracic nerves

4th FAH – Heart
Compassionate love — Heart, spleen

4th and 3rd

Entrance and exit of energy field labyrinth and earth life force

3rd ME – Solar plexus
Instinct — Kidneys

2nd RAY – Abdomen
Emotions (including sexual) — Appendix, cecum

Lumbar nerves

1st DOH – Base of spine to feet
Physicality — Uterus, prostate gland

Sacral nerves

Coccygeal nerve

Fig. 24

physical roles appear to have ended, especially in the uterus, their energenic role is still vital to the well-being of the body. If any of these organs have to be surgically removed, the body has to find alternative means of focusing the chakras and adjusting the energenics. Fortunately our Creator made our bodies very adaptable, except for the pineal gland.

The basic colours of the energy field pathways and chakras can rarely be seen with the physical eye, except in rainbows and in the colours of the sky at sunset and at dawn. However, some people are so energenically agile they are able to see the colours of the chakras in the auras of people, plants and animals as easily as they can see physical matter and physical colours.

The three pathways which connect the energy fields of spirit and mind in the circle-cross labyrinth are vital for the transmission of the essential blueprints and programmes for physical matter from soul into the physical body and back to soul (Fig. 25).

These three connected pathways in the circle-cross labyrinth also represent the directly connected first, fourth and seventh chakras in the classical labyrinth of the energy fields. They show us how the circle-cross labyrinth and the classical labyrinth operate together. If any of these three chakras become blocked, the trans-missions may become garbled and the physical body will develop faults.

When a line is drawn on a classical labyrinth to connect the first, fourth and seventh chakras, a triangle emerges. The energy fields of the chakras are also in the formation of the classical labyrinth. If a spiral is drawn as a shorthand for a labyrinth at each point of the triangle, the triple spiral emerges.

Fig. 25 Circle-Cross Labyrinth showing the connections between mind and spirit and the first, fourth and seventh chakras

This indicates another meaning of the triple spiral. As well as representing the pure thought, light and sound of the cosmic life force, it also represents both the three joined pathways of the circle-cross labyrinth between spirit and mind energy fields and the three connected chakras in the energy fields. These pathways and chakras keep open the connections and the transmission of cosmic life force to and from soul and matter.

Each chakra is an energy field and therefore has within it the complete spectrum of light and the complete tonic sol-fa of sound of its own energy field.

It is the vibration of the sound and light created by the chakras which controls the movement and momentum (rhythm) to keep the cosmic life force and the Earth life force flowing evenly through the whole energy field and the energy field systems.

CHAPTER V

THE ENERGENICS OF SOUND AND LIGHT AND THEIR EFFECTS ON THE HUMAN BODY

The harmony of the sound within each of the chakras and pathways of each energy field is vital for the well-being of the whole energy field system, especially the human energy field systems. The energy fields should be in tune with each other. The sound controls the speed and rhythm of the movement of the flow of the two life force energies through the energy fields. Discordant sound will cause too little or too much movement of the flow, resulting in flood or stagnation in the pathways and chakras. Both are equally damaging, as flooding and stagnant water demonstrate.

Sound and light wavelengths both produce movement. The Bible story of the walls of Jericho falling to a trumpet blast is well known. The sound of a musical note can shatter glass. Most people, when they hear the sounds of a rhythmic piece of music, find all, or parts of, their bodies moving spontaneously to its rhythm.

A television programme in 2004 (*The Richard & Judy Show*) broadcast a horrific video of a scan, showing the effects of heavy metal music on the foetus in the womb. The child started to move, at first in time to the music, but after a very short time it was shaking and vibrating so violently it could hardly be seen. Not taken into account is the continuing effect of the sound of the heavy metal music on the water in the womb. The child would have spent the rest of its gestation period in a severely polluted environment.

The programme also showed a scan of the effect of the music of Mozart on a baby in the womb. The child began to move, but its movements were gentle and rhythmic and the child was obviously comfortable and soothed. The water in the womb would not have been polluted by the sound of the music. Masaru Emoto's research shows that the crystals of water are beautifully formed after it has been exposed to the music of Mozart, and completely shattered by heavy metal music.

The healing power of Gregorian chant is well known. Music for healing was known to Pythagoras and the ancient Egyptians; Maat also represented music and its balanced harmonious resonance as well as representing truth and justice.

In 1873 a British scientist, Sir William Crook, discovered light also produces movement. He invented a radiometer, a 'light windmill', which demonstrated that light from the sun and from electric light creates movement. The cosmic and Earth life forces and their sound and light provide all the thought energy we need to think, i.e. to produce our own consciousness, our own processed thought, on all levels, conscious and subconscious, and all the sound and light within it. The way we process our thought energy depends on the harmony in the energy fields, and the harmony in the energy fields depends on the way we process our thought, following the two-way movement of the labyrinths.

We can hear the sounds of our own conscious thoughts as they are processed through the mind energy field, transmitted into the energy field of matter, and into the physical body, and there transformed into physical action and movements. Our movements will be calm and controlled if our thoughts are balanced and harmonious. Contra-thought consciousness, producing anger and unbalanced fear, often results in violent contra action and movement.

The vibrations and frequencies of colours, which are wavelengths of light, can slow us down or speed us up. Blues are receding colours; they seem to move away from us. Reds, yellows and oranges on the other hand are 'advancing' colours and seem to throw themselves at us. Artists have used this knowledge in the composition of their paintings for hundreds of years. A red room can make some people very jumpy and active. The proverbial red rag to a bull stimulates the bull into action and movement, although the bull can only physically see in black and white. Blue can have the opposite effect; it is a calming, healing colour, but too much blue can make some people lethargic. The effect of colour in the environment on humans is a well-known factor in the Chinese art of feng shui. It has also been well researched by psychologists. The use of blue for boys and pink for girls goes back to Roman times and possibly earlier, and relates to the calming, harmonious effect of these wavelengths of light on our human energy fields, especially the delicate energy fields of babies.

As we can 'hear' the sound of our own thought, we can, with our physical eyes closed, 'see' thought, 'see' colour in our heads. Using our mind's eye, we can visualise people and places anywhere on Earth or in the universe; the choice is endless. The physical sound we hear with our ears produces the movements in the relevant parts of our brain and bodies to translate thought sound into our own physical sound, creating speech or song.

Words and gestures, sights and sounds, which communicate thought to us, can switch on spontaneous movements within our physical bodies. Some of these movements may cause us to laugh or cry or shout, either in excitement or anger or out of a sense of fear and danger, depending on the sound and light of the thought within the communication we are receiving.

Light creates movement in the brain which activates the optic nerves and enables us to see and therefore to move easily around and communicate with our environment and everything in it.

Sometimes the sound in our own thoughts produces gestures and movements in our bodies which we call body language. These movements are usually created from the sound of our processed thought, from a subconscious level, i.e. from our soul and spirit energy fields. They communicate physically subconscious messages about our hidden emotions. But the gestures only communicate to us and to others if there is light to enable us to see them.

Communication involves movement of processed thought within and between species. It uses both sound and light, physical and subliminal, to carry and move the processed thought. Communication only works if it has something to communicate with, and if it is a two-way exchange of ideas and information. Not only does it have to be two-way, it also has to be on a similar and compatible wavelength and frequency to work. It is an interaction of transmitting and receiving, of understanding and listening. The first part of communication is connection, and connection will not work if it is not switched on and connecting. We have to make a connection to make a communication, and we have to connect within the communication in order to fully communicate.

Misunderstanding within communication happens when one half misinterprets the words or actions of the other. One half may be on a positive wavelength and frequency, and the other may be on a negative wavelength and frequency. Something is said or done with a positive intention which is received negatively. There is a misalignment between them which garbles the intended communication. Two people can talk to each other but if one, or neither, is listening to the other, the communication between them will fail. Even if they are listening to each other, if they are connected only on a physical level, the communication and the listening will be superficial. If they are listening, but are not on the same wavelength and frequency, misunderstanding will creep in and the communication will falter. We need to be fully switched on to the same wavelengths and frequencies at all levels of consciousness, physical, mind, spirit and soul, in order to fully understand and communicate with each other. Communication can become sub-liminal. Spoken words can become unnecessary. Our usual range of connecting and communicating is on the wavelengths of the mind and matter energy fields and the physical. Using our whole range of energy fields and the thought energy in the connecting life force energies, and their wavelengths and frequencies, we are able to connect and communicate directly on the levels of mind to mind without the physical connections of the spoken word or even the seen gestures.

I have found many times that by linking mind to mind with difficult, fractious children, sending them warm, loving, positive wavelengths of thought, they become peaceful and happy. It even works with some adults!

Our internal communications system works in a similar way to our external communications system. Breakdown in the two-way connections and communications on one side, or all sides, always leads to some kind of misalignment and misunderstanding, and therefore malfunction.

As the two life force energies enter our human energy field systems, they merge with the sound and light of the consciousness, the processed thought of our energy field pathways, absorbing the programmes stored within them. The movement created by the combined sound and light wavelengths both within and absorbed by the two life force energies carries them through the energy fields into the physical body, back into the energy fields and eventually back into the Earth and cosmos.

The chakras, and their sound and light, form the essential connections.

Cancer is the result of a monumental breakdown in the connections and communications within the human body on all levels, from the soul energy field through to the physical body. The internal equivalent of war breaks out, with the same catastrophic results, just as a breakdown in the balanced harmonious two-way connection and communication between peoples and nations can lead to war.

If correctly balanced and harmonious connections and communications between the two life force energies, especially the cosmic life force, are re-established in the energy fields and between the energy fields and physical matter, there is a good chance that balance and harmony and equilibrium can be restored in the physical body and healing and wholeness can be achieved.

Dowsing can identify which connections are blocked and/or disconnected, and which sound and light communications are missing. Spiritual healing, which is a vibrational energy therapy which accesses all wavelengths and frequencies of all the energy fields and the two life force energies, especially the cosmic life force, can repair and restore the connections and re-establish the essential two-way communications. This cannot be fully achieved by drugs alone, since the energy fields of the drugs can be alien to the human body and can therefore cause further complications unless they are made compatible with that particular unique physical body.

Our thinking, and the sound and light it produces,

stands a better chance of being on a balanced, harmonious wavelength if the thought input into our energy fields from the two life force energies is in equilibrium. Keeping in mind the energy equation $2P = N$, we need twice as much cosmic life force as Earth life force to achieve the correct balance.

If there is a block or disconnection in the ninth chakra, our intake of cosmic life force will be inhibited and the Earth life force will automatically make up the shortfall. We will then absorb into our energy fields an excess of the naturally negative wavelengths of the thought energy of the Earth life force. If, for some reason, the Earth's energy fields in our environment are also polluted and out of balance, the quality of the Earth life force will be damaged and the disharmony and imbalance in our intake of thought energy will be even greater. As more and more negative and contra-consciousness accumulates in our energy fields, our own conscious thought processing starts at a great disadvantage. We begin to feel the effects of depressing contra fear, and all its conflicting associated emotions which, in turn, upsets our own thought processing even further. Before long, the essential communicating and connecting systems linking the life force with the physical body break down, causing the cells and organs of the physical body itself to malfunction.

When we are aware of what is happening, we can take our own steps to remedy the situation. Using deep breathing, meditation, relaxation and positive visualisation, we can all consciously tune in to the cosmic life force from the source and draw it into our beings. We can unblock the ninth chakra and ensure the constant balanced flow of cosmic life force into our energy fields. We will then be able to consciously eject the contra-thought and replace it with pure thought energy. Often we only need to make a small shift in our own thinking habits to radically change our conscious thinking from contra-negative to positive, balanced and harmonious thinking, and enjoy all the enrichment which comes to our lives as a result.

Sometimes, however, we may need extra help, just as a broken leg needs a plaster cast. Vibrational healing and vibrational medicines provide the remedies which are needed to heal damaged consciousness.

Contra-consciousness flows out of our energy fields into the Earth's energy field systems, polluting not only the Earth's own life force which we access from our environment, but also weakening and unbalancing the quality of the cosmic life force as it travels through the Earth's energy field systems. The result is an imbalance and disharmony built into the two life force energies, largely caused by the contra antics of humanity, polluting the thought energy we receive from both the cosmos and the Earth. Eventually this thought pollution, with its imbalance of sound and light, disrupts the connections and communications throughout all the energy field systems on, and of, the Earth, adversely affecting not only the physical and mental health of humanity but of all life on Earth.

The polluted life force energies are also carried and absorbed by all the water of the Earth and are therefore absorbed physically by all life on Earth.

This may sound bleak, and it is bleak, if the human race goes on unchecked and unchecking in the contra way it thinks and acts. Our human-made worldwide communication systems are pedalling contra thought in huge quantities in a way not known before. We, as individuals, have to take responsibility both for the damage it causes and for putting it right. Every little helps... If *everyone* made that small shift to change from contra to balanced thinking and actions, the whole world energy picture, and with it global health and well-being, would be very quickly changed for the better.

The sound and light of our conscious thinking also affects the movement and flow of the life force in all the water content of our bodies, and controls the movement and the flow of the water itself, smooth or calm, fast or slow, turgid or turbulent. One of its manifestations is in high or low blood pressure. Subsequently, all the cells, tissue and organs of the physical body will be affected for good or ill, depending on the sound and light wavelengths and frequencies of our own thinking, both our conscious thinking and subsequently the subconscious thought processing of our own programmes. The movement created by the warm glowing thoughts of kindness, respect and compassion provides the stimulation needed for healthy growth, and keeps the body's fluids and blood moving and flowing at the correct speeds and rhythms to maintain the healthy function of our physical bodies. Through our own thinking, we have the responsibility for the health and well-being of our own bodies and we can, if we choose, initiate our own healing.

The descriptions of essential oils in aromatherapy and of scents in the perfume industry are the same as in music. They are described as 'top note, middle note and bass note' depending on the wavelengths and frequencies of their vibrations.

Scent is the physical manifestation of the vibrations of subliminal sound wavelengths of consciousness, circulating in the energy fields of the auras of matter in our environment. The scent of each individual aura is created from the subliminal sounds of the consciousness of that aura, making its own unique physical 'signature'. Scent is an essential part of the physical intercommunication systems of plants, animals and insects and, to a lesser extent, humans. It translates consciousness into the physical dimension, making it easily recognisable on a physical level. The most ancient part of the human brain is the olfactory bulb. It produces our sense of smell, which is an essential part of our environmental 'early warning' system.

Using the programme recorded in the energy fields system of the olfactory bulb, the subliminal sounds from the auras in our environment are not only received, transformed and transmitted as scents and smells, but they are also recorded and stored in the olfactory bulb so that we can recognise them. Another essential part of the programme is to transmit the subliminal sound of the scents of the environment to connect with the pineal gland to release the hormones needed to activate cells in other areas of the brain.

Our sense of smell is used to soothe us or to alert us to danger. For example, if we smell burning, it sets our internal alarm bells ringing and we instinctively know there is danger. It stimulates us into action, either to deal with the cause of the burning or to escape. The smell of a cake or of a delicious meal cooking stimulates our appetites and digestive juices and makes our mouths water. It produces movement in the water content of the body.

Scents speak to our instinct and our emotions. They communicate with the thought energy within both the Earth and the cosmic life forces. If our environment and everything in it is in balance and harmony, we may not consciously register a scent, although the subliminal sounds will have been processed. If it is registered, it will give us pleasure. The scent of most flowers communicates harmony, peace and joy. When we register their scent, our life force energies are given an extra boost which we may need to keep the olfactory bulb working at full efficiency. On the other hand, the scent of environmental danger such as toxic fumes is unpleasant. It acts like a shouted warning.

It has been known for thousands of years that perfume and essential oils from plants stimulate hormone production. They soothe and calm us, or energise and activate us. Smelling salts were widely used until the middle of the twentieth century. Their very strong smell was used to literally jolt someone back into conscious consciousness and re-establish their internal communication system, which had been temporarily interrupted, usually by some kind of shock, either physical or emotional.

The scents of plants contain the essential subliminal sounds of the consciousness of the plant's energy fields which give the plant its identity. These sounds can be used to balance and harmonise the sound of the consciousness within the energy fields of our own physical bodies. Depending on the plant, they can be used to correct at molecular and cell levels any distorted movements caused by the sound of distorted consciousness in the energy field system.

PART V
CONNECTING THE ENERGY FIELD SYSTEMS AND THE PHYSICAL BODY

CHAPTER I

INTRODUCING THE ENERGENIC CONNECTING SEQUENCE

Energenics proposes there is a sequence of molecules and their energy field systems which forms the mechanism needed to make the connections and communications network which transmits and transforms the cosmic and Earth life forces, and all the programmes for the physical function of the body, into the physical body.

The sequence is as follows:

1. the molecules of water;
2. the molecules of DNA;
3. the molecules of genes;
4. the molecules of hormones;
5. the molecules of vital-vitamins;
6. the molecules of mitochondria;
7. the molecules of chromosomes;
8 the molecules of the cells;
9. the molecules of neurotransmitters.

Our physical bodies are made from the atoms of the ninety-two natural elements of the Earth, which fuse together to form molecules. The first and simplest and most important molecule is H_2O, two hydrogen atoms fused with one oxygen atom to form water. Water is crucial to life: no water, no life. Water itself is a form of energy and is constantly moving and flowing. We know it is a very good conductor of electricity, which forms part of both cosmic and Earth life forces. Moving water, en masse, produces huge amounts of energy which we can, and do, harness for our external material use.

The water created in our bodies in the form of blood, lymph, cerebral, spinal and body fluids, is continually being used and also naturally evaporates. Therefore it needs constant replenishing to keep it clean and flowing.

Flowing water absorbs more oxygen than stagnant water. When we drink water we are maintaining and, where necessary, increasing its flow within our bodies, enabling our body fluids to absorb more oxygen, energising them and strengthening the connections between the energy field and chakra systems of the water molecules and the energy field systems of the whole human body.

However, at the very beginning of my work as a dowser and a healer, I discovered that water from the tap was harmful to me. I was very surprised, and so was the dowser who double-checked my findings. I subsequently found that tap water was a significantly harmful factor in the health of approximately ninety-five per cent of the people I dowsed for, about 400 over a period of approximately five years. Unfortunately, water absorbs all energy and consciousness it contacts. If the Earth life force is polluted, or the ley lines are unbalanced in the environment of the reservoir, the water we drink will carry the polluted life force into our bodies. Eventually this will have a detrimental effect on our health, as its contra-consciousness causes interference in the body's own energy field systems.

The effect of Earth consciousness on water is one of the key important reasons why healing the Earth is so important. It shows how what we do to each other, and to the Earth, we eventually do to ourselves. The sooner humanity cleans up its act, the better it will be for the health of individual humans, you and me.

So what can we do in the meantime? Dr Emoto's researches, and dowsing, both show the beneficial effect on water of giving it conscious, loving, positive thought. Dowsing shows the auric energy field of a tumbler of water expands hugely by simply saying 'Thank you' to the water and meaning it. Dowsing (and my own experience) also shows that harmful consciousness in water is reduced by boiling or by the process of carbonating. The agitating action of the bubbles rising through the water has the effect of releasing some of the contra energy held in the water, making it relatively harmless.

The atoms of the other elements which make up the molecules of our body tissues also need constant replenishment from the Earth, as well as from the programmes held in the main energy field system of the body. This is why we need to eat. In order for our food to have maximum benefit, its energy field systems should be compatible with our own energy field systems. Allergies and food sensitivity occur when they are not. This is why dowsing to access the energy field systems of both the food and our bodies is so valuable in these situations. Each human body is unique. What is harmful to one person may not be to another. Dowsing eliminates the guesswork and gives accurate information for each individual.

The cosmic and Earth life forces use the energy field systems of the water molecules to transmit the entire programme for the development and maintenance of the whole physical body from the body's main energy field of matter into the energy field systems of the DNA molecules. From there, they are transformed and transmitted and recorded into the two strands of the physical DNA molecule.

Included in the programmes held by the DNA are instructions for dividing the programmes into small parts and for delegating the parts to their appropriate genes.

The genes do not create the programmes they hold, nor the details they need to activate and maintain the programmes. These originate, as all the programmes originate, in the main energy field system of the body and are transmitted into the DNA and gene molecules by the cosmic and Earth life forces.

Each gene holds the 'recipe' for the formation of the hormone or hormones which set in motion all the chemical processes needed to start, carry out, complete and maintain its part of the programme for the physical body. Each gene also holds the 'recipe' for a class of molecules I shall call vital-vitamins.

CHAPTER II

THE ROLE OF HORMONES AND VITAL-VITAMINS IN THE ENERGENIC CONNECTING SEQUENCE

The hormones and the vital-vitamins fit, key, together in a formation similar to the Greek key pattern. They work together as the classical and circle-cross labyrinths work together; the one needs the other. Their combined energy fields safeguard their connections to the processes they control, so maintaining a smooth and continuous 'production line'.

For example, hormones required to produce proteins for cells need a vital-vitamin in order to stay connected to the process. This ensures the production of the proteins is uninterrupted. A deficiency of the vital-vitamin will eventually lead to a deficiency in the effectiveness of its hormone. The hormone will gradually become disconnected from the processes, causing a breakdown in the production of the protein. The protein-dependent cells will begin to deteriorate and, eventually, will be unable to regenerate.

The energy field systems of the molecules of the hormones and vital-vitamins are connected to the chakra systems of the main energy field system of the whole physical body. Vital-vitamins are connected to the pathways of the chakra energy fields. Hormones are connected to the chakras of the chakra energy fields.

Vital-vitamins are a small and very important group of molecules I have identified by dowsing.

Vitamins are a group of separate molecules which have little in common with each other but which, in small amounts, are essential, vital, for the normal healthy functioning of the body. They were discovered at the beginning of the twentieth century. Their name is derived from '*vita*', the Latin word for life, and 'amine' because the first to be discovered were in food, and when identified found to belong to a chemical group known as 'amines'. Although to qualify as vitamins they must be provided by our diet, three are synthesised in the human body. They are vitamin D, niacin, and vitamin K (D A Bender, *Nutritional Biochemistry of the Vitamins*, 1992).

The dictionary definition of 'synthesise' is, 'To put together, or combine into a complex whole' and 'To make up by combination of parts or elements'. Both vitamin D and vitamin K are fat soluble: they need fat to synthesise and to work efficiently.

I have called the group I have identified 'vital-vitamins', from 'vital' meaning essential, and 'vitamin', since four are listed as vitamins. Vital-vitamins are extra-essential vitamins. The five vital-vitamins are:

- vitamin K_2 (menaquinone);
- vitamin C;
- vitamin B6;
- vitamin B12;
- sodium chloride (salt).

Salt, sodium chloride, is also found in the body and in food but it is not normally classed as a vitamin. Its importance for humans has been known since very ancient times. Roman soldiers received part of their pay in salt, hence our word 'salary'. Europeans traded salt for gold with African tribes. Salt was widely used to preserve food to store for winter use. At present, salt is having a bad press. Salt is essential, but it is a neat example of too much of a good thing.

The energy fields of the five vital-vitamins are connected into the energy fields of the nine main chakra systems of the human body. I was surprised there appear to be only five, since there are nine main chakras.

Dowsing shows the vital-vitamins are connected as follows:

- chakra 1 – vitamin B6;
- chakra 2 – vitamin B6;
- chakra 3 – vitamin B12, sodium chloride and vitamin C;
- chakra 4 – vitamin B12 and vitamin C;
- chakra 5 – vitamin B12 and sodium chloride;
- chakra 6 – menaquinone (K_2) and sodium chloride;
- chakra 7 – menaquinone (K_2) and vitamin B12;
- chakra 8 – menaquinone (K_2) and vitamin C;
- chakra 9 – menaquinone (K_2).

The chakras' own energy fields need to be aligned and synchronised with the chakras of the main energy field system for the vital-vitamins to function correctly. Misalignment has the effect of disconnecting them. Vital-vitamins also form the vital link between the hormones and mitochondria (see Part V, Chapter IV). Without the vital-vitamins, hormones and mitochondria cannot connect and communicate with each other to release, activate and maintain the essential and correct chemical reactions needed to produce, activate, maintain and regenerate neurotransmitters and cells and their organs.

If the energy field system of a vital-vitamin becomes disconnected from its chakra, the hormones, whose energy fields are connected to the chakras of that chakra's energy field, also become disconnected. In effect, the hormones become switched off. It is a reaction similar to the blowing of a light bulb triggering a fuse, which cuts off the electricity supply, so all the appliances connected to the electricity supply on that circuit cannot function.

CHAPTER III

THE PHYSICAL AND ENERGENIC ROLE OF THE VITAL-VITAMIN MENAQUINONE (VITAMIN K_2) IN THE HUMAN BODY

There is a huge amount of research and knowledge about the physical structure and properties of vitamins C, B6 and B12, and sodium chloride. My definition is perhaps not so well known since it involves their energenic function as well as their physical structure.

Vitamin K was not discovered until 1974, and it has been much less researched until recently. It is thought to be synthesised in the gut and in the liver, although it does occur in a variety of foods, especially lettuce hearts and broccoli. About twenty per cent of the body pool of vitamin K is found in the liver. Vitamin K is divided into three main parts:

- K_1 (phylloquinone): needed to help blood to clot and used to help haemophiliacs.

- K_3 (menadione): the synthetic version of vitamin K, used in the pharmaceutical version of vitamin K. It can be toxic.

- K_2 (menaquinone): the least well-known part of vitamin K.

In 1988, at the very beginning of my work as a medical dowser, the first person I dowsed to check for vitamin and mineral deficiencies had been severely dyslexic as a child and, in the 1970s, had been diagnosed and helped by Professor T R Miles, MA, PhD, FBPsS, of Bangor University. At that time, Professor Miles was one of this country's leading experts on dyslexia. One of the vitamin deficiencies I found was vitamin K. I had only learned of the existence of vitamin K a few months earlier. Further dowsing showed that the vitamin K deficiency was a significant factor in the cause of the dyslexia, and that vitamin K was very important in brain function, but that this aspect of vitamin K was not known to science and medicine at that time (1988).

Coincidentally, the next two people I dowsed for vitamin and mineral deficiencies were also dyslexic and were also deficient in vitamin K. The third person I dowsed had had a severe stroke eighteen months previously. She was also deficient in vitamin K. As I gained more knowledge and information about the three parts of vitamin K, I learned through dowsing that it is menaquinone (K_2) which is vital to brain function. My dowsed information that the neurological function of vitamin K_2 was unknown was subsequently proved to be accurate when, in 1995, Dr Philip Taylor did a literature search on the then-recent published papers on vitamin K and its role in the body, held at the British Library at Boston Spa, Yorkshire. He could not find any reference to any role played by menaquinone in neurological function. D A Bender's book *Nutritional Biochemistry of the Vitamins*, published in 1992, made no mention of any connection of menaquinone and the brain. In it he writes '...the extent to which menaquinones are biologically active is uncertain' (© Shearer et. al. 1974 and Shearer 1990).

In 1996 neither the laboratories at St Mary's Hospital Manchester nor the Haematology Department of Manchester Royal Infirmary knew of any link between vitamin K and the brain, or of any known orthodox test for menaquinone. There is no human-made scientific instrument which can match the sensitivity of dowsing.

As my work as a dowser and a healer progressed over the years, I found more and more people with neurologically related illness coming to me. With the exception of two, they were all deficient in menaquinone. The two exceptions were both cases of multiple sclerosis. Although they were not deficient in menaquinone, for some reason it was not functioning correctly. I now know menaquinone was not deficient but was disconnected, which had the effect of switching off its dependent hormones.

Everyone who came to me for healing was dowsed for vitamin and mineral deficiencies as part of their treatment. From 1988 to 1996, out of a total of 729 patients, I dowsed and recorded ninety-three cases of menaquinone deficiency. They came from England, Australia and Canada; the age range was from two months to ninety-one years. Forty-four were male, and forty-nine were female. Sixty-nine people came with a range of diagnosed brain disorders. These were:

- stroke;
- brain tumour;
- Bell's palsy;
- Alzheimer's disease;
- Parkinson's disease;
- polio;
- meningitis;
- multiple sclerosis (MS);
- myalgic encephalitis (ME or chronic fatigue syndrome);
- epilepsy;
- grand mal convulsions;
- dyslexia;
- Tourette's syndrome;
- autism;
- Asperger's syndrome;
- head injuries;
- behaviour disorders.

Closer examination of the history of the other twenty-four non-neurological cases found by dowsing to be deficient in menaquinone revealed evidence in twenty-two cases of either undiagnosed dyslexia, a past neurological illness, or accident, for example polio, concussion or very difficult births. The histories of the other two cases did not reveal any apparent neurological problems, past or present, but both had received high doses of steroids for the treatment of arthritis. Dowsing indicated that the high doses of steroids were the cause of their menaquinone deficiency. Subsequently, I recorded two more cases of patients who had received chemotherapy treatment for cancer (one for breast cancer, one for leukaemia) who were deficient in menaquinone. Dowsing confirmed that chemotherapy, and not cancer, was the cause.

It would appear that without sufficient vitamin K_2, menaquinone, the brain does not function efficiently and does not renew damaged cells in the same way cells in the rest of the body can regenerate themselves. Therefore it appears that vitamin K_2 is necessary for the efficient functioning and healthy cell renewal in the human brain, which in turn is responsible for the healthy and efficient functioning of the rest of the human body.

I continued to explore, via dowsing, the role and importance of menaquinone. At the same time I was exploring the way the energy components of the human body worked. As the theory of Energenics grew, my understanding of the role of menaquinone grew with it. I came to realise menaquinone played an important role in the energy/matter connections of the human body.

It has never seemed logical to me that cells in the brain cannot renew themselves, or regenerate, as cells in the rest of the body renew and regenerate. Menaquinone deficiency seems to be the key to that situation. Dowsing shows that without menaquinone, the hormones cannot unlock the chemical programmes in the chromosomes of the cells of the brain, and cell mitochondria does not function at full efficiency. Without the hormone–menaquinone–mitochondria key, neurotransmitters cannot be formed or be activated. Without sufficient menaquinone, the production of the enzymes is disrupted and therefore the biosynthesis of the cell protein is disrupted. Eventually, the affected cells will either not be able to regenerate or will regenerate incorrectly.

The programme for the synthesis of menaquinone and the menaquinone dependent hormones is 'written' into the eggs of the mother and into the semen of the father which fertilise the egg, and is assimilated into the programme of the energy field systems of the DNA and genes of the new embryo. It is transmitted into the energy field system of the pineal gland, which forms at a very early stage in the embryo's development. If either the mother or the father is deficient in menaquinone, this can affect the amount and quality of the menaquinone which will be synthesised in the foetus and ultimately in the new human being throughout its lifetime. The development of the brain cells could be affected before birth to a greater or lesser degree, depending on the amount of the deficiency and the effect of that deficiency on its interdependent hormones, especially secretin. The role of the pineal gland, which is known to be a crystalline structure, is to receive from the energy fields *all* the programmes for the physical function of every part of the human brain and the human body, and transform and transmit them to their relevant parts of the brain and the body. The pineal gland also records and transmits the 'recipes' for all the hormones of the body, and for all the body's biological and biochemical processes.

Menaquinone is produced within the body in two stages. It is synthesised in the brain by the pituitary gland and by the liver. (Phylloquinone – K_1 – is synthesised by the liver and by intestinal bacteria.) Menaquinone is essential for the healthy function of the pineal gland itself. Without it, the pineal gland cannot fully perform its essential role in the brain.

Vitamin K is fat soluble and needs some fat to metabolise with full efficiency. There is a risk, therefore, that a fat-free diet or a very low fat diet can lead to a deficiency of menaquinone, with subsequent adverse effects on brain function and on neurotransmitters. A low-cholesterol diet may prevent heart disease but could eventually be a factor in the cause of Alzheimer's disease. A fully balanced diet is needed for optimum health.

Nature has a wonderful way of adapting to, and coping with, abnormalities but it is not always able to overcome the difficulties and obstacles caused by human interference. Strong drugs, taken over a prolonged period of time, upset the balance of menaquinone. The energy content of manufactured synthetic drugs is too strong for the highly sensitive, delicate energy field systems and their chakras within the brain and throws them out of balance. The menaquinone energy system is swamped and blocked. In effect, it is disconnected. Eventually the healthy functioning of the hormones and menaquinone dependent cells and neurotransmitters in the brain are adversely affected. The pineal gland's ability to receive, maintain and transmit the programme for the synthesis of menaquinone to the pituitary gland and the liver is inhibited, causing a deficiency of menaquinone.

A severe virus attack can also cause similar problems. ME, a menaquinone-deficient illness, often begins after a severe viral infection.

The energy fields of the liver are also unbalanced by strong drugs, including alcohol, which adversely affects the liver's ability to synthesise menaquinone (and phylloquinone). Eventually the neurotransmitters in the gut, needed by all the nerves of the spinal column, will be unbalanced and will malfunction.

As well as synthesising menaquinone, both the pituitary gland and the liver also need menaquinone to enable them to perform all their programmes and functions.

Recently, more conventional scientific research is being carried out on vitamin K. The following quotation was found among the information on vitamin K obtained from an internet search in 2002: 'Vitamin K is one of the most exciting vitamins of this decade. By keeping bone calcium where it belongs, vitamin K may help prevent heart disease, stroke, osteoporosis, Alzheimer's disease and more. Researchers are just now focusing on its potential roles in the pancreas and brain. Vitamin K is exciting because it seems to act like a hormone but shows no toxicity.'

The other vital-vitamins, B6, B12, vitamin C and sodium chloride (salt), are absorbed from our diet and are absorbed by the foetus from the mother's diet. Any deficiency of these vital-vitamins may result in disruption of the chemical and biological processes controlled by their interdependent hormones. Vitamin B12 is also needed by the parts of the brain which control physical movement, especially muscle and ligament development, use and maintenance. It is needed to connect the neurotransmitters, both in the brain and in the gut.

CHAPTER IV

THE ROLE OF MITOCHONDRIA, CHROMOSOMES, CELLS AND NEUROTRANSMITTERS IN THE ENERGENIC CONNECTING SEQUENCE

The next stage in the link between the energenic and physical mechanisms of the body is mitochondria. Mitochondria are formed from a collection of molecules which bond together to produce an energy generator and adaptor, a 'battery' for each cell. The combined energy fields and their chakras of the molecules which have bonded together to form the mitochondria process in the cell adapt the life force energies flowing through them to the particular wavelengths and frequencies needed to receive, transmit and maintain the flow of information from the hormones into the chromosomes and out of the chromosomes into every part of the cell.

The energy fields of the vital-vitamins play an important role in mitochondria. They form the connection between the hormones and the mitochondria molecules, ensuring the continuous flow of the necessary programmes needed to keep the cell operating at one hundred per cent efficiency. In effect, the vital-vitamins keep the mitochondria generator fully charged. If the vital-vitamin breaks down, or becomes disconnected, eventually all the processes needed for the healthy functioning of the cell break down.

Using the energy field systems of the hormones, vital-vitamins and mitochondria, the programme needed for a cell to form, function and regenerate is transmitted from the genes into the chromosomes of the cell. Each chromosome will be responsible for its own part of the total programme for its cell. Chromosomes are like mini genes. Chromosomes are to cells as genes are to DNA.

The chromosomes together form the equivalent of a brain for the cell. They are located in the cell's nucleus. Between them, the chromosomes will record, store and release all the information needed for the healthy function and regeneration of the cell and its ability to bond correctly with other cells. As well as holding the programme for the information of individual cells, the chromosomes also hold the programmes for the formation of the groups of cells which eventually form all the tissues, muscles, bones, organs and glands of the body, including the brain, and also including the blood, lymph and body fluid systems, and their containers.

Neurotransmitters are a group of molecules which form the cells of the nervous systems. They, and their energy fields, are used to transmit information from cell to cell, organ to organ within the body, in a system similar to a telephone communications network. Neurotransmitters have a special function in the body. They connect with both the energy field systems and life force energies, and with the separate energy system known as the meridians. The meridians are the body's equivalent of the ley lines in the Earth (see Part VIII).

All nine parts of the connecting mechanism must be in place, connected and communicating two-way before any cells can be constructed. They have to remain in place, connected and communicating two-way from and to the cells into the main energy field systems for the cell to be fully and efficiently activated, maintained and regenerated.

All the atoms and molecules which make up the physical body each have their own complete energy field system. Their own soul, spirit, mind and matter energy fields contain their own particular part of the whole programme. This also applies to all the cells, tissue, organs, systems, and so on, which evolve from the atoms and molecules.

All these separate energy field systems are constantly connected to the whole programme in the main energy field system of the body: soul to soul, spirit to spirit, mind to mind and matter to matter. There is a continual two-way exchange of cosmic and Earth life forces between them all. Therefore if the main energy fields are out of balance, the other subsidiary fields will be thrown off balance, and vice versa; a faulty energy field in a molecule will show as imbalance in the main energy field and its chakras.

The molecules and atoms of a vitamin or mineral only become deficient if their energy fields become disconnected from the main energy field system. The interruption and therefore deficiency in the supply of the life force energies depletes their energy fields and disrupts their own programmes so that they can no longer play their full part in the whole programme for the whole physical body.

Taking extra supplies of the deficient vitamin or mineral orally helps the situation. However, it is only completely resolved when the energy field system is repaired, the chakra unblocked and the vitamin or mineral is reconnected, rebalanced and harmonised back into the whole programme. This can be done very simply using a dowsing/healing technique. The problem can only be completely resolved by using an energy/vibrational therapy since it is caused by an energy/vibrational fault.

PART VI
ENERGENICS AND THE PSYCHE

CHAPTER I

AN EXPLANATION OF THE 'SUPERNATURAL'

If we understand the construction and functions of the cosmic and Earth life force energies, and the individual energy field systems of soul, spirit, mind and matter, and their chakra systems, we can then understand the phenomenon we call the psyche. When we fully understand the psyche, we can understand how dowsing works.

The circle-cross labyrinth, the classical labyrinth and the triple spiral show clearly the importance of the connections between the mind and spirit energy fields, and their first, fourth and seventh chakras in the transmission of the life force energies through the energy field system from soul through to physical matter and back to soul.

The cosmic life force enters the energy field system through the soul energy field. Once it is in the system, the cosmic life force also absorbs and transmits from soul through to physical matter all the blueprints and programmes held within the consciousness of the energy fields. Although every energy field has its own direct access to cosmic life force via the ninth chakra, only the soul energy field has direct access to the cosmic life force through both the ninth and the third chakras to the source, the Creator-God.

Simultaneously, the Earth life force enters the energy field system in the opposite direction through the third chakra of the energy field of matter. The Earth life force also absorbs the consciousness of the energy fields and transmits the blueprints and programmes from physical matter through to soul.

During our physical lives on Earth, we have easy, constant access to the wavelengths and frequencies of the pathways and chakras of the energy fields of mind and matter, especially their outer pathways of 'physical' consciousness.

The soul is the most remote of our energy fields. Most of us are not consciously aware of it, unless we are able to use our mind energy field to access the spirit energy field in order to make the connection to soul. Yet the soul energy field and our blueprint for our mental and physical existence contained in its consciousness is crucial to the well-being of our physical bodies and therefore our physical lives. Perhaps the original purpose of the religions was to help and guide us to enable us to access spirit and soul more easily, using the consciousness of mind and therefore consciously to keep open our direct access to the Creator-God and the cosmic life force in our physical lives.

When we understand the mechanics of thought in the life force energies, and consciousness in the structures of the energy fields and their interaction, the phenomena we call 'supernatural' becomes natural; 'supernatural' is in fact an accurate description of that part of our being which is operating on higher vibrations and frequencies than those of our physical consciousness, our physical bodies and our physical world, but is essential to it. The supernatural part of our energenic system holds the key to unlocking our understanding of the physical processes of our physical bodies and lives.

CHAPTER II

THE ENERGENIC CONCEPT OF THE PSYCHE

The word 'psyche' comes from the complex Greek word '*psuche*', meaning soul, life, spirit, breath. By 1658, psyche was used to mean 'the mind'. Had soul, spirit and breath become mistaken for mind? Had they become relegated to philosophical concepts? Although Descartes famously said 'I think, therefore I am', he and Newton separated the mind from the body. They concentrated on the physical body regarding mind as a physical phenomenon.

Today, we only seem able to comprehend our lives, our bodies, our world, in physical terms as 'matter', especially in science and medicine. Even the immeasurable content of the universe, now recognised by science, is described as 'dark matter', or 'antimatter'.

The constant flow of the cosmic life force through all the energy fields of creation, absorbing their consciousness, creates a communications system which extends throughout the universe. It extends throughout the planet, throughout all life on the planet, throughout humanity, throughout each individual, and back to the origin of the life force, the thought energy of the Creator.

The Earth's own life force, evolved from the cosmic life force, also flows through all life on Earth, absorbing consciousness from all the energy fields of all life on Earth. It produces another communication system which also connects with all life on Earth, including humanity and the Earth itself.

The psyche is the continuous connecting thread made by the cosmic life force and the Earth life force. They are entwined together but flow separately and in opposite directions through all the energy field systems of all life on Earth, including humanity.

Our individual human psyche is part of this same communication system, formed by the wavelengths and frequencies of the two life force energies flowing through, and between, all the energy field systems and their chakras, both within the physical body and in the aura. The map of the psyche is the same as the map of the life force energies, and of thought itself. It is the circle-cross labyrinth. There are three wavelengths in the psyche: the wavelength and frequencies of the cosmic life force, the wavelength and frequencies of the Earth life force, and the wavelength and frequencies of the combined cosmic life force and Earth life force.

The wavelengths of the cosmic life force will give access to all wavelengths and frequencies of all the consciousness of all the energy fields and energy field systems in the universe, in the cosmos and including the Creator-God. It therefore also includes spirit and angelic dimensions. It gives access to truth and to wisdom. Since it is outside of time, it gives access to past, present and future truth and wisdom, and therefore guidance. Its limits are boundless, but only if we have permission to use it.

The wavelengths of the Earth life force can give

access to the consciousness of the Earth itself and the Earth's own energy fields. It is needed to find water and minerals in the Earth, and lost objects. It is widely used for finding water supplies for farming and in the geological prospecting industries. It is also used militarily for finding caches of weapons, and so on.

A combination of cosmic and Earth life force is needed to access the energy field systems and all their consciousness of all life on Earth, that is: humanity, the animal and vegetable energy field systems of nature, known as deva energy, and the mineral energy field systems known as elemental energy. The combined wavelengths of the two life force energies are needed for diagnosis and healing for all life on Earth, including humanity and the Earth itself.

Every energy field has its own wavelength and frequency. Using the psyche and the chakras of the mind energy field and the energy field of matter, a human being can tune in to receive or transmit information from the conscious consciousness of the mind/matter to the sub or superconscious wavelengths and frequencies of the soul and spirit energy fields, and vice versa. Using the mind energy field and its chakras, we can tune in to the psyche to transmit or to receive any information from any wavelength and frequency of any energy field provided we have the permission of the consciousness of that energy field to connect, just as radio hams can transmit and receive messages from and to anywhere in the world if they are connected.

Some people are able to connect into the wavelengths and frequencies of the psyche very easily and naturally, just as some people are naturally gifted musicians, dancers, artists or so on. We say they are 'psychic'. It is not always meant as a compliment. Or they are diagnosed as having this or that syndrome. Understanding the psyche and using it responsibly is very important for our physical and mental health and well-being.

It is important for a healthy psyche that the ratio $2P = N$ is maintained in the energy fields and between the cosmic and Earth life force energies flowing through the energy field systems. This can be achieved by meditation and visualisation. Some problems labelled 'psychotic' can arise if the ratio breaks down.

CHAPTER III
USING THE PSYCHE TO ENRICH OUR LIVES

Ancient Celtic peoples believed we have seven senses. In addition to sight, touch, hearing, smell and taste, using the psyche we can have mind to mind communication, and mind to spirit and soul communication. The communication system of the psyche extends beyond our own minds, spirits and souls to all other wavelengths of mind, spirit and soul in the Earth, of life on Earth including humanity, and in the universe, the cosmos, back to our Creator, if we have permission. For the Celts to include these two extra senses with the five physical senses implies they must have used them in their everyday lives as they would use sight, touch, hearing, smell and taste.

Telepathy is an ability to use the psyche to enable us to connect the consciousness of our own mind energy field with the consciousness flowing through another person's mind energy field, enabling us to communicate mind to mind, using the psyche connections. This ability is part of the normal programme needed by all mothers and babies (human and animal), so that the mother and baby can communicate with each other without words, enabling the mother to know the baby's needs and the baby to communicate its needs. It is stronger in mothers than fathers because the baby's energy field system has been connected to the mother's energy field systems by the life force energies during its life in the womb. Mother and baby will have absorbed some of each other's consciousness. Animals and plants can also communicate with us mind to mind, using the psyche, and we can use the psyche to communicate with them.

Most important, the psyche gives us our own direct link to the Creator-God, to the 'still small voice' we call conscience. We use the psyche when we pray and when we meditate, speaking and listening to the Creator-God, transmitting and receiving, the two-way flow of the labyrinths and the life force energies.

Dowsing is a simple, elegant tool to enable us to access any part of the communication circuit created by the three wavelengths of the psyche and to receive a reply. It uses the wavelengths and frequencies of the consciousness of our mind and matter energy fields to connect to the psychic wavelengths needed to give us access to the wavelengths and frequencies of the consciousness of any other energy field anywhere on the psyche network, on the Earth, of the Earth, in the cosmos and including the Creator-God, provided we have permission to make the connection. Dowsing is the simplest, most sophisticated cosmic radio computer ever devised.

The difference between the psyche internet and the digital internet is that the psyche internet is fed by information from the Creator about all creation, and its consciousness is held in the universal consciousness of the energy fields of the cosmos, and is therefore always the truth. The digital internet is human-made and therefore has error. Any faults in information received via the psyche are due to human misinterpretation and misunderstanding of the information, and not to the information itself.

CHAPTER IV

AN ENERGENIC EXPLANATION OF HOW DOWSING WORKS

If we are to use our mind energy field wavelengths fully, we have to concentrate our thought energy and our consciousness for longer periods of time than normal. We have to learn how to control the flow of the cosmic and Earth life forces as they travel through the connections in and out of the mind energy field into spirit and soul wavelengths, back again into mind and matter and into the physical body. Normally the flow is so fast we are not aware of having any contact at all with our spirit and soul wavelengths, with our sub or superconsciousness. It is outside of time! If we are to become aware, we have to use the mind/matter/physical matter connection to transform it into our physical awareness. This is the role of the dowsing tool.

Focusing and concentrating our dowsing questions on the dowsing tool is a simple way to hold and concentrate our conscious thought for much longer than normal to enable us to make the necessary connections. We can also achieve this through meditation. Dowsing is a form of interactive meditation and prayer. The dowsing response to the questions asked is shown through the dowsing tool used. This is usually a hand-held pendulum or rods. Sometimes, depending on the person's sensitivity and experience, the tool is part of the dowser's own body, for example the hands or finger, or even the blinking of the eyes. The response of the tool gives the dowsing signal which shows the answer to the question. For example, if the dowsing tool being used is a hand-held pendulum, the 'yes' response is often shown by a clockwise swing, a 'no' response by an anticlockwise swing, and a 'don't know' response by a sideways or to-and-fro movement. These responses can vary from person to person so the individual's own dowsing responses must be checked and verified before dowsing begins.

The area of the physical brain which enables us to be consciously aware of using our psyche communications link is the pineal gland and its energy field system, which receives and stores all the programmes and consciousness needed for the function of the autonomic and sympathetic nervous systems.

All consciousness has within it thought, sound and light. The sonic resonance of the sound within the consciousness of the question, whether spoken or thought, vibrates from the questioner to the consciousness within the energy field system of the object of the question, and back to the energy field system of the questioner, through the connecting life force wavelengths of the psyche. This interaction produces the responding harmonic sonic resonance which will either be harmonious with the question, producing the 'yes' signal, or inharmonious, producing the 'no' signal, or neutral, producing the 'don't know' signal of the hand-held dowsing tool.

If the human body is used as a dowsing tool, the

vibration of the sound of the response within the interconnecting life force wavelength triggers that part of the programme held in the pineal gland which is needed to create the involuntary movement of the part of the body being used as a tool. It follows, therefore, that we all have programmed into us the ability to dowse, if we want to use it.

Provided our energy fields and their chakras, especially the ninth and third chakras, are in balance and harmony and fully working to maintain the correct ratio of the cosmic and Earth life forces through the whole energy field system, and the energy field system is securely connected to the energy field system of the pineal gland, we can all dowse accurately.

If we are easily able to tune in to the cosmic wavelength, we will be able to tune in to a combination of the cosmic and Earth wavelengths and all that they access, but we may not be able to tune in to the Earth wavelength alone. This accounts for why some people, including myself, cannot dowse to find water, minerals or lost objects.

When we are dowsing on the cosmic wavelength, or the combination of cosmic and Earth wavelengths, we need to ask for protection for the connections with our own energy field system. The energenic connections needed for dowsing are disrupted or blocked by contra-thought and consciousness, both our own and/or contra-consciousness absorbed into our mind/matter energy fields from external sources. This may be the reason why some people say they cannot dowse. Anyone, everyone, can dowse. As with all our skills, natural or learned, practice makes perfect. We can use dowsing to enable us to access our own spirit and soul wavelengths, sometimes referred to as our 'higher selves'. Dowsing is a useful tool to enable us to sharpen our intuition and to check the accuracy of our intuitive thoughts.

Before using the cosmic wavelength and/or the combined cosmic and Earth life force wavelengths of the universal psyche for dowsing, we must obtain permission to tune in to these wavelengths and have permission to use our own psyche to tune in to the psyche of the energy field system of the object or subject of the dowsing. We can do this by using our verified dowsing response to ask not only if we have permission to dowse, but also if we have permission to proceed from the subject of the dowsing. This applies whether it is dowsing for a blade of grass, a human being, the Universal consciousness, or the Creator-God. Having obtained permission, it is important not to exceed its remit.

If we access, dowse, on these wavelengths of the psyche without permission, we will have a faulty connection and any information we receive will be inaccurate, which will rebound back to the dowser. The Creator has made the dowsing communication system safe from abuse.

Dowsing is only as good as the questions asked and since the questions can only be answered by 'yes', 'no' or 'don't know', they need to be phrased with this in mind. Its limits are our own limits and our ability to use creatively our mind energy fields, thought energy and conscious consciousness, to formulate the right questions accurately and precisely. For example, there is a subtle difference between 'Can I do...?' and 'Should I do...?' and the dowsing response to those questions will reflect that subtlety. The answer to 'Can I...?' may be 'Yes', but the answer to 'Should I...?' may be 'No'. This example demonstrates the importance of using truth with wisdom.

Sometimes we may want or need another dowser to check our information. If so, it is important to ask someone who works on the same wavelengths and frequencies we are working on and whose energy field system has a sonic resonance compatible with our own. How do we know if the dowsing should be checked and who to ask? By dowsing!

As with other aspects of life, if knowledge is being sought about a complicated subject, sometimes two or more heads are better than one for formulating the best questions to arrive at the accurate answer. A crucial part of dowsing is interpreting the answers correctly in order to arrive at the truth.

Fairy stories and myths contain the remnants of much long-forgotten knowledge. The priests and priestesses of the ancient oracle were dowsers. Is the origin of the magic wand a dowsing rod with a crystal attached to the end of it to enhance its efficiency?

The Church outlawed dowsing in the twelfth century, saying it was connected to the devil. It is exactly the opposite. When we tune in to the cosmic life force, our individual connection with the Creator-God is strengthened and gives us a direct line to the ultimate truth and wisdom. This is very empowering for the individual, which is not what power-hungry institutions want.

The dowsing tool is a very useful, effective, healing tool for 'lasering' the healing energy of the cosmic life force from the source into areas where it has become disconnected and/or depleted so that these areas are accurately reconnected and replenished.

Dowsing is a wonderful diagnostic tool. It is so sensitive it can pick up malfunctions of the energy field systems before they have manifested in the physical body, and it can be used to repair any damage.

This book is not about how to heal or how to dowse. There are many excellent books available on these subjects.

PART VII
THE ENERGENICS OF CONCEPTION
AND OF DYING

CHAPTER I

CONCEPTION, GESTATION AND BIRTH

There are only two sure things about our lives on Earth: we are conceived and physically born, and we physically die. Energenics, together with an understanding of the psyche, the two life force energies and the eternal cosmic energy fields of soul, spirit and mind, can help to explain the energy processes of conception and dying.

A new human being is conceived when the human egg is fertilised by the human sperm. Energenically, the Earth life force integrates the two energy field systems of matter of the egg and of the sperm. Fertilisation occurs when the cosmic life force brings a 'new' combination of soul-spirit-mind energy fields from the cosmic energy fields and transmits and integrates them into the newly integrated soul, spirit and mind energy fields of the combined energy field systems of the egg and the sperm.

The cosmic and Earth life forces flowing through the newly integrated energy fields of soul-spirit-mind carry their combined consciousness, blueprints and programmes into the newly integrated energy fields of matter of the egg and the sperm, and the new energy field of matter for the fertilised egg is formed. The new energy field system, with its new blueprint and pro-grammes for the new human being, is in place. It is connected to the physical matter of the fertilised egg by the water of the fluids surrounding it in the uterus.

The remainder of the new energenic connecting system of molecules is formed from the new programmes in the new energy field system of the fertilised egg. The first molecules to evolve are the DNA and the genes.

Using its new blueprint and programmes, the newly fertilised egg, the blastocyst, physically splits several times, and the human embryo begins to develop in the water of the protective sac at the centre of the uterus.

Each embryo is unique, including twins, and each one is eternally connected to the cosmic dimensions of the wavelengths of soul, spirit and mind by the cosmic life force. The energy fields of mind and matter of identical twins are connected, but they have separate spirit and separate soul energy fields.

The new incoming cosmic soul-spirit-mind energy fields bring to the new energy field system of the embryo their own consciousness, information and programmes, possibly absorbed and collected over aeons of time in the universe and on Earth.

The energy field systems of the egg and of the sperm also bring to the new energy field system of the embryo all the consciousness, information and programmes gathered over the present lifetimes of the mother and of the father, including their conscious consciousness at the moment of fertilisation, and all the previous existences of their soul-spirit-mind energy fields. They will also contain consciousness and programmes absorbed from the energy field systems of previous generations of the families of the mother and of the father. This is how family likenesses and traits, and sometimes diseases, are passed from one generation to another.

The new main energy field system and its chakras resonate both around and within the new human being in the uterus.

The cosmic and Earth life forces circulating through the energy fields of the foetus also absorb consciousness from the energy field systems of the mother. Unfortunately this may include residues of stress and trauma suffered by the mother before, during or after conception and through the pregnancy. Depending on the severity of the stress, its contra-consciousness may be transmitted into the energy field systems of the baby and become part of its deep subconscious. This may affect the baby's own developing blueprint and programme but the results may not show in the physical body until later in life, sometimes much later.

The energy fields of the developing foetus are very delicate and are programmed to absorb the adapted cosmic and Earth life force energies transmitted to it through the waters of the womb. Polluted water will inhibit the transmission of the life force energies to the developing cells and organs of the foetus. I have already mentioned the devastating effect of contra physical sound, such as heavy metal music (Part IV, Chapter V). However residues of the ultrasound of scans during pregnancy are equally harmful to the developing child.

CHAPTER II

THE ENERGENICS OF DYING

In our Western civilizations, one of the greatest fears we humans have is a fear of what happens to us when we die. Our attitude to dying colours our living. If this fear can be removed, it can make a huge difference to the balance and harmony of our lives and the way we live our lives. It can bring a tranquillity which is of great value to our mental and physical well-being.

The core of our beings is the immortal, eternal combination of our soul, our spirit and our mind energy fields, together with all the consciousness these energy fields have processed at conception, in the womb and during our lifetime on Earth. To help our understanding, it is useful to remember that during our physical lives, the main energy field system of a human being including all its chakra systems, and the cosmic and Earth life force energies flowing through them, resonates simultaneously in the aura and within the physical body. The two life force energies transmit the accumulated consciousness of the energy fields, containing all the programmes for the physical function of the body, to and through all the subsidiary energy field systems of the body, from molecules onwards. The energy field systems of the molecules of the water of the body are used to make the first connection for transmitting the two life force energies into the physical body.

The physical body dies when its connecting mechanism to the energy field systems breaks down irretrievably and it can no longer receive and process the two life force energies from the cosmos and from the Earth. When this happens, the two life force energies which have been circulating in partnership, but in opposite directions, through the energy field pathways and chakras, separate.

The main core of our being, the three main energy fields of soul, spirit and mind and all their consciousness, separate from the main energy field of matter and from the Earth life force and therefore from the Earth. The soul, spirit and mind energy fields remain connected to the cosmic life force.

The fourth main energy field of the system, the main energy field of matter of the whole physical body, together with all the subsidiary energy field systems of the physical component parts of the physical body, and all their consciousness from atoms and molecules onwards, remain connected to the Earth life force. They return to the Earth and the Earth's own energy field wavelengths. These are the wavelengths generally known as the astral plain.

Using the Earth life force and the cosmic life force which is part of, and within, the Earth life force, and which is circulating through the Earth's own energy field systems, the physical matter of the body gradually disintegrates back into its atoms of the ninety-two natural elements of the Earth and rejoins the atoms of the Earth: 'ashes to ashes, dust to dust'. This is also what happens to other animal and plant life on the planet.

Perhaps we have an innate knowledge of these processes when we pray for someone who is dying. When we pray, we are instinctively reaching out to the Creator-God and the source of the cosmic life force. We are bringing in cosmic life force to rebalance Earth life force, facilitating the separation of the two life forces so that the main energy fields of soul, spirit and mind can easily make the transition to the cosmic wavelengths, and the remaining energy fields to the Earth wavelengths. The physical human has made the transition from physical life to life which is known as 'life in spirit': spirit forms the connection between soul and mind.

During our eternal lives in this cosmic dimension known as spirit, the soul energy field continues to be the keeper of the complete programme for its spirit and mind, and is the most important receiver of the pure cosmic life force. Mind and soul energy fields communicate with each other through the spirit energy field, and mind and spirit also have a direct link to the cosmic life force through their ninth chakras. All three energy fields are connected to the eternal psyche wavelengths of the cosmic life force. Therefore they are able to communicate with any other energy field connected to the psyche. This means that it is possible for a physical person, with permission, to use the psyche link to connect mind to mind, spirit to spirit, soul to soul with a person in spirit, if the spirit is also able and wishes to connect.

During our physical lifetime on Earth, our soul and

spirit energy fields gradually absorb consciousness from the mind and matter energy fields which have direct access to our physical bodies and our physical lives. So soul, as well as mind, will have an imprint on its consciousness of the physical body and the physical consciousness of our lives. This is how and why clairvoyant mediums can 'see', using their mind's eye, what a spirit looked like and can describe its physical appearance and character when it was living in the physical dimension of Earth.

If, when a person dies, their consciousness is weighed down with excess fear and/or contra-consciousness, the Earth life force will be too strong for the soul, spirit and mind energy fields to separate from the main energy field system of the person because the cosmic life force in their energy field system will be correspondingly too weak to separate from the Earth life force, and will be unable to transmit the soul-spirit-mind energy fields to their right dimensions and wavelengths in the cosmic energy fields. The soul-spirit-mind energy fields will stay connected in the circle-cross format with their energy field of matter and remain attached to the Earth life force in the Earth's own energy fields. The body will disintegrate as usual but instead of only the energy field of matter being connected to the Earth's energy systems, the whole main energy field system of the person will be attached to the Earth's energy field systems and will be carried along by the Earth life force. It may be deposited on to the energy field systems of other places, people or belongings, sometimes fleetingly, or it may stay attached to the environment where it had lived or died in physical life. Remembering the light property of the Earth life force is black, these spirits will appear to be in darkness or in a grey twilight and become 'lost' in their wrong wavelengths of energy and environment. These earthbound spirits are known as 'spirit attachments'.

It is very important to rescue spirit attachments, and not only for their own well-being. They have an extremely unbalancing effect on the host energy fields and consciousness. In addition to the contra-consciousness which has kept the spirit attachment earthbound through its connection with the Earth life force, it adds to and continues to upset the balance and harmony of the Earth life force and the consciousness of the Earth ley lines. This has consequent harmful effects on the flora and fauna, and especially on humans, in the environment of the spirit attachment, i.e. where the earthbound spirit has become attached. They can and should be helped by a special form of healing which heals and transmits them into their right dimension in the cosmic wavelength and clears and cleanses the Earth environment of any of their contra-consciousness left behind in the Earth life force.

What is a Ghost and how is it Different from a Spirit Attachment?

When the main energy field of matter of a human or animal, and its consciousness, merges with the Earth's own energy field of matter, its consciousness normally also becomes part of the consciousness of the Earth and therefore the Earth life force. The energy field of matter of the physical body and its consciousness, animal or human, has impressed upon it the form of the physical body as it was in life, but not necessarily as it was at the time of death. It will project the part of life when the consciousness in the energy field system, and therefore the energy field of matter of that person, was strongest. If this consciousness is particularly strong, the person's energy field of matter may not be able to be completely assimilated into the Earth's consciousness, and will remain separated from the Earth's consciousness, usually in the place where the physical person lived and/or died. It is this separated consciousness that is a ghost.

A spirit attachment consists of the whole energy field system and its consciousness of a person. It includes the displaced soul, spirit and mind energy fields which have become tied into the Earth life force because the cosmic life force is/was too weak to carry the spirit, and its soul, spirit and mind energy fields into their right dimensions and wavelengths of energy. A spirit attachment can attach to any energy field system, not only the Earth's and the Earth life force. Its presence is always unbalancing and therefore potentially harmful since its attachment is usually due to shock and trauma of some kind.

If the projected consciousness of the energy field of matter, the ghost, has good positive vibrations, the Earth and therefore the Earth's life force in that place will remain in balance and harmony and can be beneficial. If, however, trauma, shock and their associated excess fear is involved in the consciousness which has resulted in the ghost, the Earth life force in that place will be unbalanced by the ghost contra-consciousness and will have a detrimental effect on the lives and health of the people living and working there.

This situation can also be easily remedied by healing, by the healer connecting sufficient cosmic life force to neutralise the contra-consciousness of the ghost so that it becomes harmoniously assimilated back into the Earth's consciousness, and the Earth life force is rebalanced and harmonised. It is a very important part of healing the Earth.

As with spirits and spirit attachments, some very sensitive, highly attuned people, especially young children and animals, can sense and 'see' ghosts and some can actually see the physical impression of their consciousness. When it is unexpected and not understood, it can be very unnerving.

Contra human consciousness in all its guises pollutes the Earth life force and therefore pollutes the Earth itself, the water of the Earth and all life on Earth. Unless it is cleared and balanced, it blocks the Earth's energy field chakras and disrupts the flow of cosmic life force through and into the Earth and all its energy systems.

One of the factors producing global warming, but of course not taken into account, is the huge amount of contra-consciousness of human 'hot air' emitted by us, and especially by the global media and the Internet.

CHAPTER III
A BRIEF EXPLANATION OF MEDIUMSHIP

Many people have an innate knowledge of life after the physical life on Earth, because it is part of our programme in the deep sub or superconsciousness of the soul energy field. Most people, when asked, can remember having some experience of sensing, seeing or hearing spirit and the wavelengths and dimensions of spirit we know as angels. Often these experiences are explained away as inexplicable.

We call our modern, mainly electronic, communications industry 'the media', the Latin plural of medium, a communicator. It passes information from place to place, person to person, computer to computer, and so on.

The title of 'medium' is usually reserved for someone who is able to use their own energy field system and their own connection to the cosmic wavelength of the psyche to consciously and physically communicate with mind, spirit and soul consciousness in the eternal dimensions of the energy fields of the cosmos, provided that spirit is able to and willing to communicate with a person who is physically alive on Earth.

Just as it takes skills to be able to be a medium, the spirit also needs the skill to be able to communicate back to Earth. The spirit may have to develop the skill during its life in the cosmic dimensions.

I use 'title' deliberately. To be a medium is a privilege and a gift. Like any other gift, it needs practice, hard work, training and commitment if it is to be fully and correctly used and appreciated.

Some people have very open and sensitive connections, not only with their own psyche wavelengths of the cosmic and Earth life forces in their own energy field systems, but especially with the psyche wavelengths and connections to the life forces and energy field systems in their surroundings and with other people. They can connect very easily mind to mind, spirit to spirit, soul to soul with other spirits and, unfortunately, with spirit attachments. If they, or their families, do not understand what is happening, these connections can be very disturbing. Sadly, these people are often labelled 'psychotic' or mad. Energenic healing, using a team of healers who understand the problems, can give very effective help to these people. Since it is a problem of disturbed consciousness, it needs to be dealt with by using consciousness, i.e. healing.

A sensitive psyche, when it is controlled and understood, is a gift, just as skills in music, dancing or mathematics are considered gifts. Very young children often have wonderful clear psyches which enable them to connect to many dimensions of consciousness, both in the physical world and the cosmic/Earth worlds of spirit and soul, but as it is rarely understood or encouraged, it usually dims as they grow older.

Autism and some learning and behaviour difficulties are often caused by spirit attachments and by disturbed and/or faulty connections in the child's psyche, and in the main energy field system and the energy field systems in the brain. Specialist vibrational medicine, and healing, should be incorporated into the help and treatment they receive.

The ancient Egyptians had a very good clear knowledge of the cosmic dimension of our energy fields, i.e. of spirit, and of the process of dying. It is shown in the illustration of Nefertari being received into spirit. The Book of the Dead shows clearly their knowledge of the continuation of the life of the soul, spirit and mind after the physical body dies.

PART VIII
THE MERIDIANS

CHAPTER I

A SHORT SUMMARY OF THE PRINCIPLES OF THE MERIDIANS AND OF ACUPUNCTURE

The meridians in the human body form a completely separate energy system from the energy field systems of Energenics. They are equally important and operate as a partnership. In physical terms, they could be described as similar to the two separate water systems in the physical body: the lymph and the blood.

Knowledge of the meridian system of energy in the human body has been handed down to us through Chinese and Japanese medicine for centuries. It forms the basis of the therapies of acupuncture, acupressure, shiatsu, aromatherapy and reflexology, and of tai chi, chi-qong and kung fu.

In the Chinese concept, chi is carried through the human body by lines of energy called meridians. Fourteen meridians connect vertically with all the major organs of the body, from the top of the head to the feet, along the arms and hands, along the spine and up the centre front of the body.

The balance and equilibrium within the chi is known as yin and yang. The chi will be unbalanced if yin and yang are out of balance with each other. Too much yin will lead to a deficiency of yang. Too much yang will produce a deficiency of yin. Imbalance in the chi will upset the flow of the chi along the meridians making it either too fast or too slow. The adverse effect this has on the physical body can be treated by acupuncture.

If the flow of chi is blocked in a meridian, it can be released at various points on the skin which relate to points on the meridians. They are known as the acupuncture points. Needles are inserted into the skin at the diagnosed points, and have the effect of releasing the chi, allowing it to flow freely along the meridian again.

Acupuncture is a diagnostic tool which recognises energy components of physical matter and provides a clinical, physical means of accessing them. It was devised to work directly on the meridians, to free them from distortions and imbalances caused by blocked energy, using the points on the meridians.

By 1992, advances in the use of radioactive traces have shown not only that meridians exist in the human body, but that they exist as mapped in ancient Chinese medicine. They show the meridians also flow in the 'spaces' between the blood vessels and cells.

The principles of acupuncture are known as the five phases and the eight criteria needed to arrive at an accurate diagnosis and acupuncture treatment. The five phases are: water, wood, fire, earth and metal. They are also known as the five elements.

The eight criteria are: yin and yang, cold and hot, empty and full, and internal and external. Each of the five phases is examined for imbalance in the four pairs of opposites which make up the eight criteria. Since

Western medicine has phased out a life force energy component in the physical body, this appears as nonsense to most Western doctors and scientists, although many are now exploring these possibilities. The important relationship of 5:8 is shown in the classical labyrinth, in the pyramids, the golden mean and the ratio between the Fibonacci series of numbers.

Just as an imbalance in the flow of traffic on the roads can eventually cause traffic jams, so the flow of chi along the meridians can become blocked. Blocked chi shows physically as pain. Continuing the traffic analogy, the tailback from the cause of the traffic jam may stretch for miles. Similarly, blocked chi may show as pain in a part of the body seemingly unrelated to the cause of the pain. We call it 'referred' pain. In fact, all the molecules, cells and organs of the body are interrelated.

There is a huge amount of knowledge and many excellent books about the meridians and about acupuncture and its allied therapies. Here is a very brief outline.

The main meridians in the human body are numbered one to fourteen. They are:

1. heart;
2. small intestine;
3. bladder;
4. kidney;
5. pericardium;
6. triple heater;

7. gall bladder;

8. liver;

9. lung;

10. large intestine;

11. stomach;

12. spleen;

13. conception vessel;

14. governor vessel.

Numbers one to twelve run in pairs on either side of the body. A fault in the meridian on one side of the body also shows on the other side.

Six meridians connect to and from the legs and feet; of these, three connect from the head to the legs and feet. They are classed as yang. They are the bladder (three), the gall bladder (seven) and the stomach (eleven).

Three meridians connect from the feet to the trunk of the body. They are classed as yin and are the kidney (four), the liver (eight) and the spleen (twelve).

Six meridians connect to and from the hands. Of these, three connect from the hands and arms to the head. They are classed as yang. They are the small intestine (two), the triple heater (six) and the large intestine (ten).

Three meridians connect from the trunk of the body to the hands. They are classed as yin and are the heart (one), pericardium (five) and the lung (nine).

The thirteenth meridian, known as the conception vessel, starts near the anus and runs up the centre of the front of the body, neck, throat and chin, to just below the bottom lip.

The fourteenth meridian, the governor vessel, starts at the coccyx and runs up the spine, up the centre of the back of the body, to the neck and head, over the top of the head to the centre of the forehead, the nose, to the top lip, and finishes on the centre of the top gum inside the mouth.

Every meridian has a number of points placed at various intervals along the meridian. These are the points used in acupuncture. One of the points on each meridian is a 'source point' which keeps that meridian in balance. It is similar to a datum point.

The meridians and the energenic energy field systems are connected by the main chakras.

The circadian rhythms in the body, which control our body clocks, are controlled by the flow of energy in the meridians.

Japanese shiatsu follows similar principles to Chinese acupuncture. Instead of using needles, the blocked life force energy, *hado*, is released by applying gentle pressure on the acupuncture points of the meridians both on the skin and at deeper levels within the body. Shiatsu means 'finger pressure' but other parts of the hands and the elbows, the knees and the feet, are also used to apply the pressure to the body. Although the name shiatsu is relatively modern, dating from around 1900, its origins go back thousands of years.

Aromatherapy massages the essential oils into the body along the meridian lines. This releases blocked energy and corrects the speed of the flow of chi along the affected meridians.

Reflexology is another ancient Eastern energy therapy. It is thought to have originated about five thousand years ago in Egypt. The energy of every organ in the body is reflected in the feet and hands via the meridians. If pressure on a part of the foot produces pain, it indicates a malfunction in the organ reflected in that part of the foot. Gentle massage relieves the pain and helps to heal the affected organ by releasing the blocked *hado*, or chi. Reflexology is being widely used in the West. Practitioners are working with doctors in hospitals and hospices with very beneficial results.

CHAPTER II

HOW ENERGENICS CONNECTS WITH THE MERIDIANS

The Energenics hypothesis proposes that meridians are the body's equivalent of the Earth's ley lines and their energy composition is very similar. They both reflect the consciousness of their physical structures and are energised by them. The meridians reflect the consciousness of all the energy field systems of all the molecules, cells, neurotransmitters, tissues and organs in the physical body. The meridians *do not* carry the life force energies – that is the function of the energy fields – but they are used to enhance the life force energies, as the mirror facets of a lighthouse lantern enhance the light given out by the lamp inside. Meridians resonate on a wavelength of energy which is between the energy field systems and physical matter. They are, therefore, a wavelength nearer to physical matter.

This enables meridians to act like a telecommunications system for the whole physical body, keeping all parts of the physical body in communication with each other. This communication system is used by the cranial nerves, neurons and neurotransmitters in the brain, gut and spine, to transfer instant information needed for the smooth operation of the autonomic nervous system, and for communicating within and between the cells and neurotransmitters. If there is a problem anywhere in the physical body, it will be reflected and communicated in the meridians.

Each meridian is constructed in a similar way to the energy field pathways and to the Earth ley lines. They are each made of the seven strands of the wavelengths of sound and light of the tonic sol-fa and the spectrum. If we could see the meridians, I believe they would look like spiralling rainbow ribbons. The polarity of each of the seven strands of the ribbon should be positive, positive, negative, neutral, positive, positive, negative.

The source point of each main meridian is a vortex of energy in the form of a classical labyrinth. It is not an energy field so it does not have chakras. If the source point is in balance, the whole meridian will be balanced.

The points used on the meridians for acupuncture occur where the spiralling 'ribbon' twists to change direction.

Sound and light reflected from the organs and resonating through the meridians will be distorted if the subsidiary energy field system of any organ, cell or molecule is distorted. Depending on the severity of the distortion, the spiralling ribbon of the meridian tangles or knots at the turning point of the spiral. It becomes out of tune. If it becomes knotted, the energy flow will be blocked at that point and the resulting build-up of energy behind the knot will manifest in the physical body as pain or inflammation.

Pain represents an emergency telephone call by the cells of the organ via the neurotransmitters, communicating that all is not well. Pain is directly related to the meridians and is a physical manifestation of an energy phenomenon. The meridians block as they become tangled and knotted by the distorted energy reflected from the organ. Energy (chi) builds up behind the blocks and causes pressure. The knots and blocks in the affected meridians distort the information being sent and received by the neurotransmitters and the result is inflammation, physical pain and/or discomfort.

Since meridians only resonate between the wavelengths of the energy field of matter and physical matter, when using the meridians to treat a physical malfunction only some of the energy symptoms of the physical problems are being addressed. The therapies of the meridians, acupuncture, acupressure, shiatsu, are as valuable today as they ever were. But they are only a part of the energy picture.

Imbalance in the meridians, which can be detected by dowsing, is the effect of the cause of disease and the resulting disease, but it is not the cause itself. However, blocked meridians are the cause of the effect of pain.

For a lasting solution to our physical problems, I have found the energy field system and its chakras need to be healed first, followed by clearing the meridians. The meridians cannot flow if any of the chakras are malfunctioning. The knowledge of chakras and the knowledge of meridians have been linked together since very ancient times.

Chinese culture has long understood that just as our internal 'environment' of the cells and organs within our bodies should be in balance and harmony, so the external environment of our homes, workplaces, schools and hospitals should be in balance and harmony. The two are inseparable.

The meridians in the feet, whether flowing down into the feet from the body or up from the feet into the body, connect with the ley lines in the Earth. The Earth ley lines recharge the meridians with more electromagnetic chi from the Earth. All is well in the meridians if the ley lines in the Earth are in balance and harmony.

Unfortunately any disharmony and imbalance echoing in the Earth's ley lines will be relayed through our meridians directly into the organs of the physical body. These distortions are in addition to any distortions to the Earth life force energy caused by pollution of the energy fields of the Earth. In effect, due to the meridians, we receive a double dose of polluted Earth energy. At the same time, the meridians discharge their energy through the feet into the Earth. All is well in the ley lines of the Earth if the energy discharged is balanced. If it is polluted, it will add to the Earth's energy pollution.

The effect of the distortions of Earth life force energy and of the Earth ley lines on the physical body is known as geopathic stress. Sometimes its effect is felt immediately; sometimes it takes a steady 'drip, drip' over a period of time before the effect of the resulting imbalances becomes apparent. In my experience, it is always an important factor in all forms of ill health, especially cancer. Occasionally it is the only factor. The Chinese system of feng shui is designed to help to keep the energies of the environment of home and work-place in balance and harmony with their occupants (see Part III, Chapter VIII).

PART IX
THE CAUSES OF DISTORTED ENERGY FIELD SYSTEMS

CHAPTER I

THE ENERGENIC EFFECTS OF SHOCK

Part IX explores the causes of the energenic problems which can lead to physical and mental ill health in humans. Energenics grew out of my work as a healer and my quest to understand how, and especially why, an illness started, how and why healing works, and why healing is sometimes blocked.

Physical matter and its energy field systems, including the physical human body and all its energy field systems, are inextricably linked. The circle-cross labyrinth shows this clearly with the symbol for physical matter at the centre, at the hub.

The circle-cross labyrinth shows how the energy fields of soul and spirit merge, and how mind and matter energy fields merge, and shows mind links spirit and matter. Therefore what affects one will affect the others. Contra-consciousness and our contra conscious thinking may affect the behaviour of physical matter. Similarly, if physical upheaval or trauma to the physical body also disrupts consciousness and connections in the energy fields of matter and mind, the whole energy field system may be affected. Eventually this may cause a distortion in the programmes for the physical matter of the body.

The two-way flow of the cosmic and Earth life forces in and out of the energy fields ensures that any fault, anywhere in any of the subsidiary energy fields and their chakras of molecules onwards, is transmitted to, and recorded in, the main energy field system of the body and vice versa. Any fault in the main energy field system will be recorded in the energy fields and chakras of the subsidiary systems.

This is why the main energy field system and its chakras form such a valuable diagnostic aid. A potential physical fault in a molecule will show in the aura of the whole body, even before it becomes physically evident in the physical body. Using the psyche connection of the life force energies, it can be detected by dowsing and put right. Most importantly, the cause of the problem can be found and remedied wherever it is in the system: soul, spirit, mind or matter, both energy field and physical.

The energy fields and the life force energies flowing through them are all basically made of thought energy, with all the various wavelengths and frequencies of sound and light of the consciousness it produces.

Human energy fields are extremely sensitive and immensely strong. They have a built-in resilience so that most contra interference bounces off without damaging them or their chakras. However, both chronic and acute disease in the physical body develops from dis-ease, i.e. discomfort, caused by contra-consciousness which leads to distortion and/or dis-ruption somewhere in the energy field systems.

If the disease is to be eradicated and cured, the root cause of the dis-ease needs to be identified, put right or eliminated. It is therefore essential to know and understand what can cause the distortions and disruptions which can lead to disease.

Even some physical injuries which, on the surface, appear to have no connection with soul, spirit, mind and matter energy fields may have their roots somewhere in a disruption in the energy field system leading to weakness in its associated part of the physical body.

The effect of shock on the human body is well known. At its worst, it can result in death. Within and around us, and on or within the Earth, shocks little and large, major and minor, are continually affecting our lives, our health and our well-being. Our resilient energenic and physical make-up enables us to withstand and overcome the effects of shock and resolve it. Problems arise when our ability, mentally and physically, to resolve shock on a day-to-day basis breaks down.

According to the *Shorter Oxford English Dictionary*, the word 'shock' was in use before AD 1150. It is an old English word meaning 'a group of sixty units'. A shock of corn was a group of sixty sheaves of corn, placed upright and supporting each other. By the fourteenth century, shock also meant 'a crowd of people, or a heap or bundle of things'.

By AD 1565, 'shock' had acquired an additional meaning, derived from the old French word '*choquer*', and the later French word '*choc*', which were used in jousting to describe the encounter of two mounted warriors charging at each other. 'Shock' came to mean 'a sudden or violent blow, impact or collision, tending to overthrow or to produce internal oscillation in a body subjected to it'. By 1614, shock also meant 'the disturbance of equilibrium, or the internal oscillation resulting from this'. By 1705, 'shock' was used to mean 'a sudden and disturbing impression on the mind or feelings, usually produced by some unwelcome occurrence and perception'.

At first glance, it looks as though the early and later meanings of the word 'shock' are unrelated. However, looking at the later meaning of 'shock' in terms of consciousness energy, we can see it would contain a 'heap or bundle' of contra-consciousness which produced/caused the sudden violent blow, either physical and/or mental, of the shock itself. The effect of the sudden violent blow, or disturbing impression, in turn produces the disturbance of equilibrium, physical and mental, adding still further to the 'heap or bundle' of the contra-consciousness of shock.

Shock to the energy field systems creates a situation comparable with the tremors felt in the Earth caused by an earthquake. Small tremors from small earthquakes are hardly felt and any disturbance is quickly rebalanced. The vibrations of a major earthquake can be catastrophic.

The vibrations of shock cause a great disturbance similar to the effect of the shockwaves created by the collision of the Earth's tectonic plates under the sea, which produces a tsunami. The effects of a physical tsunami can be felt worldwide. An energenic tsunami caused by shock can be felt throughout the energy field system and in the physical body.

The shock from physical trauma, as well as damaging the physical body, explodes into the energy fields in the aura and within the body. The shockwaves and the vibrations they produce in the energy field pathways disrupt the life force energies flowing through, which floods and blocks the next chakra. The whole energy field is disrupted in the aura and within the body. The organs of the physical body may begin to malfunction in the area of the blocked, swamped chakra.

In my own experience, the onset of a serious disease, for example cancer in the physical body, can usually be traced back to shock from trauma which may have happened several years, or even many years, before the illness began but is directly connected to it.

Large shock can be built up from the steady 'drip, drip' of little shocks, caused by unresolved stress and its persistent contra-consciousness of worry and anxiety. The build-up of excess contra-consciousness can eventually have a harmful effect on the human body, causing the essential connecting mechanisms between the energy field systems and the physical body to break down.

A jolt is a small shock caused by a small amount of stress. It can be beneficial. Sometimes the life force energy flowing through the energy field systems becomes stagnant and needs something to move it forward. If we have become stuck in certain behaviour and thinking patterns, we may need a jolt to move us forward and away from the old redundant patterns into new ways of thinking, into new and renewing consciousness. In the physical world, the proverbial remedy for fixing something mechanical is to first of all shake it or bang it! We use a short, sharp shock to help someone overcome and move out of hysteria caused by a large shock, for example the jolt of the sonic energy of smelling salts.

The balance ($2P = N$) within an energy field and within its chakras can be upset by the 'internal oscillation' caused by shock, mental or physical. If the shock is severe, it can disturb the equilibrium between all the energy fields of the energy field system and cause a breakdown in communication between the energy fields and its chakras. The life force energies are unable to flow freely through the system and the chakras block. The life force energies build up behind the blockage and spill into the other chakras and pathways, upsetting their balance, harmony and equilibrium. Other energy fields in the system are affected when the disturbance reaches the third chakra, the entrance and exit of the energy fields, or the eighth chakra, which holds the equilibrium between the energy fields, or the first, fourth and seventh chakras. It is most serious if the ninth chakra is blocked, preventing the intake of cosmic life force.

A malfunctioning organ in the physical body may need a surgical operation. The operation will cause shock in the energenic systems of the body. This can be resolved by using energenic therapies such as healing and flower essences (see Part X), together with the usual physical remedies.

CHAPTER II
THOUGHT FORMS

Thought forms are the remnants of our contra thoughts and thinking, the bogeymen, the ghosts we build up for ourselves in our minds, especially after shock and emotional or physical trauma. They are made from stored fragments of distorted consciousness and their unbalanced and inharmonious light and sound will continue to upset the equilibrium between the energy fields and the balance within each energy field. They will continue to produce the internal oscillation of the shock.

Eventually thought forms settle like dust in the energy fields of the chakras, creating a situation similar to dust in the mechanism of a clock or watch. Unless the thought forms are cleared away, they gradually accumulate, settling into the chakra most affected by the trauma. The affected chakras will be unable to carry out their function of receiving, transforming and transmitting the two life force energies through the energy fields. If the chakras of the energy field of matter are affected, they will be unable to supply sufficient life force energy to the molecules of the hormones and vital-vitamins connected to the chakra, and the essential chain of communication between the energy fields and physical matter will begin to break down.

If the chakras are working efficiently, they are able to receive the thought forms and, using the balanced life force energies of the cosmos and the Earth, transform them into harmless, balanced consciousness which integrates harmoniously with the consciousness in the energy field systems.

If the thought forms are very large and strong with excessive contra-consciousness, the chakra may not be able to fully process them. If the thought forms are not fully processed, their residues stay in the chakras, clogging and silting, eventually causing disruption to the chakra mechanisms and the whole function of the chakra. This adversely affects the consciousness transmitted into the next pathway and its chakra. In a domino effect, the whole energy field and its chakra systems are thrown out of balance and harmony. Should the silting continue, and if the third chakra (i.e. the entrance and exit of the energy field labyrinth) becomes blocked, the flow of the life force energies between the energy fields will be obstructed. The equilibrium between the energy fields will be disrupted and, eventually, the whole transmission of the programmes through the energy fields is damaged. When this happens, the *dis*ease originating from the shock, or shocks, becomes disease.

Severe shock, resulting in huge thought forms of contra-consciousness, can completely block the entire energy field system very quickly and the result is death.

Some dreams, especially nightmares and disturbing dreams, are manifestations of thought forms we have produced during waking hours which are then released during sleep. It is as though sleep washes and cleans the conscious and subconscious consciousness of the mind energy field. It enables the debris of thought form to be released and brought forward from all the pathways of the energy field to be cleared and eliminated out of harm's way by the cosmic life force as it exits the mind energy field by the third chakra, and before it enters the third chakra of the energy field of matter.

Sleep gives us the opportunity to regularly empty our mental rubbish bins and eject the bogeymen we have created for ourselves with our own worry and stress thoughts: 'Sleep that knits the ravelled sleeve of care'. This is one of the reasons why sleep is so important, especially for the young and the very young. If their bogeymen of stress, anger and worry thoughts are not dissolved away naturally through sleep, they can grow and gather and lead to physical and mental problems later on, often manifesting as behavioural problems.

Thought forms which are ejected from the energy fields during sleep can accumulate, like thought-dust, around the pillow area of the bed. If a person is sensitive to them, they will disturb sleep. The disturbed sleep causes more fear and disruption, escalating into a downward vortex of fear as more and more thought forms are created by the person. They become jammed into the chakras of the energy fields of the brain. The delicate mechanisms of the pineal and pituitary glands and the hippocampus are the first to be affected. Hormones and vital-vitamin connections are disrupted and insomnia develops.

Native Americans make their dream catchers, which

look like spider webs, to catch and dispose of dream thought forms.

All thought forms can be detected by dowsing. Healing is the most effective way of evaporating and eliminating thought forms. They, and their contra-consciousness, must be returned to the source of all thought, all energy, the Creator-God, to be dissolved, cleared and cleansed and their distorted consciousness replaced by pure thought energy from the cosmic life force. I have found the easiest way is to simply say the Lord's Prayer with this intent. The Lord's Prayer was originally written as a healing mantra and transcends all religions. It probably has its origins in the Essene tradition, going back for thousands of years. Evensong and prayers at bedtime probably had their origins in an innate knowledge of the release of thought form during sleep, i.e. at night, and how to clear and cleanse them away. The prayers were, and are, extremely practical and effective.

Panic attacks are caused by the jamming together of many smaller thought forms of worry and anxiety into one large and complicated thought form which blocks the chakra system and prevents sufficient cosmic life force from passing through the mind energy field to correct the imbalance of the Earth life force which results. The chakras associated with the brain and their related hormones are the first to be affected, followed by the fourth chakra. The physical effects may show as palpitations, breathlessness and, at worst, heart attack and/or asthma.

Some long-term thought forms are fed into the human mind energy field, generation after generation, for centuries. They have evolved from stories of man's inhumanity to man, and through stories which became legend, which became myth. The thought forms which have evolved from the continuous telling of these tales have become archetypal. They have become embedded in the collective psyche of humanity, sometimes undermining individual free will. They can adversely affect the collective behaviour of humanity in deed and word, feeding human's inhumanity to humans and to other life on the planet.

The Earth's own energy fields, and the ley lines, are thrown into disarray from shocks caused by natural phenomena such as earthquakes, floods, avalanches, landslides, and so on, and from the resulting thought forms created by humans caught up in these events. More disarray to Earth energies is created by shocks caused by human activity such as excessive building, mining and roadworks, and the trauma caused to flora and fauna of the Earth from the excessive use of pesticides, intensive farming and the industrialisation of animal and plant husbandry. All of these shocks and their residues of thought forms have exactly the same effect on the energy fields of the Earth, and subsequently on the energy fields of its water and its flora and fauna, as shocks have on a human being and on humanity. Eventually the Earth's own energy fields are thrown out of balance as their chakras clog with thought form.

When great horrible deeds are perpetrated, such as wars, the Cathar massacres, the Holocaust, the excesses of revolution, the African wars and massacres, the tragedy of 9/11, and the massacre and mistreatment of animals which happened in the UK during the foot and mouth epidemic of 2001, the shockwaves are so immense they penetrate to the very core of the Earth. They penetrate to the core, the centre, of the labyrinth of the energy field of matter of the Earth. The resulting huge upheaval of distorted consciousness disrupts the Earth's energy field and physical matter connections, first with water and then with all life on Earth. Unless it is released and healed, the Earth's equivalent of cancer spreads over the planet, taking various forms. Some examples are: the foot and mouth epidemic, AIDS in Africa, famine, the increase in cancer in young adults, the excesses of crime and vandalism, drug taking and bullying, and the rise in terrorism.

If the consciousness of the ley lines contains contra-consciousness, reflected from the physical features on the Earth's surface, natural and/or human-made, the ley lines will attract more contra-consciousness to them since like attracts like in consciousness.

Thought forms attracted to and attached to ley lines can become mixed with the Earth life force and may clog the third and ninth chakras of some human energy field systems, especially in the mind and matter energy fields. This will inhibit the intake of the Earth and cosmic life force into these energy field systems. If the chakra is already silted by the person's own thought form, the invading thought forms will add to the problem in that area of the body. This is another cause and effect of geopathic stress.

CHAPTER III

MIASMS

Occasionally, residual memory of the actual shock and trauma which produced thought forms settles into the energy field system which forms the aura, even if the thought forms associated with the shock or its trauma have been eliminated.

This 'blot' or stain of contra-consciousness on the energy field is called a miasm. For example, a person has a serious illness or accident early in life and, although he/she recovers, a contra memory or imprint of the illness stays in the aura of that person, usually in the mind energy field. It is a situation rather like spilling cream on to a carpet. The cream can be removed, but some residual grease from the cream may remain on the carpet. Depending on how much it was trodden in, the greasy stain left on the carpet gradually attracts more and more dirt, getting worse unless it is specially cleaned and treated.

The aura is weakened at the point where the miasm has settled, causing a void. The void is very similar to the black holes in the universe. The suction caused by the void is like a whirlpool, pulling in unbalancing contra-consciousness, since like attracts like in consciousness. The miasm forms a barrier which prevents the two life force energies from circulating through the energy field at that point, causing further imbalance.

The void created by a miasm enables unwanted 'intruders', for example more thought forms, bacteria, viruses, and so on, to infiltrate the weakened energy field system in the aura. The aura, which normally protects the physical body, is unable to fulfil its role and the internal energy field systems of the body become vulnerable to more passing intruders, causing acute and chronic illness.

The structure of the void caused by a miasm is an inverted classical labyrinth. Therefore it has a two-way flow. What goes in will eventually come out. Are black holes in the universe made from accumulated polluted Earth life force (hence their blackness), discharged from the Earth's energy field system into the cosmos?

The inward flow of the miasm takes its contra-consciousness into the energy fields of the aura at the point where it attaches. In effect, it 'stings' the aura.

On the outward flow, the miasm ejects from the aura some of the consciousness of the damaged energy field, just as a sting from an insect can sometimes draw blood from the body. The miasm brings polluted energy in and pulls good energy out, so making room for more polluted energy to enter. The cycle continues until the miasm is eradicated. The severity of the damage to the auric energy field system will depend on the size of the miasm. The larger and deeper the miasm, the more damage it will inflict.

Eventually the miasm may penetrate so deeply into an energy field pathway it is carried into the energy fields of the molecules of the energy connecting mechanisms of the physical body. If this happens, it may affect the genetic structure of the body, causing the beginnings of genetic interference, depending on where the miasm settles. When this happens, the miasms themselves can be passed to succeeding generations.

If they are not resolved and eradicated, miasms which are caused by events in babyhood, childhood and early adolescence may slowly develop over the years and eventually contribute to the causes of illness and disease later in life, for example cancer, depression.

Consciousness can only be healed by consciousness and the pure thought of the cosmic life force. Miasms can only be eradicated by energenic-based therapies and remedies.

Case Study

Jean, aged forty-nine, was suffering from depression. She woke every morning with a deep, unidentifiable fear which prevented her from leading a normal life. During healing it emerged that when she was six months old, her mother became pregnant and was very ill, and Jean was sent away to be looked after by her mother's sister until her mother recovered. Dowsing indicated this was the root cause of her present fear. When the miasm and the thought forms caused by this trauma in her babyhood were cleared, using energenic healing and flower remedies (see Part X, Chapter III), her present fear and its associated depression cleared and Jean was able to lead a normal life again.

At present the only way to detect, locate and diagnose miasms is by dowsing, or by a healer sensing the voids in the auric energy fields. Checks must be made to ensure that the life force energies are not being blocked by a person's own excess contra thought patterns. The cause of the miasms must be resolved. Miasms are one of the main reasons why healing is sometimes not effective. If sufficient life force cannot enter and circulate through the energy field systems and the body, neither can the healing cosmic life force. Provided the healer is aware of the problem of miasms, especially miasms in the soul energy field, and asks for them to be cleared, cleansed and healed, the healer can be used to eradicate all the miasms and repair the damaged energy fields, if that is the choice of the patient.

Other unwanted intruders, sometimes drawn into the energy field system by miasms, are distressed, earthbound spirits which are lost and/or their thought forms. I believe these spirit attachments are one of the key triggering factors for many 'psychotic' mental illnesses such as schizophrenia, autism and Alzheimer's disease.

Miasms can attach themselves to any part of the human energy field system, to the energy field systems of any matter including the Earth itself, and can be stored there.

The following are the categories of miasms which affect humanity.

PLANETARY MIASMS

These are stored in the Earth's own consciousness, in the Earth life force energy. If our energy fields are sufficiently strong and balanced, they will be filtered out by our main third chakra in the energy field of matter, which is the entry point for the Earth life force into our energy field systems. Planetary miasms are responsible for the outbreaks of epidemic illnesses such as influenza, plague, the common cold and, now, AIDS. They are drawn to us by our own miasms or excess contra thought patterns and consciousness. If the third chakra is not strong enough to repel them, the miasms attach to the Earth life force flowing through the energy fields of the molecules of the connecting mechanism between the energy fields and the physical body. This starts with water, which via lymph and blood has direct access into all cells of the body.

The contamination disrupts the programmes for the function of the hormones and vital-vitamins. Gradually the immune system and the physical structure of the body weaken, making us more vulnerable to passing viruses and harmful bacteria.

The Earth's planetary miasms are caused by the shockwaves of trauma on and to the planet, both human-made and natural. They are caused by the effects of war, revolution, human inhumanity to human, excessive building activity, mining and quarrying, explosions, especially underground atomic testing and volcanic eruptions, and earthquakes in areas of human habitation. In addition, the excess fear surrounding cancer, syphilis and tuberculosis have now caused planetary miasms.

What we do to the Earth, we do to ourselves. Earth disrupts humans, disrupts Earth, disrupts humans...

The healing and eradication of the Earth's planetary miasms are especially important for healing the Earth and the Earth's own energy fields, and therefore for healing people, animals and plants.

INHERITED MIASMS

If the trauma which caused a miasm is very deep and intense, the miasm may penetrate and settle somewhere in the soul energy field.

The miasm will cause interference in the chakras' ability to receive, transform and transmit the life force energies and the programme through the soul energy field. The interference resulting in a distorted programme will eventually be carried through the whole energy field system, and the communicating connecting link into the physical body. The fault will be registered in the molecules of the DNA and genes, and in the energy field system of the pineal gland which records and holds the whole programme for the function of the physical body. The result will be a weakening or distortion of the physical body in the area of the disrupted chakra. For example, if the miasm is lodged in the fourth chakra of the soul energy field, some parts of the body associated with the main fourth chakra (the chest, lungs, spleen or heart) are likely to be affected.

If this deep, intense miasm is not cleared and cleansed away in the person's lifetime it, and its consequences, will be carried forward into the energy fields of the next and succeeding generations, until it is cleared. It will become an inherited miasm.

Should the inherited miasm settle in the third chakra of the soul energy field of the new embryo, although it will not block the entrance to the energy field, it will inhibit the intake of cosmic life force into the whole energy field system of the embryo, upsetting the balance of the life force equation $2P = N$. This may result in further interference and distortion in some part of the programme in the embryo's own soul energy field.

Case Study

A man is gassed in the fighting in the First World War. As a result of this trauma he suffers from chest problems for the rest of his life. After the war, he marries and has a son. The son develops asthma. Eventually the son marries and has a daughter, who also develops and suffers from asthma. When the miasms she had inherited from her grandfather and father were identified and cleared and her energy field system was restored and healed, her asthma attacks were alleviated. I have found that if both the paternal and maternal grandfathers of second-generation children retain miasms from the First World War, the risks to the grandchildren are increased.

My dowsing indicates asthma is one of the diseases connected with faulty genes caused by inherited miasms. The faulty gene cannot be corrected unless the inherited miasm is dealt with and cleared and cleansed away. This can only be achieved by the vibrational therapies of healing, and flower remedies.

Flower remedies can help to dissolve and remove any residual deep-seated thought forms associated with the inherited miasms (see Part X, Chapters I and III).

The programme and the blueprint which provides the information for the DNA and genes must be corrected in the energy field of soul. As with all healing, the permission of the soul will be needed before any healing can take place. This can be done using dowsing (see Part VI, Chapter IV, and Appendix I). It may be that the soul which has absorbed the inherited miasm and its resulting defects has chosen to link with those defects in order to learn and grow from the physical experiences of the life which will evolve as a result.

If inherited miasms are not eradicated, over a long period of time they become archetypal, and their associated thought forms become archetypal memory banks in the energy field systems of the Earth and of humans. As well as affecting health, they can affect behaviour and attitudes of people. Although they may not affect an individual, they show in the 'group psyche', for example in national and peer group characteristics. This is what happens in deep-seated cultural behaviour which can interfere with a person's own free will and affects the way they think.

All of these conditions can be detected by dowsing and, with permission, healed.

POLLUTION MIASMS

Miasms can be caused by the shock and trauma of heavy doses of pollution. Or they can be caused by the slow 'drip, drip' effect of pollution, especially the residues from radiation, excess electromagnetic energy, petrochemicals, heavy metals and drugs, including chemotherapy and vaccination.

The risk of miasms from vaccination is twofold. The vaccine itself is usually beneficial but sometimes leaves a miasm if it is very strong and the recipient is very young. The injection (i.e. the piercing of the body) used to vaccinate also disrupts the energy fields, both within the body and in the aura at that point, especially if they have already been weakened by miasms.

Most British babies today are born with electro-magnetic miasms and therefore can have considerably weakened auras and energy fields. This is due to the effect of ultrasound scans on the delicate energy fields of the baby during the mother's pregnancy, in addition to any unresolved miasms the baby may have inherited. The more scans the baby has, the greater the risk. This makes the child very vulnerable to pollution, both physically and energenically. During gestation, miasms can more easily penetrate to soul level and permanently upset the baby's energenic and physical blueprint, sometimes to such an extent the foetus aborts. Making a bad situation worse, most babies and young children are wheeled around in buggies and prams, which seem to be designed so that the child is at the level of, and at the mercy of, any passing traffic exhaust fumes.

Mobile phones, televisions and computers give off excess electromagnetic energy and have become another source of pollution miasms. Young children watching television or DVDs and using computers for hours each day, and people who spend much of their lives working with computers, are particularly at risk because the main ninth chakra can be blocked by excess electromagnetic energy. The block often occurs in the entrance/exit of the ninth chakra's energy field labyrinth, i.e. in the third chakra of the ninth chakra. This will lead to a deficiency and an imbalance in the cosmic life force circulating through the entire energy field system, especially in the energy fields of mind and matter. The result may be an excess of Earth life force causing contra-consciousness which can lead to stress, aggression, inattention, and so on. A strong balanced ninth chakra will prevent this from happening.

The ninth chakra is the key to our well-being. It maintains the balance in all the energy fields, from the main energy field system and its chakras to all the subsidiary energy field systems and chakras of molecules onwards, especially the molecules of water in the body.

Children's energy fields are very sensitive, and therefore children are most at risk from the effects of radiation and electromagnetic contamination in the ninth chakra. If the contamination disrupts the energy field systems of the molecules of water in the brain, some brain function may be adversely affected.

OUR OWN MIASMS

Our own acquired miasms include trauma associated with our own past births, past lives and past deaths. These miasms and our inherited miasms have usually penetrated to soul-spirit energy fields and may affect the blueprints for our physical development. The blueprint may be intact but the miasm distorts its transmission. When the miasm is removed, the distortion can be corrected and normal transmission resumed.

During our lifetime we can acquire additional miasms from traumatic events which may have happened to us. The first can be the trauma of conception and of birth itself, and any trauma which occurred when we were in the womb. This includes not only the physical trauma of scans I have already mentioned, but also emotional trauma suffered by the mother during pregnancy. In addition, miasms can occur from events in babyhood and childhood and throughout our lives, and from accidents and illness. A remedy miasm has also been identified (Gurudas 1983) caused by people taking too much of a drug, or homeopathic remedy, and by chemotherapy.

This information on miasms applies to the Earth itself and to everything on and in the Earth, animal, vegetable and mineral. It also applies to our personal possessions, especially jewellery. It is well known that we leave an imprint of our consciousness on our possessions. We also leave an imprint of any miasms we may have and they can have a harmful effect on us, or on any subsequent owners, or on the environment where they are kept, unless they are cleared and cleansed.

CHAPTER IV
ENERGENIC TIES AND ENTANGLEMENT

Sometimes, if we become very emotionally attached to another person or to a possession, including a pet, or to a place, its energy fields can become entangled with our own energy field systems. The effect is to 'tie' us in to the other energy field system. Its thought forms begin to merge with our own thought forms, and vice versa. As a result, the sound and light of our own consciousness is distorted. The balance and harmony of our own energy fields and the equilibrium of the energy field system is upset. The chakra nearest to the tie can become blocked, which disturbs the speed and rhythm of the flow of the cosmic and Earth life force energies through the energy fields. Eventually the physical body may malfunction in some way, often resulting in physical and/or mental pain.

Energenic ties can prevent the energy field system from receiving sufficient cosmic life force energy and can prevent healing and other vibrational therapies from being absorbed, unless the healer is aware of and can dissolve the associated thought forms and dis-entangle the ties.

If someone is very worried, that is, fearful and anxious, about us, the worry and fear thought forms they produce on our behalf can become entangled into our own energy fields, causing damage and disruption which can make the situation they are worried about even worse. Concerned, loving care without fear about someone is very different and is helpful and beneficial to the person involved.

A physical analogy of an energenic tie of consciousness is an animal roped and tethered to a post. It wants to be free but cannot get away, causing it fear and frustration. The post holding the tether can be uprooted or damaged by the strain on the rope tied to it. So when healing ties, we need to ask for healing and freeing for both ends of the tie. The 'rope' of the tie is usually made of a string of thought forms which need to be dissolved and returned to the source for clearing, cleansing and reprogressing: the cleansed, recycled thought content is returned to where it belongs, either the cosmos or the Earth.

Healing consciousness ties between humans makes the difference between being roped, 'tied', together and holding hands. Ties take away individual free will. Holding hands makes a caring connection that anyone can let go at any time of their own choosing.

If someone who is energenically tied to another person dies, the emotional ties that were created during the lifetime of the deceased person can remain in place. This can happen even though the spirit of the deceased person is in its right wavelength and dimension. Bearing in mind the ties are made of distorted consciousness, the possible added anguish of separation and its associated thought forms can make the tie stronger. Equally important, the 'pull' of the tie can distort the energy fields and chakras of the living person.

Sometimes one-way ties may have been formed as a cry for help from a deceased person in spirit with a living person. The spirit may still be suffering from contra-consciousness associated with the circumstances of its transition (i.e. dying) process and still needs healing.

If the tie is attached to the energy field of matter of a living person it may result in some form of physical breakdown of the body in the area controlled by the chakra or chakras distorted by the tie. If this is in the area of the fourth and/or seventh chakra, it may trigger a general health breakdown in the bereaved person, perhaps even causing the syndrome we know as 'a broken heart'.

When the tie, or ties, and their associated thought forms are attached to the mind energy field of a sensitive, living person, that person can experience all the projected contra-consciousness of the mind energy field of the deceased person in spirit. If this happens it may result in uncharacteristic severe depression which does not respond to normal treatment.

The only way to identify and remedy the effect of these one-way ties is by dowsing and specific energenic healing to sever and eliminate the ties and dispose of the thought forms. Then the resulting symptoms of both the deceased person in spirit and the affected living person can be dealt with. Even with healing, the symptoms will persist if the ties remain in place.

Ties from spirit attached to the mind energy field of a living person can be severed and cleared by one specialist healer. However the aftermath in the living person may take longer and may need two or more healers working together. It is a situation similar to dealing with a flooded house: the rain and the flow of water stops and is pumped out, but the cleanup and repair operation takes longer to be completed before the house is returned to normal. The house cannot be cleaned and repaired until the water has been eliminated.

These forms of spirit ties are different from spirit attachments. A tied spirit is in its right dimension attached to the cosmic life force and the cosmic energy fields, but it has formed the ties by its own contra-consciousness projecting into the energy field system of someone living.

A spirit attachment is not in its right dimension and wavelength. It is attached to and trapped in the Earth life force. However, if it also becomes tied by its own contra-consciousness to the energy field system of a living person, it can be doubly dangerous. The consequences for that person's own mental and physical health can be very serious. This is one of the causes of schizophrenia, especially drug-related schizophrenia. It can only be fully remedied by specialist energenic/spiritual healing using two or more healers working as a group. Bearing in mind that, in terms of consciousness, like attracts like, there may be contra-consciousness in the energy field systems of the affected person which has drawn the spirit tie to it. This possibility must be checked and dealt with to prevent a recurrence of spirit ties.

Potentially the most dangerous ties we can have are those we construct ourselves to our own thought forms, consciously or subconsciously. They need to be dissolved and eliminated because they prevent us from moving forward from contra-thinking, and its consciousness and actions, to balanced and harmonious thinking and its subsequent actions.

Our own thought form ties can lock us into behaviour we call addictive habits. They can be little or large, helpful or unhelpful. They are only harmful if they eventually disrupt our lives. It is our ties to our own thought forms which make the habits difficult to break if we want to. One of the consequences of these ties is a weakening of the energy field systems which will inhibit the flow of the life force energies, especially if the thought forms have settled in the third and/or eighth and ninth chakras, with a potential disruption somewhere in the physical body especially in the kidney and diaphragm area.

The solution is to strengthen the main energy field system, and therefore subsequently the subsidiary energy field systems of the organs, using healing, meditation, visualisation and vibrational therapies to dissolve and eliminate the ties and the thought forms. All the physical massage therapies, for example aromatherapy and reflexology, also disentangle ravelled meridians caused by a malfunctioning organ or organs.

Gentle healing and massage, together with appropriate flower remedies, would be immensely helpful if they could be given soon after birth, especially if the birth had been complicated.

CHAPTER V

PSYCHO-TOXICITY

Psycho-toxicity is a form of thought, consciousness, poisoning. It can be inflicted deliberately, as in a curse, or it can be unintentional, rather like food poisoning. It is an endemic toxicity brought about by the thought forms and contra-consciousness created by other people's thoughts and ideas about another person. It is caused by antipathy, anger, fear, maliciousness, from one person or persons to another, or others. The thought forms are distributed like fine dust throughout the main energy field system in the aura of the person or persons under attack. These thought forms are particularly dangerous because they pollute the life force energies of the psyche, as well as the consciousness of the energy fields.

In common with all thought forms, self made and projected, the psycho-toxicity is gradually sucked into the vortices of miasms. They also eventually become tangled into the chakra energy fields at all wavelengths of the energy field system from soul to the energy field of matter. As well as the aura, this includes all the energy fields within the physical body from molecules onwards, so damaging the recipient's mental and physical health.

Since the psycho-toxicity is in the aura, not only do the victim and the perpetrator need to be cleared, cleansed and healed, but also other people who may have been unintentionally influenced by the thinking of the perpetrator towards the victim. Psycho-toxicity in a group psyche is the root cause of racism and religious intolerance. The contra-consciousness of the person, persons, or group's own toxic thought forms draws more contra-consciousness to it and makes a bad situation worse for the victim. If a person already has miasms and is then attacked by psycho-toxicity, the toxicity will more easily penetrate into the physical body, especially the brain.

Psycho-toxicity can be cleared by using the circle-cross labyrinth, which is a map of the psyche, and by specialist healing.

CHAPTER VI
ALIEN ENERGY

The *Shorter Oxford English Dictionary* defines 'alien' as 'belonging to another place or person'.

In Energenics, my definition of alien energy is 'energy which has infiltrated into an energy field system from elsewhere, and is incompatible with that system's own wavelengths and frequencies'.

Bearing in mind that all energy, including alien energy, contains wavelengths and frequencies of thought, sound and light, alien energy disturbs the harmonic resonance of the consciousness of the energy fields it infiltrates. It is always disruptive to some extent and is therefore potentially harmful. It can affect any energy field system on, or of, the Earth, including the deva energy field systems and psyche of the species of flora and fauna of the Earth and their collective psyches. Alien energy is especially disruptive to the energy field systems of humanity, both individual humans and the collective human psyche.

Other than the cosmic and Earth life force energies, any energy which has come in to an energy field system from elsewhere and is compatible and in balance and harmony with that system, is *not* classed as alien energy. In fact, it can be beneficial and necessary to counteract the effects of alien energy. Examples are the wavelengths and frequencies of vibrational medicines such as flower essences, essential oils, homeopathy and the healing life force energies channelled through a healer into another person, place, plant or animal, or the Earth. It is essential the healer is connected to and is channelling cosmic life force, as well as harmonious Earth life force. In the case of humans it is particularly important that the healer's own energy field systems are resonating harmoniously with whoever is to receive the healing, otherwise even the healing energies may intrude on that person's free will, at some level, usually on the wavelengths of soul and spirit, i.e. in the deep subconscious.

The most obvious example of alien energy is extra-terrestrial energy, i.e. unconnected with the Earth, which has infiltrated into the Earth's own energy field systems from another place in the universe, and is not compatible with the Earth and life on Earth. It does *not* include the energy of the sun, Sirius, the moon, the planets and constellations which form cosmic ley lines with the Earth and which should be compatible and in harmony with the Earth.

Extraterrestrial alien energy is the most disruptive and causes the most distortion to the Earth and life on Earth. It finds its way into and onto the Earth through the voids and damage to the Earth's protective aura and its chakras, especially the ninth chakra. This damage is caused by the effect of shocks, miasms, thought forms and psycho-toxicity in the Earth's energy fields, usually as a result of contra human activity, sometimes over aeons of time.

Energenics has shown me that humanity is the cause and architect of its own troubles. This is not a new idea. In the New Testament, Revelations 13 especially the last verse, 13:18, indicates that six hundred three score and six (666), which is often regarded as a code for the devil, refers to 'a man'.

The Creator-God, having given us free will, can only intervene when we ask for help. Sorting out the mess we have created, often using God as an excuse for mayhem, sometimes has to cause anguish and pain, rather like an operation which has to be performed by a surgeon on the human body when it has gone drastically wrong.

Alien energy which infiltrates the Earth's energy field system acts like a jamming device. It clogs the chakras, preventing the Earth itself from absorbing sufficient cosmic life force to produce the correct balance of yiang and electromagnetic chi needed in the Earth life force energy. The result is unbalanced Earth life force which will be detrimental to all life on Earth, including humanity, in the area of the infiltration.

This is a very watery planet. The unbalanced Earth life force and the alien energy are absorbed by and stored in the water of the Earth. This upsets the harmonic resonance of the water molecules which in turn not only further disrupts the Earth's own consciousness but also carries the disruption to life on Earth. Water forms the first part of the essential link connecting life force energy to physical matter. If water is disrupted, the whole connecting communicating mechanism between the energy fields and physical matter is disrupted, with potentially serious conse-quences for matter. When contaminating energies from physical and energy pollution caused by human activity go directly into the water of the Earth, into the seas, rivers, streams and ponds, they have the same effect and are equally damaging.

If the Earth, its water, its energy fields and its life force are discordant and contaminated, it spells trouble for life in the water and on the Earth, especially humans. Unfortunately some plants and animals we use as food are not immune and pass their vulnerability and the alien energy they have absorbed on to us. The most affected are wheat, potatoes and some fish, farmed and wild. Many people are noticing a sensitivity to these foods, which often shows as aching joints or headaches, depression or digestive problems.

People living or working in areas of distorted Earth life force and the unbalanced ley lines resulting from it gradually absorb the alien energy and the distorted Earth life force into their own energy field systems. This form of alien energy is always disruptive. Sometimes it can be extremely harmful, causing geopathic stress. In my experience, it is always a significant factor in any form of chronic mental and physical illness, especially cancer and leukaemia. Sometimes it is the only cause of an illness.

Occasionally the Earth's own uncontaminated energy becomes alien to us if we visit another country, or even another part of our own country. This happens when the Earth life force in the place we are visiting does not resonate harmoniously with our own energy field systems and the Earth life force within them. Until we adapt, we may feel depressed or ill in the new environment, giving us the symptoms we aptly call 'homesickness'. The Earth life force we have absorbed from another place may not show as 'alien', that is, disruptive, until we return to our home environment and renew our intake of 'home' life force.

On the other hand, being with people and visiting places can have invigorating and beneficial effects on our mind and matter energy fields, for instance when we are on holiday or with uplifting friends. These compatible energies, although belonging to another place or person are not classed as alien in Energenics.

CHAPTER VII
SPIRIT ATTACHMENTS

Another cause of disrupted life force in Earth and human energy field systems is the condition known to healers as spirit attachment (described in Part VII, Chapter II, and Part IX, Chapter IV). It is important it is accepted and understood since it is one of the causes of schizophrenia, autism, behaviour disorders and so-called psychotic mental illness. The problems it causes cannot be fully resolved by drugs alone. It is easily detectable by dowsing, as well as by specialist mediumship.

Spirit attachments are usually of human origin but sometimes the soul, or spirit energy fields of the deva wavelengths and the mineral structure of the Earth are displaced, usually due to the distorting effects of physical pollution in the Earth's own energy fields, and therefore in the Earth's own life force.

The spirit attachment may be fleeting and may voluntarily move on quickly. We even have a phrase for it: 'I don't feel myself today!' Problems arise when the attachment becomes stuck and tied and entangled into another energy field system and cannot move away. The toxicity of the spirit attachment and its accompanying consciousness and thought forms has a very adverse effect on its 'host's' energy field system, and therefore on the physical body and consciousness of the host.

If the psyche of the human host is very sensitive

(for example, a child) the spirit attachment's energy fields and consciousness can override the host's own energy fields and consciousness. The host can sometimes 'hear' the thought-sound of the attachment's consciousness and mistake it for their own processed thoughts, i.e. thinking. Alternatively, they know it is not their own thinking and that it comes from another spirit. They think the guidance comes from a high source, angelic or even 'god', when of course it is from a very low source. Without the cosmic life force, it is cut off from the Creator-God. The spirit is usually a human who was very troubled in the physical life and death, which is why it is now a troubled soul, lost in the Earth's energy field systems. Sometimes the excess anger and fear of the attachment's thought forms and consciousness spills into the consciousness of the 'host' and upsets behaviour patterns. This is what happens in some mental illness, in some children with severe behaviour problems and in schizophrenia.

We have had very good results for patients when the spirit attachments and other alien energy and thought forms have been released, dealt with and healed. It is also an essential part of Earth healing.

This is specialised and important work for energenic healers. Two or more healers who work on similar and harmonised wavelengths and frequencies of consciousness are needed to work together to solve and heal the problems of spirit attachment and their consequences. Before and during the healing process, all healers involved must ensure they have permission to do the work, that they are working on the highest and best wavelengths and that they are well protected with cosmic life force.

CHAPTER VIII

THE ENERGENIC EFFECT OF THE ALIEN ENERGY OF VIRUSES

The energy field systems of viruses are formed from extraterrestrial energy as well as cosmic life force. Therefore, they are not compatible with the energy field systems of life on Earth. They are not of this planet, but they are easily drawn into the energy field systems of the Earth and life on Earth, especially humanity, through the damage caused by miasms in the energy fields. The energy fields of matter are especially vulnerable to viral attack.

The great plagues that have afflicted the Earth over centuries were caused by excessive viral extraterrestrial energy, drawn into the Earth through great miasms, and shock inflicted by war and human mayhem. Examples are the Hundred Years War and the Black Death in the fourteenth century, the Great Plague following the English Civil War in the eighteenth century, cholera worldwide, the great influenza epidemic following the First World War, polio following the Second World War, and now AIDS.

The virus does not infiltrate the Earth life force but is absorbed by the water of the Earth, including water vapour in the air, and is carried directly into the body via water. Because water is the first essential link in the energy communication and connection with the body,

322

it immediately disrupts the essential communication between the energy field systems and the physical body causing interference in our programme for the immune system.

The virus is drawn directly into the physical body through the nose and mouth and is absorbed and stored in the water content of the body. If the energy field systems of the physical immune system are working well, it will also be expelled from the body via the water systems and no harm is done. If the immune system becomes overloaded, the discordant energy of the virus will begin to interfere with the connection communication link between the energy field of matter and the physical body.

The first energy field systems within the human body to be affected are those of the natural organisms of our bodies, causing them to grow and expand, throwing the body and its immune system out of balance and harmony. This is why antibiotics appear to be helpful. They bring the proliferating bacteria back into balance by destroying the surplus overgrowth. What is needed, in addition to the antibiotics, is a vibrational remedy to clear, cleanse and eliminate any remaining alien energy of the virus and to give healing to the affected bacteria to restore their energy field systems to harmony and equilibrium and to heal the affected physical parts of the body.

If the body is already weakened by geopathic stress, the energy field system of the virus, with its alien extraterrestrial content, may not be completely eliminated through the energy and water systems of the human body. If it settles into the energy field systems of the brain, the working of our essential microchip, the pineal gland, will be disrupted. In addition, the water molecules of the cerebral fluid will become polluted. The consequences will be felt throughout the brain and the body. This is one of the factors in the cause of ME and, sometimes, of Alzheimer's disease. The programme for the production and performance of the hormones and vital-vitamins menaquinone and vitamin B12, needed for all healthy brain function, is disrupted. The hippocampus is eventually damaged and can no longer efficiently perform its vital role as our memory bank.

We often develop immunity to viruses and their alien energy in our own area or country, as plants and animals develop immunity, but this does not necessarily give us immunity to viruses in other areas or parts of the world. There are many examples of people travelling around the world who return home with strange illnesses and diseases, which sometimes take years to eradicate using conventional physical methods.

CHAPTER IX

THE ENERGENIC EFFECT OF THE ALIEN ENERGIES OF POLLUTION, CONTAMINATION AND DRUGS

The effect of any alien energy which infiltrates the energy field systems of the human body is similar to its effect on the planet. It disrupts the cosmic and Earth life force energies flowing through the energy fields, and consequently disrupts the whole energy field system, and eventually the physical body. The programmes being transmitted into the physical body become garbled, like interference in a television or radio programme.

At worst, the programmes for the cells and organs become completely scrambled in the area of the physical body connected to the damaged part of the energy field system, and cancer and tumours can develop. The disruption will show in the main chakras of the physical body even if the damage is at molecular level. The normal function of the lymph is to clean and clear pollution from the water content of the cells and organs. It only fails if it is overwhelmed by the amount of pollution. Sometimes it is overwhelmed by the pollution caused by the alien energy of the drugs used as treatment.

When the energy field systems of the human body

are strong and healthy, the chakras will automatically deal with interfering alien energy by transmitting it through the system, eventually ejecting it out of the soul energy field in the aura before it can do any damage. The problems arise when, and if, the alien energy field systems block any part of the chakra system. How do we find out? By checking the energy fields of the main chakras using dowsing.

Alien energy also comes from any form of contamination, from any kind of pollution, whether it is from matter or energy. It can find its way into our energy field systems through our food and drink, and through drugs of any kind, including alcohol, chemotherapy, radiotherapy and vaccinations. It can come from plants, animals and insects, and from the contra-consciousness of thought forms created by other people. If the Earth life force is polluted by Earth pollution, alien energy can come from the Earth itself. Genetically modified crops create alien consciousness within their energy fields, which is discharged into the energy field systems of the Earth, subsequently polluting the Earth life force, the whole environment and everything living in it or on it.

The energy field systems contained in the food we eat and in the liquids we drink need to be in harmony with our own energy field systems. If, for any reasons, the food and/or drinks are discordant, the energy we absorb from them will be disruptive and potentially harmful and therefore produce the physical and mental symptoms of food allergies and sensitivity. One of the origins of the blessing of food and saying grace before a meal was to bring the food and drink into harmony with the body, making them more beneficial to us and eliminating any harmful effects they may otherwise have had.

Since each human being is unique, the best, most accurate, efficient and simple way of discovering which foods may contain incompatible alien energy for an individual is by dowsing.

The interference caused by the alien energy from drugs causes the side effects of drugs. Although the physical content of the drug may be beneficial, its energy field system and consciousness is alien because the natural composition of its ingredients has been changed and the natural programmes have been disrupted.

Excessive use of drugs, including alcohol, can lead to dangerous imbalances in the psyche. The alien energy of the drug swamps the cosmic life force and blocks it from the psyche, leaving only a reinforced connection to the Earth life force and anything and everything which may be attached to it: miasms, thought forms, earthbound spirits, extraterrestrial alien energy, and so on. Drugs may bring about an altered state of consciousness but it will become contaminated consciousness.

In these situations the only whole way forward for the drug taker is for the psyche to be cleared and cleansed energenically and vibrationally. This allows the cosmic life force to be reconnected, restoring the equilibrium and balance to the energy fields. Depending on the severity of the contamination, at least two or more healers are needed for this work with each patient. Physical medication alone is not enough for a lasting remedy for drug-induced psychosis and schizophrenia.

If alien energy, thought forms and miasms, and all the distortions and disruptions of the energy field systems of the human body are not cleared and cleansed away, they eventually reach the soul energy field. The original blueprint for all the programmes needed for the upkeep and healthy functioning of the entire physical body is stored in the soul energy field and will become contaminated. This is how disruptions to the energy field systems received in babyhood, childhood and early life, unless they are corrected and healed, can eventually have far-reaching consequences, significantly contributing to the causes of degenerative diseases which appear much later in life.

All of these contra energies can be detected by dowsing. At present, this is the only way they can be found. They can then be cleared. The energy field systems can be cleansed and repaired using vibrational remedies and therapies and energenic healing. When this happens, the physical treatment of the physical symptoms of disease is even more effective. Harmful side effects of drugs can be minimised and the disease is unlikely to reappear because the cause of it will have been dealt with.

When the embryo/foetus is subjected to ultrasound scans, its delicate energy fields are bombarded with very strong energy, causing immense strain on its whole energy field system. The chakra system may break down and the flow of the cosmic life force will be blocked. The foetus may die. It may develop malformation to a greater or lesser extent if the essential connecting sequence between its energy field system and physical body is distorted. Residues of the sound energy which is used to make the scan are absorbed by the water of the womb and the foetus lives in a polluted environment for the remainder of the pregnancy. Depending on the inbuilt strength of its energy field systems, the foetus's energy fields may or may not be able to adapt to the alien energy it has been exposed to.

If the foetus cannot fully adapt, its programme, recorded in the soul energy field, may become distorted, resulting in some damage to the child. The baby will be born with damaged and/or weakened energy fields which will be unable to provide sufficient protection from the environmental hazards we are all exposed to.

Dowsing indicates the incidence of the huge increase in childhood asthma is directly related to the general use of ultrasound scans in pregnancy. My own research has shown that pregnancy scanning in the UK was started in about 1979 and by 1983 it was in general use. There was a general rise in asthma before 1983 but a huge rise in asthma occurred from 1983 onwards.

As the generation of children born with weakened energy fields become parents themselves and their children are subjected to ultrasound scanning, the incidence of damaged energy fields in children will be compounded in the future. Based on dowsing, I believe the increasing incidences of autism, hyper-activity and obesity in children are directly linked to the damage caused to the energy field systems of the child due to the overuse of ultrasound scans in pregnancy, allied with the damage to the energy fields during the vaccination process. These factors also increase children's vulnerability and sensitivity to the alien energy of food additives, and the effects of chemicals, preservatives, herbicides and pesticides in food production.

As well as radiotherapy, ultrasound and ultrasound scanning equipment, other examples of the sources of polluting alien energy are the emissions of electro-magnetic energy from televisions, microwaves, computers, the computer mouse and mobile phones. These emissions become harmful if the equipment is used excessively, and contribute to the formation of miasms. The excess electromagnetic energy upsets the balance of the electromagnetic chi and yiang energy within the Earth life force flowing through the energy field systems of the recipient. This leads to further imbalance between the cosmic and Earth life forces. The excess of one leads to a deficiency in the other.

I have already mentioned that a small circle-cross diagram attached to electronic equipment significantly reduces its emissions of polluting electromagnetic energy.

Similarly, we have found that healing and/or a large dose of the flower remedy known as Rescue Remedy, used immediately after an ultrasound scan, radio-therapy or X-rays, neutralises the harmful energy of the treatment (see Part X, Chapter III).

As well as the clamour of our own unruly contra thoughts, there is an immense amount of contra noise pollution in our modern western world. It is difficult to find a very quiet environment for very long. Aircraft or traffic noise usually breaks in sooner or later. The subliminal aspects of physical noise pollution can have a serious polluting effect on the yiang wavelength of the Earth life force. The alien sound distorts the sound within the cosmic life force and the Earth's own consciousness, and prevents them combining to form yiang energy. The result of too much noise is paradoxical: it causes a deficiency of yiang, the sound energy within the Earth life force. The deficiency is compensated by extra electromagnetic chi and the Earth's own consciousness. The whole balance, harmony and equilibrium of the Earth life force is disrupted, with potentially serious consequences for all life on Earth, especially humans.

Part IX of the Energenics hypothesis has described the problems which can occur in the energy field systems and the psyche of a human being. The effects of these problems cause mental disease and physical disease and ill health in the human body.

Energenic problems need energenic, vibrational solutions. Part X outlines these solutions. They have all been studied in depth, and have been successfully and widely used for many years, sometimes for thousands of years.

PART X
SOLUTIONS: HEALING AND VIBRATIONAL REMEDIES

CHAPTER I

HEALING

The art of healing is almost as old as humanity. The ancient Egyptian goddess Isis was shown as a healer. Two thousand years ago the healing work of Jesus of Nazareth and his disciples was documented in the New Testament. Today, healing is sometimes known as the laying-on of hands, faith healing or spiritual healing. Reiki is also another form of healing, first used in Japan about two hundred years ago.

Healing is complementary to conventional allopathic medicine. It is not 'instead of' conventional medicine. Used in partnership, they enhance each other.

The role of the healer is to identify the problem in the energy field system of the patient and to clear and cleanse and reconnect and replenish with the cosmic life force. This will restore balance and harmony within each energy field, and equilibrium and synchronicity between the energy fields. I find dowsing is an invaluable tool for identifying and locating the problems and the faults caused by the problems, and for ascertaining they have all been solved. Sometimes the problems in the energy field systems which have led to the malfunction of the physical body and/or the mind can be solved quickly, but often it takes time and patience.

It is the mind energy field which transmits the cosmic life force, i.e. the healing energy, into the energy field of matter and the physical body. It is the mind which forms the connection between the deep sub-subconsciousness of soul and spirit, and the conscious consciousness of physical matter and the physical world. If conventional medicine recognised this immensely important, vital connection, it would be a huge step forward in the whole field of healing and medicine. It is the mind processing the cosmic and Earth life forces, our thought supply, which activates the physical brain, not the other way round.

If the mind energy field is polluted with contra-consciousness, the whole energy field system and eventually the physical body will be affected. One of the causes of autism is faulty connections between the energy fields and between the connecting mechanisms into the brain.

A healer is able to access and use the psyche and the mind energy field to make the necessary links with the energy field systems of the patient. This enables the healer to connect and transmit the cosmic life force into and through the whole of the energy field systems of the patient, both in the aura and within the physical body. The ability to do this is inherent in all of us and we could all use it, not only for healing for other people but, equally importantly, for healing ourselves. The efficacy of the mind exercises of visualisation and meditation is well known.

Having first made the connection with the Source, the cosmic life force and the patient, we need to ask for healing for the root cause of the problem and for the effect of the cause. Therefore we need to ask for healing on all wavelengths and frequencies of the following:

- the main energy field system and its chakras;
- all the subsidiary energy field systems;
- the whole energenic connecting sequence of molecules, especially water, and its complete connection to the physical body;
- the meridian system;
- the physical body itself.

The healer is using consciousness and the pure thought energy of the cosmic life force to reconnect the patient with the source of all healing, the Creator-God. Thought, both the pure thought of the Source, the cosmic life force and the consciousness of the Earth life force, and the consciousness of the processed thought of the energy fields are outside of time and space. Therefore the physical distance between the healer and the patient is of no consequence. Healing works equally well when the healer is at a distance from the patient. The healer and the patient may be in different parts of the world, the country, a building or on the other end of a telephone. This form of healing is known as distant (or absent) healing.

Occasionally, a healer may be asked to send distant (or absent) healing to a friend or relative and the patient may not be consciously involved. The healer must not proceed without the permission of the patient on some level: either conscious, subconscious or sub-subconscious, i.e. on the wavelengths of mind or spirit or soul or all three. To do so could trespass on some wavelengths of the patient's choice and free will. This is equally important whether for premature babies or elderly adults. In my experience, distant healing is especially beneficial for babies and children.

The importance of the mind energy field, both of the healer and the patient, to facilitate healing brings us to the placebo effect. 'Placebo' comes from the Latin verb meaning 'I shall please'.

It is accepted that thought is the basis of the placebo effect, but both the placebo thought and its effect are dismissed as of no consequence by most of science and conventional medicine. In fact, it is crucial to the healing process, both conventional and energenic.

The effect of the consciousness of both the prescriber and the patient should be taken into account when assessing drug trials. It should be remembered that contra-consciousness is stronger than positive consciousness and will weaken the beneficial properties of the drug or treatment.

Sound in Healing

The sound within consciousness is vital to healing. It is needed to ensure the two life forces flow throughout the energy field systems and their chakras at the right speed and rhythm, not too slow, not too fast.

The beneficial effects of the music of Mozart and Bach and of Gregorian chant are well documented. What is not so well documented is the hugely adverse effect contra sound has on the human body and the water systems of the body, especially the brain. If there is sound pollution in the energy field system of the water molecules in the cerebral fluid and blood, the water is unable to fulfil its essential function of connecting the Earth and cosmic life forces, especially the cosmic life force, into physical matter. When this physical matter is in the brain, the consequences can be very detrimental to normal brain function.

Sound pollution can begin before birth. I have already described the evidence of the effect of heavy metal music on the foetus in the womb (Part IV, Chapter V and Part IX, Chapter IX). Antenatal depression and the sound of its contra-consciousness in the mother can also have serious consequences for the child, both before and after birth.

Some healers are able to physically 'tone' with the patient to bring balance and harmony to the sound of the consciousness within the energy field systems and the life force energies. It is equally effective for a healer to 'visualise' the sound of the relevant note of the tonic sol-fa for each chakra. The mind energy field of the healer seems able to transmit the note which is audio-visualised into the mind energy field of the patient at the best wavelength and frequency to benefit the patient.

Light and Colour in Healing

The colours of the light within consciousness are as important to the energy field systems and therefore to healing as sound. The wavelengths and frequencies of the colours of the spectrum are the same as the wavelengths and frequencies of the colours of the energy field pathways and their chakras (see Part III, Chapter IX and Part IV, Chapter V). They vibrate around and within all physical matter: animal, vegetable and mineral.

Each colour of the spectrum is a wavelength of light. The millions of frequencies (vibrations) within each of these wavelengths give all the variations of each colour in the whole of creation. Some are visible to the physical eye and some are usually invisible to the physical eye but visible to the 'third eye', the mind's eye.

I have found by dowsing that we each have a dominant colour in our energy field system which shows in our aura. Some people can see this vibration of colour around a person with their physical eyes. A woman I know sees people as 'a yellow person' or 'a green person', and so on. She has always seen these colours from childhood and regards it as quite normal. My own dominant colour is blue. If I am feeling 'off colour' and I boost blue into my aura, I immediately feel better – energised!

The vibrations of the wavelengths and frequencies of the colours of the clothes we wear and of the colours we have around us in our homes are very important. They contribute to our well-being when they are compatible with the vibrations of our energy fields. If they are not compatible, or if they are too strong or too weak or out of balance, they contribute to our feelings of being 'off colour'. The energising or debilitating effects of colour in the workplace, schools and hospitals has been well researched.

Spectacles with coloured lenses have been found to help children and adults overcome some of the problems caused by, and causing, dyslexia.

Dowsing shows that each organ of the body has its own dominant colour, which is reflected into its root meridian. The meridians form internal spiralling rainbows.

If the aura is out of balance and harmony and deficient in colour, the rest of the body's energy field systems will also be affected. Any imbalance in the organs is reflected into the meridians and into the aura of the whole body.

The energy field system and chakras of the aura can be corrected by concentrating on each colour of the pathways in turn, and by visualising the colour surrounding the whole body. I find this is easiest to do with the colours of the spectrum in front of me and using a pendulum.

Dowsing shows that by energising the dominant colour in the aura, even if it does not appear to need it, the rest of the spectrum of colours in the aura will be brought back into balance and harmony. It is therefore helpful to know which colour we can literally 'breathe in' and visualise permeating the whole physical body and aura to combat being, and feeling, 'off colour'.

If we think of every wavelength and frequency of colour when we are correcting the energy fields and chakras of the aura, this automatically has the effect of balancing and harmonising the colours of the subsidiary energy fields of the molecules, cells and organs, the meridians and all the chakras. However, dowsing and experience have shown that balancing and harmonising the organs and the meridians does not automatically clear the aura or the chakras.

We should also check that white is in balance and harmony, and black is in balance and harmony. White is the colour of cosmic life force; black is the colour of Earth life force. Both black and white are vital for our health and well-being. They each contain all the colours; if one of the colours is too strong or too weak, it will affect the purity of the life force.

Colour healing is equally effective when used in distant healing.

Crystals in Healing

The use of crystals and gems in healing are forms of light healing. Many healers use their properties of receiving, transforming and transmitting the light of the cosmic life force into and through physical matter. The energy field systems of the atoms and molecules of the crystals are able to connect directly with the subsidiary energy field systems of the atoms and molecules within the body. The chakras and energy field systems and the cosmic and Earth life force in the gems and crystals neutralise polluting contra-consciousness and are able to bring balance, harmony and equilibrium to damaged energy field systems.

It is important to heal, i.e. to clear and cleanse and to revitalise the crystals with pure cosmic life force on a regular basis, or they may become saturated with contra-consciousness and may begin to transmit that into the energy field systems they are meant to be helping. This can be done by 'walking' a classical labyrinth to recharge the energy field systems of the crystals. They can be cleared and cleansed physically by using salt and water to strengthen their connections with the cosmic and Earth life force energies and by leaving them in a sunny position.

There are many excellent books on crystal and gem healing.

The physical body is a collective manifestation of the energy fields of soul, spirit, mind and matter, and their consciousness, but sometimes the physical body is damaged beyond repair, or we may have come to the end of our allotted span on this physical Earth. Experience has shown that even if the physical body cannot be repaired, repairing the energy fields brings peace, tranquillity, courage and strength to the person involved. The person is made whole, even if the body is not. When the time comes, healing can make the transition from the physical life into spirit easy and peaceful. Healing occasionally needs to continue when a person has physically died, and has moved from the physical life into spirit.

Energenics is based on all the cases I have worked on since 1988, either alone or in partnership with other healers. Although the cases number about 3,000 they would be regarded as anecdotal by mainstream science and medicine. Every human being is unique and has its own unique consciousness linked into the life force of the cosmos and of the Earth, so there can never be an accurate basis for double-blind tests, even if they are scientific. Ultimately the proof of the pudding has to be in the eating.

Healing is an art, and art is subjective. Science is objective. Modern medicine needs to embrace and combine both subjective healing and objective science, respecting both since they are equally important. Since each human being is unique, medicine should never be wholly objective.

CHAPTER II

HOMEOPATHY

Homeopathy is well known and widely used and studied and there are many books written about it. Briefly, it was discovered and founded by a German doctor, Samuel Hahnemann of Leipzig, between about 1796 and 1810, and works on the principle of 'like cures like' – '*similia similibus curantur*'.

The property of water to memorise, that is, to hold consciousness, is used to hold the consciousness of the energy content of the physical matter of the substance involved, even when all physical trace of the physical substance has been eliminated from the water. This has been demonstrated and proved by the research of a French scientist, Jacques Benveniste.

Homeopathy is a vibrational medicine which can be taken physically. It uses the subsidiary energy field systems and consciousness of the molecules of the substance needed to energenically repair a similar but damaged substance in the physical body. It heals on the wavelengths and frequencies of the main and sub-sidiary energy fields of mind and of matter and their chakra systems, with subsequent benefit for the conscious 'physical' mind and the physical body of the patient. Homeopathy is also very effective when transmitted vibrationally through thought, as in distant healing.

At present the only way of measuring the effectiveness of homeopathy is by so-called anecdotal evidence. There is a mass of it worldwide, accumulated over 200 years of continuous and successful use. It is the only valid way of assessing homeopathy, since it works on each person's unique consciousness. It therefore suffers from the non-understanding of most conventional science and medicine because of the impossibility of measuring its worth by conventional scientific methods. Even some practitioners of homeopathy seem not to fully understand this and advocate more 'scientific' research.

CHAPTER III

FLOWER ESSENCES OR 'REMEDIES'

The *Shorter Oxford English Dictionary* says an essence is 'that by which it is what it is'. It is also 'an extract obtained by distillation or otherwise from a plant (or drug) and containing its specific properties in a reduced form'.

The energenic essence of a whole plant or tree is contained in the collective consciousness of its whole energy field system, and the cosmic and Earth life forces flowing through. They are all gathered together in the flowers of the plant or tree. This is the essence which can be transmitted into water and preserved in the water to use as the flower essence, or remedy. A flower essence is purely an energenic, i.e. vibrational, remedy.

Essential oils are also sometimes referred to as 'essences'. Both dictionary definitions apply to the essences of the essential oils. The difference between the flower essences of the remedies and the essences of essential oils is that the essential oils also contain the physical essence of the physical properties as well as the energenic essence of the whole plant or tree.

The first thirty-nine flower essences were discovered and used by Dr Edward Bach between 1930 and 1936. He called them flower remedies. Many more have been found and used with great effect since.

Dr Edward Bach was a Harley Street physician who came to realise and understand that the root of all disease was in the dis-ease within the psyche. Using himself as a guinea pig, Dr Bach discovered the flowers of thirty-eight plants and trees which could deal with all the then known causes of contra human emotions. His work has been very well documented by the team of dedicated people who worked with him. He made a thirty-ninth remedy, the famous Rescue Remedy. It combines four of the flower essences into one symbiotic remedy. The Bach flower remedies have been used continuously since the 1930s by millions of people worldwide with great success.

Edward Bach's aim was to discover a simple, effective, totally safe method of healing which anyone could use, whether they were medically qualified or not. He succeeded totally. His original flower remedies remain the definitive collection.

All flower essences are effective on all the wavelengths and frequencies of the whole energy field system. There are now thousands to choose from, worldwide. Dowsing to find the right one and the best dosage helps to ensure accuracy and saves time, effort and money. However, if you prefer, there are excellent highly experienced flower essence practitioners. Flower essences are also used by some doctors. They are safe and gentle; they produce no side effects, and are particularly valuable in the treatment of all forms of mental depression. The only complication which might arise is caused by the small amount of alcohol used to preserve the flower essences. This can easily be avoided by using the essence on the skin or as a light spray around the body into the aura, or added to a bath. They can also be received vibrationally through thought, as in distant (absent) healing. Sometimes these methods are even more efficient and effective ways of using flower remedies than taking them orally, especially for children and babies.

Flower essences are made by using the ability of water to absorb and remember consciousness and its sound and light. The consciousness of a plant, tree or shrub is transferred into water, usually by floating its flowers on a bowl of water and leaving them in the sun for a few hours. Sometimes they are made by boiling the flowers in water. The essence is sealed into the water by adding a small amount of fruit alcohol, either brandy or vodka, which also acts as a preservative. This preserved essence is known as the stock or mother essence, and can be used either directly from stock or diluted.

Flower essences are even more effective if the prescriber and the user, but especially the prescriber, trust and understand them and know the wavelengths and frequencies of the energy field systems which need to be cleared by the remedy.

If the person making, selling, giving or prescribing the essences does so with the thought of total trust in them and their efficacy, the essences will be even more effective. The positive thought for the good outcome will add to their strength.

Conversely, contra-consciousness is also transferred into water. If, when making a flower essence, the maker has doubts about it working, these contra thoughts will also be absorbed by the water and the essence will not be so effective, or may not work at all. Any faults in a flower essence can easily be detected by dowsing.

When the treated water of the essence is taken or absorbed by a human, or a plant or an animal, the essence of the flower and its immunity to any pollution of the Earth's life force is absorbed into the energy fields and water systems of the body. Similar offending thought forms and miasms to which the plant has built an immunity are dissolved and removed from the chakras and the energy field systems of the patient. As the thought forms are dissolved and eliminated by the flower remedies, the chakras unblock. Harmony and balance are restored to the energy fields and to the flow of the two life forces flowing through them. The vital connections between the energy field system and the physical body are restored, and the physical body begins to recover as its correct programme is once more transmitted though the molecules and into the restored hormone and vital-vitamin connections by the cleared and cleansed chakras. We now know this applies not only to humans but also to plants and animals, and even to the planet. There are specific flower essences for specific types of thought form and the contra emotions which caused them.

The remedies clear and cleanse the consciousness of the person using them, setting up the right conditions for that person to receive and respond to healing, whether it is vibrational healing or conventional medicine.

In my view, dowsing is needed for really accurate diagnosis and prescription when the deep, deep levels of the sub or superconsciousness of spirit and soul are being cleared. It helps to confirm the instinctive soul to soul, spirit to spirit, mind to mind communication between the healer, the plant and the recipient. Interestingly, when Edward Bach was discovering his remedies, radiesthesia, or medical dowsing, had not been introduced into England. Instinctively he used his own body and psyche as the dowsing tool.

The consciousness of each human is unique. Therefore the way each flower essence works for each person using it is unique. As in homeopathy, trying to press flower essences into the usual double-blind scientific mould for testing is useless and completely misunderstands how they work.

The use of consciousness stored in water as a medicine to heal is not a new idea, or even a 200-year-old idea! In her book *Great Works of Egyptian Art*, Elizabeth Longley (1996) shows a photograph of a statue of a priest holding a stela of Horus dating from about 300 BC. The statue is now in the Louvre, Paris. In her book she says, 'The statue is covered with magical formulae and simply by drinking water poured over it, a patient could be cured. Stelai, like this, sometimes in bronze, were often set up in public places. Drinking the water poured over them gave protection against reptiles or could heal stings or bites.' We should remember the Egyptians had an advanced knowledge of medicine and the structure of the human body both physically and energenically. When you do not understand, or have forgotten the energenic principles behind the treatment, you would think of it as superstition or magic, or even nonsense.

There is a whole genre of flower essences waiting to be 'switched on' and used to heal the clogged chakras of the Earth's energy fields, and to release and dissolve the contra archetypal thought forms, miasms and memory banks which have transferred from the Earth into nations, into people.

Some national flowers may be able to be used as flower essences for their own nation. For example, the rose of England; the thistle of Scotland; the daffodil of Wales; the shamrock of Ireland. Others which we have discovered are magnolia for unconditional love and forgiveness, bluebell for deep, extreme grief, and Madonna lily for eliminating extreme fear, often associated with fire, and for restoring trust.

Certain orchids thrive on alien, extraterrestrial energy, especially the orchids of the South American Andes. This makes their flower essences very effective antidotes to viral energy, both for individuals and in epidemic conditions. Once the virus has been neutralised and eradicated, the damage it caused and the damaged consciousness which attracted the virus to it can be dealt with.

Flowers and plants for Earth healing are used vibrationally. The trust of the transmitter and the prescriber is vital. New flower remedies, when they have been identified, need to be connected by thought through the consciousness of the psyche of the person making them, tuning in to the psyche of the plant. Their effectiveness will be enhanced or diminished by the quality of this exchange of consciousness. This applies to all new flower remedies, whether they are for people, deva energies, or the Earth. In effect, we must ask the permission of the plant to use it.

If a flower which is already used as a flower remedy has an extra dimension of healing within it, but this is not known, it will not be effective on that wavelength until it is consciously discovered and communicated. Only one person needs to make the discovery and communicate it to one other person in order to 'switch it on' worldwide. That aspect will then become effective wherever, whenever, and to whomever it is needed when the remedy is taken or transmitted with trust.

For example, Edward Bach's most famous remedy, the Rescue Remedy, relieves all symptoms and thought forms caused by mental stress, and physical and mental shock. It now also relieves stress at molecular level caused by the alien consciousness of drugs. Rescue Remedy can be used to correct, neutralise and cleanse away the harmful energies and distorted consciousness which cause the side effects of drugs, including vaccine and alcohol. If Rescue Remedy is taken about ten to fifteen minutes after taking the drug, or shortly after the vaccination, it will prevent any harmful side effects and restore the body to balance, harmony and equilibrium.

If this is the outcome needed, it should be in the mind of the person taking the Rescue Remedy for this purpose, or in the mind of the person prescribing it or sending it vibrationally. However, even flower essences have their limits! Alone, they may not be able to be effective if a person is using drugs to excess.

If it is asked, and permission is given by the plant,

the life force energy in a flower will be released to anyone needing it while the plant is growing. For example, walking through a bluebell wood could be very healing and soothing for anyone needing bluebell essence for extreme grief at that time.

Homeopathy can be used to heal some miasms but only on the wavelengths of the energy fields of mind and matter. If used to excess, homeopathy itself can cause a miasm. Flower essences heal miasms on all wavelengths of all the energy fields – matter, mind, spirit and soul. They have no harmful side effects. If they are wrongly used, or used to excess, it is merely wasteful of the essence.

Flower essences are healing-in-a-bottle. Sometimes the essences alone are sufficient and other forms of healing and medication may not be needed. They can be used by anyone at any time. Not only are they complementary, they can enhance the efficacy of conventional medicine and drugs. Flower essences should be recognised as the medicines of the twenty-first century.

Flower essences heal the root causes of disease, as well as helping to heal the disease itself. Without them, we are usually only treating the symptoms of disease. For example, the cause of the illness may go back to what appears to be a long-forgotten stress, felt as a baby or small child, such as the fear felt by the baby during a long and difficult birth but the stress is still there in the supersubconsciousness of soul and spirit.

When the symptoms and the causes of disease are treated together, true health will emerge.

Case Study

Sally had suffered all her adult life from premenstrual tension, with severe pain and bleeding every month. Her menstrual cycle was a nightmare, and she was often bedridden for one or two days every month. She agreed to be a guinea pig for my theories.

I dowsed she needed a physical vitamin B6 supplement and three Bach flower remedies. The flower remedies were to clear the blocks from the chakra systems of chakras one and two, and from the energy field systems of the disrupted hormones, and to facilitate reconnecting the corrected hormones. The vitamin B6 was to connect with chakras one and two, and to connect with the hormones of chakras one and two to activate the correct programme in the uterus for a healthy menstrual cycle. I asked her to visualise this happening as she took the B6 supplement and the flower remedies. I did not send any healing. It so happened her usual menstrual cycle coincided with the full moon.

The first month she reported little change. Her second period came two weeks early and was slightly easier.

Her third period was three weeks after the second and showed a considerable improvement. By the fifth month she had established a changed menstrual cycle of twenty-eight days away from the full moon, and with very little discomfort for the first time for many years. Eighteen months later, she had established and maintains a normal tension-free, regular, comfortable menstrual cycle, away from the full moon.

This case is interesting because it shows how inter-related we are to the Earth, the moon and the cosmos. In Sally's case, the moon's cycle was not compatible with her own cycle.

Five people have used this therapy, tailored by dowsing for their own needs. The success rate is one hundred per cent.

In this case study, there were two very important added factors: the positive trust we both had that the therapy would work, and especially my trust that the information I was using was accurate.

Thought energy of the cosmic life force and the consciousness from the Earth form the two life forces essential for all our physical existence. Therefore it is logical that we can enhance and direct their flow through our bodies using our own positive thought and consciousness processes.

CHAPTER IV

ESSENTIAL OILS AND AROMATHERAPY

Perhaps humans first discovered the therapeutic effects of the scents of certain plants when they were used as firewood or kindling. 'Perfume' comes from two Latin words, *'per'* meaning 'through' and *'fumare'* meaning 'smoke'. As well as being the main ingredient of perfumes, essential oils are very powerful, effective healers, and have been in continuous use for many thousands of years. They were known to the ancient Egyptians and the Babylonians. Exodus 30 in the Old Testament describes two recipes given to Moses by God. The first is for an anointing oil to be made of myrrh with other oils and spices, 'after the art of the apothecary' (Exodus 30:23–24). The second recipe is for a holy perfume made of sweet spices and pure frankincense also 'after the art of the apothecary', to be used only in the tabernacle (Exodus 30:34–38).

The New Testament tells us that the three wise men brought gifts of gold, frankincense and myrrh to the infant Jesus. They were the three most valuable gifts that could be given. Myrrh was more highly prized than gold in the ancient world.

In the latter part of the twentieth century, essential oils have become valued again. The Aborigines of Australia have introduced us to tea tree oil, which is used by the dental profession in Australia. It is a natural antibiotic and one of the few antidotes to the superbug MRSA. Lavender oil is another natural antibiotic.

When gently massaged into the skin, the tiny molecules of the essential oils are absorbed directly into the bloodstream through the vascular layer of the skin. They are a gentle natural form of ultrasound treatment.

Each of the varying scents of trees, flowers and plants is unique to its species. Energenically, their subliminal sounds, distilled into the essential oil, can produce the varying wavelengths and frequencies needed to make corrections and adjustments to the consciousness within the energy fields, especially of mind and matter. They can also correct the speed and rhythm of the flow of the life force energies through the energy fields, both in the aura and within the physical body. The sounds within the essential oils modify the sounds within our consciousness which may have caused disruption to the flow of the life force energies and therefore to the transmission of the programmes needed for the function of our physical bodies. The clamour of our thoughts may need quietening and slowing down. Or they may need a louder jolt to move them forward if they have become too slow and apathetic.

The scents of essential oils are divided into three categories, known as top note, middle note and base note.

Top note oils usually have a strong scent which dissipates quickly.

Middle note oils have a fairly strong scent which

resonates and lasts for longer than the top note oils.

Base note oils have a more subtle scent than either top or middle note oils, but they resonate and linger for much longer.

Essential oils are usually used in combinations of all three notes, to strike the right chord to achieve balance and harmony.

They can be used in several ways. They can be massaged gently into the skin, diluted in a suitable vegetable oil known as a carrier oil, on average a dilution of ten drops of essential oil to twenty milli-litres of carrier oil. A few drops of undiluted essential oils can be added to hot water and inhaled, and they can also be added to bath water. During massage and in inhalation, the essential oils are absorbed directly into the area of the body which needs help, so the help is immediate with no harmful side effects; only the toxins are dealt with. In addition, the meridians are corrected and disentangled by the massage and the healed energies of the body's organs. When the essential oils are added to bathwater, the effect of the sound of their absorbed consciousness on the water enhances their healing properties. The subliminal sound of the scent is absorbed by the whole aura of the body, and is transmitted into the subsidiary energy field systems within the body.

There are many excellent highly trained aromatherapists and there are many informative books on aromatherapy. The oils should be purchased from reputable sources to guarantee their purity and strength. Once again, dowsing can give invaluable guidance.

CHAPTER V

FOOTNOTE

Acupuncture, shiatsu, reflexology and massage are extremely effective vibrational therapies. They are very widely known, studied and used. Although they work in partnership with Energenics, they connect with the separate energy system of the meridians. Therefore I have not included them in this book.

PART XI
EPILOGUE

Thought, with all its wavelengths and frequencies from the source, the Creator-God, is the uniting activating energy of the cosmos, the universe, the Earth and everything on, in and of the Earth. It forms the thought, sound and light of cosmic life force, the one continuous thread which links, underpins and activates all creation. Earth life force and consciousness evolve from it. Energenics shows how thought energy and consciousness are organised in the cosmos, on Earth, and in the energy field systems of physical matter of the Earth and of life on Earth, especially humanity. It proposes that the term 'energy' used by healers and dowsers encompasses cosmic life force, Earth life force and the consciousness which evolves from them, and affects them, as they are processed through all the individual energy field systems of all life on Earth.

I hope Energenics takes away the fear, suspicion, misunderstanding and mystique which seem to surround the words 'spirit', 'spiritual' and 'psychic'. I hope it helps us to see them as they are: integral parts of our bodies, our lives and our living, empowering us to heal ourselves and others, to be healed, and to take responsibility for ourselves and our own lives.

The story of the Holy Grail has resonated with us for centuries. Its mystery never seems to lose its appeal to young and old alike. Does the story of the quest for the Holy Grail encode the quest to understand the nature and the construction of the energy which fills and powers the universe and all matter in the universe?

Was the secret, the key, found by the nine original Knights Templar? The story of King Arthur and the Knights of the Round Table, and their quest for the Holy Grail, dates from that time.

The first, and memorable, lecture I heard on the classical labyrinth was given by Richard feather Anderson in 1993 at the Diamond Jubilee Conference of the British Society of Dowsers at York. He plotted a graph of the distances of the pathways to and from the centre of the labyrinth. The resulting shape of the graph is the shape of a chalice (Fig. 26).

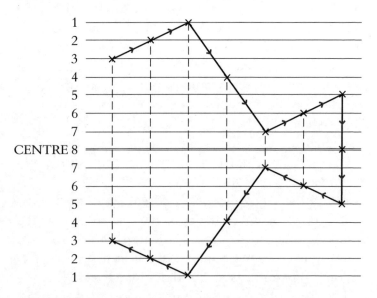

Fig. 26 A graph of the distance of the pathways of the Classical Labyrinth to and from the centre, showing the shape of the chalice

Energenics proposes that the classical labyrinth is a map of the structure of the energy fields which support matter. The energy fields carry the cosmic and Earth life forces into and out of physical matter. Each energy field is like a chalice for the life forces which flow into and out of it, as wine flows into and out of a chalice.

The circle-cross labyrinth is a map of the flow of the cosmic and the Earth life forces. Together they form the 'wine' of life flowing into and out of the 'chalice' of the energy fields. Without this 'wine', nothing is and nothing can be. The circle-cross labyrinth and the classical labyrinth need each other. The wine needs the chalice, and the chalice is of little use if it is empty.

I believe the two maps together help to solve the riddle of the construction of the energy within an atom, and the construction of the underlying, underpinning energy of the Earth and the universe. It is complicated and, at the same time, incredibly simple.

As well as helping us to understand and solve the problems of *dis*ease and its resulting disease, will this knowledge enable us to access the limitless supply of cosmic energy to use in our conventional use of the word 'energy', without plundering and ruining our beautiful home, planet Earth?

Truth and wisdom were the highest twin concepts of the very ancient Egyptian culture and were represented by Maat and Thoth. They were regarded as an inseparable partnership. Some years ago, I was wondering how to describe 'truth'. What is truth? What is wisdom? This is the answer I received:

Truth is right-mindedness, balance and harmony. What is right, balanced and in harmony may not be at some time in the future. Nothing is ever static. All grows, develops. What is true for you may not be true to someone else at that time. The future has many scenarios but all true steps taken in good faith build up the overall harmony and balance.

Wisdom is the insight into, the understanding and the mindfulness of the wider issues of the implications of truth. As with the circle-cross, truth and wisdom should never be separated.

Energenics is my truth at this time. It will grow as the knowledge, understanding and wisdom of medicine, science, healers and dowsers accumulates and combines. When we all work together, respecting each other and our truths with kindness and compassion, the benefits for the Earth, all life on Earth and especially for humanity, will be enormous.

APPENDIX I

DOWSING: A SHORT EXPLANATION OF ITS HISTORY AND ITS USES

Most people associate dowsing with searching for water, oil or minerals. In fact, its uses are infinite. The dowsing tools are usually hand-held rods or a hand-held pendulum which can be any size or shape. The dowsing tool facilitates an interaction between the dowser's own mind and the subject of the dowsing causing a movement in the tool which signals either 'yes/positive' or 'no/negative' or 'don't know/neutral'. Asking and phrasing the right questions so they can be answered 'yes' or 'no', and dowsing to verify the correct interpretation of the answers received by the dowser, is crucial to the accuracy of the overall outcome of the dowsing (see Part VI, Chapter IV).

Dowsing has been known and continually used by humans for thousands of years. Its origin dates back to the twin concepts of the god Thoth and the goddess Maat in the earliest times of ancient Egypt. Thoth represented wisdom, knowledge and science; Maat represented truth, justice, balance and harmony. One of her symbols is a plumb line and bob, i.e. a pendulum.

There is an early reference to dowsing in the Bible in Exodus 17:5–6, which tells us Moses 'smote the rock with his rod and water came forth'. The dowsing rod was an essential piece of equipment for ancient nomadic peoples and was treated with great care and respect. It is referred to in Psalm 23:4: 'Thy rod and thy staff, they comfort me'. Dowsing was known as divination, that is, 'of the divine'. Along with the study of mathematics, it was an essential part of the curriculum of education for the sons of the rich and influential people in ancient cultures. Although dowsing was outlawed in Europe by the Christian church in the Middle Ages, it continued to be used for detecting ores in the mining industry and for finding water.

Pendulum dowsing was used in India in the twelfth century AD. It was introduced into Europe by a German academic, Professor Antoine Gerboin of the University of Strasburg in 1799.

At the end of the nineteenth century, Abbé Mermet of France began to use pendulum dowsing for scientific and medical purposes. He called it radiesthesia. In 1935 he published a book: *Principles and Practices of Radiesthesia*. Today, radiesthesia is used widely by the medical profession in France and in other European countries for diagnosis and prescribing. This aspect of dowsing was introduced into the UK by a surgeon, George Laurence, in 1939. Albert Einstein was known to be very fascinated by dowsing. Now dowsing in all forms is used all over the world.

From 1987 to 1989, Professor Hans Dieter Betz, professor of Physics at the University of Munich, was financed by the Ministry of Research Department of the German Government to conduct experiments into the dowsing phenomenon to see if it could be proved according to an accepted scientific model whether dowsing exists and works. He and his team, using one hundred dowsers in carefully controlled experiments, successfully proved that dowsing does exist, and works. When looking for water, they found scientific instruments scored a thirty per cent success rate, and dowsing scored a seventy per cent success rate. 'Unconventional Water Detection' by Professor Betz was reported by him at the International Congress of the British Society of Dowsers at York, July 1993.

At the same Congress, Dr Alexander Dubrov, Research Fellow of the Library of Natural Sciences of the Academy of Science of Russia and the Institute of Traditional Medicine, reported on the important part played by dowsing in Russia, where it is known as biolocation. It is used in all aspects of science, medicine, engineering and geology, and is recognised by their government. High-level courses in biolocation are widely available and used by hundreds of graduates from all branches of science. It is used in scientific and practical research and saves large amounts of time and money. Professor Dubrov's lecture was published in the *Journal of the British Society of Dowsers*, September 1993, vol. XXXV, no.241.

APPENDIX II

DRAWING A CLASSICAL LABYRINTH

The late Donovan Wilkins showed me this simple method of drawing a classical labyrinth. He was a famous professional dowser from Cornwall who earned his living by finding and accessing water supplies.

The labyrinth can have either a right-hand opening or a left-hand opening. Dowsing can decide if the opening should be on the left or on the right. If there is any doubt, put the opening on the right.

1. Draw an upright cross with the equal horizontal arms slightly shorter than the equal vertical arms. The space on the paper, or on the ground, above the top of the cross and beyond each of the two horizontal arms of the cross must be sufficient for seven pathways.

2. Draw a semicircle, or cup shape, in the corner of each of the four sections made by the cross. The space

between the line of the semicircle and the lines of the cross will be the measurement decided for the width of the pathways.

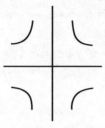

3. Make a dot halfway between the two points of the semicircle and an equal distance from the base of the semicircle and the corner made by the joining of the lines of the cross. This will be the basic construction for the labyrinth.

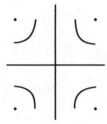

4. Join up the parts of the basic construction of the labyrinth in the sequence shown by the numbers on the next diagrams.

To draw a right-hand labyrinth, join up the numbers moving always to the *left*. Start at the top of the cross, marked 1, move across to 1 on the top of the semicircle in the top left-hand section made by the cross. Take the top of the semicircle in the top right section of the upright of the cross (marked 2) and draw over the top of the cross to the left. Join 2 to 2 (the dot in the centre of the top left-hand semicircle). Still moving from right to left over the top of the cross, join 3 to 3, and so on, until you have connected 8 to 8. The labyrinth is now complete.

To draw a left-hand opening labyrinth, draw across the top of the cross to the *right*, that is, linking left to right.

The numbers and arrows are shown here in the diagrams only to clarify how to draw the labyrinth in these instructions. Do not put them on the labyrinth you are making.

Drawing a Right-Hand Opening Classical Labyrinth

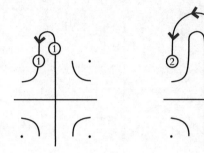

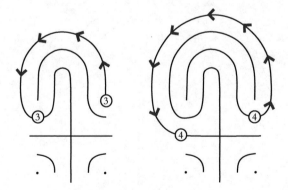

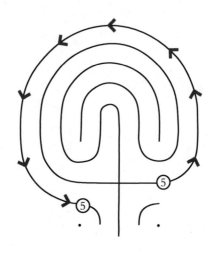

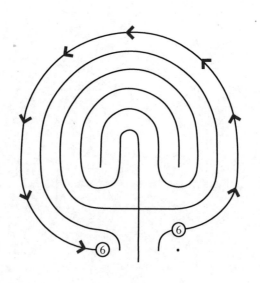

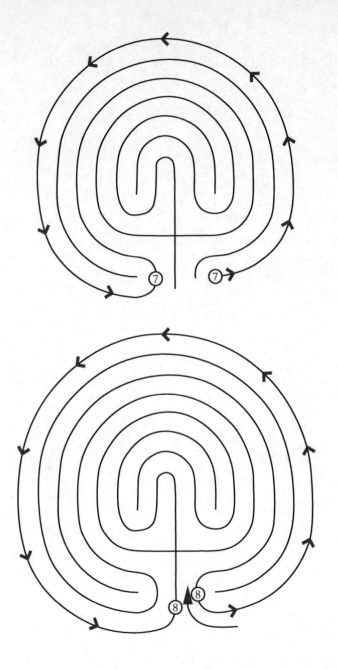

Drawing a Left-Hand Opening Classical Labyrinth

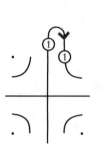

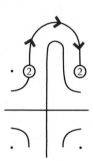

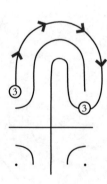

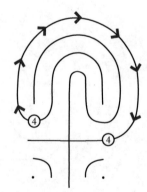

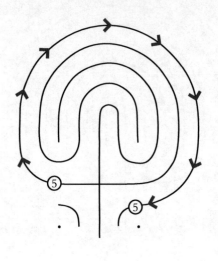

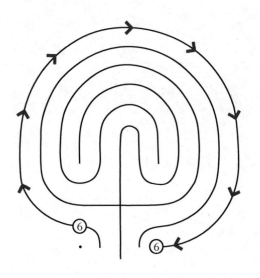

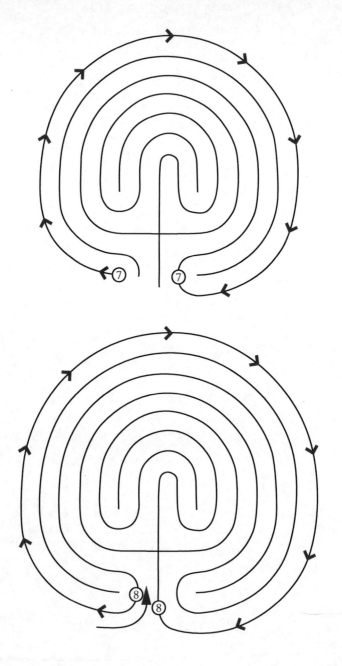

5. Your finished labyrinth (right-handed opening) will look like this. It should be drawn as evenly as possible:

Or left-handed opening:

Painting or Drawing a Labyrinth on the Earth

Measurements should be in imperial units. Metric measurements should *not* be used, as they are not in harmony with the Earth.

Remember, the space on the ground above the top of the cross must be sufficient for the width of seven pathways. Ideally the spaces between the lines of the pathways should be nine inches, but this should also be checked by dowsing.

Therefore the minimum space needed on the ground for the top of the labyrinth will be 7 x 9 inches = 63 inches, *plus* the width of eight lines, each one approximately 0.5 inches = 4 inches. This makes a total of approximately 67 inches above the top of the cross, or approximately six feet.

The space needed for the width of the labyrinth will be 2 x 7 pathways *plus* the centre = 15 pathways x 9 inches = 135 inches *plus* 16 lines x 0.5 inches = 8 inches. The minimum total width needed = 143 inches or approximately twelve feet.

Dowsing will verify the best position and orientation of the labyrinth on the ground, and whether it should have a right-hand or a left-hand opening/exit.

A Drawing of the Circle-Cross Labyrinth

BIBLIOGRAPHY AND FURTHER READING

All word definitions are taken from the *Shorter Oxford English Dictionary*, Clarendon Press, third edition, 1973.

'Psyche' is also taken from *A Pocket Etymology of Medical Terms* by Declan Anderson & Richard Buxton, published by Bristol Classical Press, 1981.

Part I

Achterberg, Jeanne, *Woman as Healer*, Rider, 1990

Coates, Callum, *Living Energies*, Gill MacMillan Ltd., 1996

Hope, Murry, *Ancient Egypt: The Sirius Connection*, Element Books, 1990

Lamy, Lucie, *Egyptian Mysteries*, Thames & Hudson, 1981

Seem, Mark, *Acupuncture Energetics*, Thorsons Publishing Group, 1987

Szekely, Edmund Bordeaux, *The Teachings of the Essenes from Enoch to the Dead Sea Scrolls*, The CW Daniel Co. Ltd, 1978

Part II

Charpentier, Louis, trans. Fraser, Sir Ronald, *The Mysteries of Chartres Cathedral*, RLLKO, 1997 (2006)

Wallace-Murphy, Tim & Hopkins, Marilyn, *Rosslyn, Guardian of the Secrets of the Holy Grail*, Thorsons, 2002

Part III

Bachler, Käthe, *Earth Radiation*, Holistic Intuition Society, 2007

Emoto, Masaru, *Messages from Water*, Hado Kyoikusha Co. Ltd, 1999

Emoto, Masaru, *The Hidden Messages in Water*, Hillsboro, Oregon, Beyond Words Publishing Inc., 2004

Gordon, Rolf, *Are You Sleeping in a Safe Place?*, Dulwich Health Society, 1988

Journal of the British Society of Dowsers, vol. XXXVII, no.258, December 1997

Mann, W Edward & Hoffman, Edward, *Wilhelm Reich – The Man Who Dreamed of Tomorrow*, reprinted 1990 by Crucible, an imprint of Aquarian Press (part of the Thorsens Publishing Group)

Winchester, Simon, *Krakatoa: The Day the World Exploded*, Penguin Books, 2004

Part IV

Campbell, Don, *The Mozart Effect*, Hodder & Stoughton, 1997

Lacy, Marie Louise, *Know Yourself Through Colour*, Aquarian/Thorsons, 1989

Lacy, Marie Louise, *The Power of Colour to Heal the Environment*, Rainbow Bridge Publications, 1996

Le Mee, Katherine, *Chant*, New York, Bell Tower, 1994

Part V

Bender, D A, *Nutritional Biochemistry of the Vitamins*, Cambridge University Press, 1992

Shearer, M J, McBurney, A & Barkhan, P, 'Studies on the absorption and metabolism of phylloquinone (Vitamin K_1) in man' in *Vitamins and Hormones*, 1975, no.32, pp.513–42

Shearer, M J, 'Vitamin K and Vitamin K-dependent Proteins' in *British Journal of Haematology*, no.75, 1990, pp.156–62

Part X

Gurudas, *Flower Essences and Vibrational Healing*, Cassandra Press, 1983

Longley, Elizabeth, *Great Works of Egyptian Art*, Parragon Book Service Ltd, 1996

Morgan, Dr Brian and Roberta, *Brain Food*, Pan Books Ltd, 1987

Tisserand, Robert, *The Art of Aromatherapy*, The CW Daniel Co. Ltd, 1977

Weeks, Nora, *The Medical Discoveries of Edward Bach, Physician*, The CW Daniel Co. Ltd, 1940

Worwood, Valerie-Ann, *The Fragrant Pharmacy*, London, Macmillan, 1990

Appendix I

Journal of the British Society of Dowsers, September 1993, vol. XXXV, no.241

Neilson, Greg & Polansky, Joseph, *Pendulum Power*, Destiny Books, 1977, 1987

ACKNOWLEDGEMENTS

First I thank all my family, friends and patients. They have taught and given me so much over the years.

I especially thank Helen Beck for her enormous generosity in giving me her time, patience, encouragement and expertise, and for transcribing my book into electronic form, and to Harry Beck for his patience during what became a long process.

I also thank these special people who have helped and supported me and in their various ways have helped to make *Energenics* possible:

My husband Peter for all his patience during the writing of *Energenics*;

My daughter Wendy for her painting, which is reproduced on the front cover of this book;

The late Maire Dewar, my early healer mentor, who introduced me to Trevor and Christine Chidlaw, and to Nora and Alan Froude, and Alan Dawes. This book would not have been possible without their love, support and sharing of knowledge over the years.

Dr Marjorie Cotton and Rosemary Hudson, who encouraged and supported me in my research into menaquinone and my first steps in writing;

Richard feather Anderson for introducing me to labyrinths in his lecture to the British Society of Dowsers' Diamond Jubilee Conference, York, in 1993, and the late Donavon Wilkins, who first encouraged me to pursue my theories which evolved into Energenics;

Gill Shaw, Jennifer Round and Geeta Russsell for always being there;

Stephanie Lyons for her support and for sharing her gifts and her knowledge;

Jane Higginbottam, Lianne Campbell, Jyotish Patel and Pam Matfin for their challenges, their trust and their sharing, which have enabled me to learn so much over the years;

Dr Philip Taylor for his advice, patience and guidance, helping me to choose and use a computer;

Dr John Briffa for his support and encouragement, and for his help and advice, which enabled this book to come to fruition;

Rosemary Kay for reading the first draft of my book;

Lorna Read for editing the first draft of *Energenics* and for her valuable comments and advice;

Peter Eyles, Jodrell Bank and the Department of Solar Physics at St Andrew's University, for generously giving their knowledge and their time;

All the people at Athena Press for their work and expertise in producing this book and for publishing *Energenics*.